Rash

Rash
A Memoir

Lisa Kusel

WiDo Publishing
Salt Lake City

WiDo Publishing
Salt Lake City, Utah
widopublishing.com

Cover design by Zoë Linn Anderson
Original artwork by Terje Adler Mørk
Book design by Marny K. Parkin

ISBN 978-1-937178-84-0
Library of Congress Control Number available upon request

Printed in the United States of America

For Loy,
my Buddha baby

Contents

Well, do not swear. Although I joy in thee,
I have no joy of this contract tonight.
It is too rash, too unadvised, too sudden,
Too like the lightning, which doth cease to be
Ere one can say "It lightens." Sweet, good night.
This bud of love, by summer's ripening breath,
May prove a beauteous flower when next we meet.
Good night, good night! As sweet repose and rest
Come to thy heart as that within my breast.
        —William Shakespeare, *Romeo and Juliet*

"What really happens to expats? Do they ever truly assimilate, feeling like
they belong to their adoptive cultures, or do they go over to the dark side
like Colonel Kurtz building their own twisted version of empire?"
        —Anthony Bourdain

Part 1:
The Bali Jar

ONE NIGHT MY HUSBAND, VICTOR, TURNED TO ME IN BED and said, "Sweetie, I think I need to do something different."

I was so engrossed in reading *The Line of Beauty* that I only half-heard him and thought perhaps he was referring to sex. But then I saw he had his finger stuck inside *Three Cups of Tea*.

"Okay. Like what?" I asked right away, not wanting to lose the moment. A potential deliverance from the mundane floated, like steam from a cup of chai tea, under my nose. I gestured at the book. "You want to go to Afghanistan and teach in one of those schools?" Victor had been teaching middle school for over fifteen years, first in private schools then public. He was the most passionate and principled teacher I knew.

"No. I'm not going to drag us to Afghanistan—not with a six-year-old—and by the way, the story takes place in Pakistan."

"Okay, not *Pakistan*, but somewhere else, maybe? You could teach anywhere," I said, clutching at what I thought could be a turning point, a crossroads, a pivotal moment. I pushed the covers off and sat up. "When we first met, you said that someday you wanted to go teach in another country, remember? Why not do it now?"

Now, because I had just spent two years writing what I thought was my best novel yet, only to have it rejected by ten publishers. My agent suggested I let it sit in a drawer for awhile and go start a new novel. Wouldn't it be marvelous if I wrote my new better book in some exotic locale, perhaps somewhere with an ocean view?

"I mean Loy is the perfect age to learn other languages," I added because I didn't want him to think it was only about me.

"Yes, she is."

"Think about it, Victor," I pushed. "There isn't anything about our life right now that would keep us from leaving, right?"

He leaned back against the pillow and stared out the window. I threw my book onto the nightstand and followed his gaze out toward the bright landscape swathed in a full moon's glow. I could make out dozens of oaks on the long stretch of Sierra foothills beyond our fence line, broccoli-like with their leafless curly branches and long thick trunks.

"Yeah. Yeah, I agree that it should be now, because in ten years I'll be, what, fifty-six," he said. "But not there. Not some place that's dangerous." At the mention of the word, *dangerous*, our old cat Rex began furiously licking his back paw.

I reached over and took Victor's hand; his strong kind hand that had held mine for going on fourteen years. "You're totally in a place with teaching where you can try something out of your comfort zone; something that could make a real difference."

"You're right. I am. Let's try to figure out how we can do that," he said, giving me a hurried kiss before opening the book again, the book I decided to have bronzed someday. "Good night."

"Good night," I replied, suddenly energized. Thrilled that my husband, my life partner, my would-be hero, was up for having an ADVENTURE, *if* the right one pulled up, that is.

The promise of paradise fell into my family's lap on an afternoon in early spring. I was languidly swinging back and forth on the front porch of our blue house on the hill in Nevada City, California, watching the woodpeckers peck at our siding, when the mailman drove his truck up the long steep driveway. Rex snoozed in the sun beneath a naked oak tree. He was deaf enough not to notice the engine approaching. Old enough not to bother raising his ragged head when the mail guy hustled up the steps, handed me my mail, and shot back down to his truck before I could even ask him how it was going.

I tossed the propane bill and two special offers for satellite TV aside and opened the latest issue of *Brown Alumni Monthly*. I wasn't technically a Brown University alum, since I'd only gone to graduate school there in the late eighties, but I liked seeing what *real* Ivy-leaguers had done with their lives—as opposed to what had become of us groovy California state university kids.

I skimmed around the classes from the 1980s and saw that someone named Mark consulted with Fortune 500 companies on corporate social responsibility. Wendy was recently promoted to chief marketing officer at her D.C. law firm. Good for her.

Rex was suddenly beneath me, sliding the side of his face along the insole of my hanging foot. He meowed, then jumped into my lap and batted my face. I read on while rubbing my palm back and forth along the hard nubs of his vertebrate.

Stephen was practicing acupuncture in San Raphael, while Professor Hannah taught geography at Oregon State University. Scott and Kristen had just welcomed their fourth child, and Brad and his family had just moved to Bali to help start a brand new Kindergarten through 12th-grade school.

Bali.

I said it aloud: "Bali."

My mouth played beach ball with the word.

My brain filled with images of orange flowers and blue-green seas.

I put Rex on the ground and ran to the computer to look up the school in Bali, trying to focus on the words instead of the cerulean skies and swaying palm trees that washed across the pages. *Innovative ecological and sustainable education . . . the buildings will be constructed out of bamboo . . . organic gardens will be planted throughout the campus . . .* I quickly clicked over to JOBS and when I saw they needed a

7th/8th-grade teacher, I hooted into the air, immediately sending the link to Victor. I knew he wouldn't read any personal email until he got home from teaching, but I was too excited not to send word ASAP.

"The director is in my Brown alumni magazine," I wrote. "It looks amazing, right? Just like what we were talking about!"

I spent the next hour Googling John Hardy, the founder of this Green School. Born in Canada in 1949, he dropped out of school due to supposedly undiagnosed dyslexia. In the Seventies he traveled to Bali where he learned traditional Balinese jewelry-making techniques. He got so good at it that he opened his own factory and hired a legion of Balinese artists to forge his silver designs, which were sold in upscale stores like Nordstrom and Neiman Marcus.

In 2007 he sold the company—called *John Hardy*—for how much was not revealed, but a few business articles alluded to something like $150 million.

There was a piece in *The New York Times* with pictures of him and his gorgeously fit second wife Cynthia, and their two adorable daughters Carina and Chiara in their lavishly designed wooden house overlooking a lush river valley.

When I heard Victor's car coming up the drive I looked past the computer and watched Loy unbuckle herself from her booster seat and jump out of the car. Victor hoisted his heavy daypack onto his shoulder then reached into the backseat to grab Loy's small pink princess pack. In perfect stillness she waited for him to take her hand.

As they walked up the railroad-tie staircase to our front door I imagined my beautiful family standing together with John Hardy's beautiful family amidst all that tropicalness.

"Victor! Come in here now!" I yelled from the computer desk in the den as soon as they entered the house. "Look at this," I said. "This school is exactly what you were talking about; a place where you can make a real difference. The students are going to come from all over the world. The curriculum is like green-colored Waldorf. It's perfect."

"From your perspective, maybe. Get up and let me finish reading about it."

"Wait, you read the email I sent you?"

"Lisa, when you put OUR LIVES WILL NEVER BE THE SAME AGAIN in the subject line, you know I'm at least going to peek."

I kissed the top of his balding head then went to go find Loy, who was sitting on the couch holding a large plastic doll, its completely bald head turned against her flat chest. "Hi, my love, how was school?"

"Good."

"You hungry? You want some cheese and crackers, or what about a smoothie?"

"After I feed my baby, yeah, I want a smoothie."

I kissed the nursing mother and went into the kitchen. I got as far as taking out the frozen blueberries and peeling a banana, before I could take it no longer and walked back into the den to stand behind Victor.

"So?"

"It looks good. Great, actually. I mean, the thing that I'm most attracted to is that it won't be just rich international kids. They plan to offer spots to local Balinese kids, too."

"Awesome."

"I'm a little concerned that they're not really clear about the curriculum, though."

"Just think about Loy!" I said as I kicked that silly doubt of his down the hallway. "She'll learn so much about other cultures. I mean, she'll probably be speaking three languages by the time she gets to middle school."

Loy appeared at the doorway. "What did you just say, Mommy? What am I speaking?"

"Nothing, kiddo," I said, pulling her and her sated baby into the kitchen with me. As I watched Loy suck blue yogurt through a straw I pictured her running through the jungle, her reddish hair streaked through with blonde highlights, her legs tan and strong.

"You want to go live in Bali?" I asked the unsuspecting Loy.

"Are you and Daddy going too?"

"Of course. We'd never go anywhere without you."

She jumped off the stool and ran up the stairs. "Yes, I want to move to Bali!" she yelled, before running toward her bedroom.

Inside the den, I found Victor typing a cover letter to the school. I read over his shoulder, perhaps making a few too many minor suggestions. He pushed the chair back and said that he had to deal with his own students' work at the moment, and if I wanted to pursue this phantom job in Bali, I should write the letter myself.

"This suddenly sounds too important to you," he added as he reached into his bag and slid out a whopping pile of student papers. "I get that you think this would be an interesting place for me to teach and, yeah, for Loy it'd be nothing but great, but what about you? What will you get out of it?"

"I, ah . . . it's Bali! How can it not be amazing? Look what happened to Elizabeth Gilbert."

"Who?"

"She wrote *Eat, Pray, Love*."

"Seriously, sweetie. What has that got to do with you?" Victor had a pen poised over an ink-smudged sheet of paper. I knew once he dug in and started correcting work I'd lose his attention, and Bali might float away like so much fairy dust.

"Well, uh, she's a writer too, and she goes to Italy then India then Bali; because she's hoping to find—"

"I don't care about her, Lisa. What do you want?"

Why *did* I want to run away from our perfect life in California? What was I looking for exactly? A change of scenery? Sure. A new place to write? Yup. What else, Lisa, what else? Why else would I want to leave our little blue house on the hill in our tiny artsy town in the mountains where we had a gaggle of friends, and Victor had a good-enough job, and I had a little writing studio on the property?

Was I afraid that if we didn't move to Bali we'd live in this house until Loy went away to college, and the thought of that unchanging scenario made me feel trapped? Was I worried that, like the sea at low tide, the passion between Victor and I had been steadily receding?

But then again, no man in his right mind wanted to make love to a woman who'd been as moody and withdrawn as I'd been the last year.

But, if we moved to Bali, my relationship (and sex life) with Victor could only improve. I'd try to spend more time with Loy. It'd be me, not Victor, she'd run to after she scraped her knee. I'd become a supermom.

If we moved to Bali, I reasoned without any real reason, I would finally find true self-love and inner peace. Isn't that what happens to people who hang out doing yoga all day with other groovy ex-patriots on some heavenly palm-jammed island? For sure, I would learn to experience the shivery synaptic snap of the moment. I'd get keener; be able to smell the purple in Loy's paintings; see the perfume wafting off the skin of beautiful women; hear the fish swim.

I would reinvent myself. I would find contentment. I would be present.

Victor and I would fall in love all over again.

Bali would make that happen. Bali. How tropical and flowery that sounded. Yes, if we moved to Bali, all would be light and golden and I'd—

"Lisa, I'm still waiting for you to answer my question."

"I think, if we moved to Bali, I'd learn how to stop searching for something new all the time and be grateful for what I have."

A mere forty-eight hours after Victor emailed his cover letter to Green School in Bali, Brad from the *Brown Alumni Monthly* emailed back, asking if he could interview him over Skype. I tried not to pace a trough into the hallway floor as they chatted back and forth for well over an hour. And then, just when I thought the conversation was slowing, Brad offered to fly Victor to Bali to check it out.

"Wait, what?" I said to him after the call ended. "He wants to fly just you down there?" A bone of jealousy got caught sideways in my throat. "Not your wife and child? How are you going to decide if it's right for all of us if we don't go, too?"

"He said you're welcome to come, and they'll pay for our hotel but not the flight."

Before I could sit down and type Sacramento to Bali into Expedia, Victor put his hand out to stop me. "I looked. It's fifteen hundred dollars a ticket."

"Yikes."

"I know."

"You're going to go, though. Right?"

He closed his eyes and rested his clasped hands on top of his bald spot: Victor's deep thinking posture. He said nothing. I said nothing. Above us Loy banged around in her bedroom. Finally, he opened his eyes and asked, "Any idea where my passport is?"

As long as Victor was flying off to Bali-land, Loy and I headed south to Disneyland. "You haven't seen your family in months. Take Loy down for a long weekend," Victor suggested as he packed. "You know I have no interest in ever going there."

"But it won't be as much fun without you." Nothing was ever as much fun without Victor.

He stopped counting out a pair of boxer shorts for each of the seven days he'd be gone. "Believe me, Lisa, as much as I know Loy will love it, I'd never use 'Disneyland' and 'fun' in the same sentence."

Three days and eight times through Snow White's Scary Adventures later, Victor Skyped me at my aunt and uncle's house in southern California.

"This place is amazing, sweetie," Victor said so loudly I had to click down the volume on the earphones. "We have to do it."

"Tell me more," I said, picturing white-sand beaches and turquoise seas. Warm tropical winds. Slowly lapping waves. Muscular men handing me drinks with—

"Well, my classroom—all the classrooms are going to be totally magical. Most of them are still being built, but Brad walked me around the site and I was blown away. I mean, the designs are like nothing you've ever seen. Everything is bamboo. Everything, even the bathrooms."

Under the YES BALI heading on the piece of paper in front of me I put a checkmark.

"And like we thought, I won't just be teaching expat kids: twenty percent of the students will be Balinese kids on scholarship."

Loy would go to school with the village children. Another YES. "Nice. Okay. What about the other teachers?"

"Brad showed me their resumes. Loy's teacher's name is Dawn. Everyone says she's extraordinary. They're smart; way more experienced even than I am—I'm sure I'll learn a lot from them. There's an older British woman, Carol—she's teaching the fifth/sixth grade class. She's been working with middle-school kids for thirty years. She knows curriculum like you wouldn't believe. And Johnny, the third/fourth teacher, is from New Zealand. He has two kids. One will be in Loy's class."

I could hear the excitement in his voice even through the long-distance haze of our Skype connection. Yet another YES BALI.

"And I'd have two co-teachers; an Indonesian teacher and another western teacher. I met the western teacher, Sara, tonight at dinner at John Hardy's compound."

"You like her?"

"She's really great. Great energy. We have so much in common."

"Uh-huh. What about John Hardy? What's his house like up close?"

"It's beautiful. Way bigger than in the pictures online. But I'm not actually staying at his house. I'm staying at the hotel on their property."

"Cool." I pictured a small cement Sheraton surrounded by palm trees.

"They have me in this weird old wooden hut. He and Cynthia had four of them shipped over from Java. I think they normally charge something like $300 a night to stay in one."

So much for the Sheraton. "What is he like?"

There was a pause. "He's a little full of himself, but maybe I'd be too if I was a multi-millionaire."

"No, you wouldn't."

"Whatever. His heart is in the right place; but I have to say, after one evening of listening to him pontificate about himself and why he knows what's best in education, I asked for reassurance from Brad that Hardy would have nothing to do with the day-to-day running of the school. And that he'd have *no* say about the curriculum."

"He was that bad?"

"Bad enough that I said I wouldn't work here otherwise."

He hadn't taken the job yet, but already Victor needed reassurance? "What did Brad say?"

"He told me there was absolutely nothing to worry about. That he would be the go-between between the school and the Hardys. That both John and Cynthia would keep their distance. And I trust him. He's passionate about the school, and he's very bright."

I started doodling little hearts under the NO BALI heading. "Is he calm? He looks calm in his online picture."

"Calm isn't the word for it. He's a Buddhist. He's even met the Dalai Lama. Oh! Guess who I'm having dinner with tomorrow night?"

"Who?" I had questions that extended beyond spiritual elbow-rubbing.

"Kartika Sukarno."

"Who is that? Another teacher?"

"No, moron," he said with a laugh. "Sukarno was the first president of Indonesia after they threw the Dutch out. Kartika, or maybe it's Karina—anyway, she's his daughter."

"Oh." Would that mean I'd be dining with dignitaries? Would I need to buy a new wardrobe?

"And I heard that Donna Karan, the designer, comes here to visit all the time. John's daughter from his first marriage works for her in New York."

Definitely a new wardrobe. "What about salary?"

"$3,000 a month, with no taxes taken out. Plus, roundtrip airfare for the three of us, which basically gives us another $4,500."

Behind me I heard Loy in the kitchen describing the Buzz Lightyear Astro Blasters ride to Aunt Sharon and Uncle Marty. "And we can live okay on that?"

"Brad said if we wanted to, we could hire a maid, a cook, a nanny, *and* a driver, and still have plenty left over."

Maids? Cooks? Wait a minute: would they be living in the house with us? Would we eat only Balinese food? What exactly is Balinese food? Would Loy still be able to eat quesadillas and drink smoothies?

Kramer, my aunt's standard poodle, ran into the dining room and started sniffing me as if he could smell the sudden ambivalence on my skin, and it smelled yummy. "Tell me about the housing situation," I said before I could get too worked up.

"They'd give us either a two-bedroom hut or a three-bedroom one, depending on the rest of the hires. Brad showed me Johnny's house— it's almost done. It's pretty wild. Really different."

We'd be living on campus with the other teachers and their children, which meant we'd have a built-in community. Okay, for sure another YES BALI.

"But I have to warn you, there's not going to be a lot of privacy. There aren't any walls. Oh, and just so you know from the start, I'd have to work really hard," Victor said. "Probably harder than I've ever worked, because there's so much that's still not in place—"

I stopped drawing hearts. "What do you mean? What's not in place?"

"Whatever. School stuff. Like they haven't created a curriculum yet. Or things like discipline policies. And no one has yet to tell me if I'll have to teach PE or music, too. That sort of thing."

Red flags began flying around my aunt's dining room. "But school starts in August and it's already May."

"I know, but honestly, these are just formalities. I get the sense that they mostly have their shit together."

Mostly? Did I just hear a hint of hesitation in Victor's usually self-assured voice?

When I didn't respond, Victor yelled into the phone, "Hey, are you changing your mind? It was your idea that I come here."

"You don't think maybe we're being a little rash?"

"Rash? Are you fucking kidding me, Lisa?" said my preternaturally patient spouse.

"Just wait—I'm sorry I said that, but I want it to be a good thing; I want us to—"

"Sweetie," he said before I could figure out what I really wanted to say. "This is a once-in-a-lifetime teaching opportunity for me. I mean, think about it. This is a very well-funded international school with a green focus in a rural setting and, on top of that, there's the incredible housing right on campus."

"Yeah, that's true," I said, although I still had many more questions. Before I could ask him to tell me what a typical day would look like for all three of us, or to at least promise me that Loy would grow up even smarter and kinder than she already was, he said, "I'm going to sign the contract tomorrow," three seconds before the computer connection in Indonesia went dead.

Two days later Victor flew home to California with the signed contract in his hand and a To-Do list four pages long. We had a total of six weeks to get ready to move to the other side of the planet.

One of the things at the top of my To-Do list was to find out a little more about where we were moving to! I have a Masters degree in cultural anthropology and have done a fair bit of traveling, yet before

I read through Loy's atlas and scrolled through never-ending websites, I realized with a pocketful of embarrassment that I knew close to nothing about Bali, or the Balinese people who lived there. I had no idea what language they spoke. I had no idea if the Balinese were polytheistic or if they'd been missionized into Christians. I had no idea if they ate spicy food, believed in Santa Claus, or were against public nudity. I had no idea what their houses looked like, how they dressed their children, or what sort of vegetables they farmed.

I had no idea that it was the Dutch who first *discovered* Bali in the 1500s (in much the same way Columbus discovered America), and introduced the island and its beauteous offerings to the western world, but that it wasn't until the 1920s that scores of international musicians, artists, and anthropologists began arriving. I'd forgotten that Margaret Mead and Gregory Bateson did much of their anthropological research in Bali in the 1930s. Walter Spies and Jean Le Mayeru, among other artists, glorified Bali's sumptuous landscape and topless native women in their paintings. Famed musicologist, Colin McPhee, moved to Bali to learn about gamelan music. Noel Coward and Charlie Chaplin visited the island together on a steamship.

Tourism exploded in the 1970s, fueled not just by antiestablishmentarianism or hallucinogenic drugs, but by the romantic notion that Bali was one of the last untouched utopias. Hipsters and movie stars, rock stars and rich jet-setters flew into the new International Airport, which opened in 1968. And many of them, according to the expat blogs I read, never left. I wondered, with not a little trepidation, whether I, too, would someday be a successful expat.

I read up on Indonesia—a country with a population of some 245 million people living across more than 17,000 islands, spread out over 3,500 miles. I made the mistake of opening the U.S. State Department's listing on Indonesia which stated: "There remains a continued threat of terrorist attacks, demonstrations and other violent actions that may affect U.S. citizens in Indonesia." And: "The general level of sanitation and health care in Indonesia is far below U.S. standards."

And this not so comforting bit: "most expatriates leave the country for serious medical procedures."

Given that Victor had already committed to the job, I tried to focus on the positives. I was psyched to find out that even though Bali is part of Indonesia—which has the largest Muslim population on the planet—90 percent of Bali's almost four million souls are Hindus, practicing not *Indian*-Hinduism per se; but rather a unique Balinese-style Hinduism that includes all kinds of beautiful rituals and festivals. I wanted to learn more about those beliefs and practices, and maybe even thread the parts that spoke to me into my own nascent journey toward enlightenment.

Whenever doubts bubbled up during those six weeks of scrambling around trying to push every detail into place, I fantasized about enjoying those phenomenal eight dollar massages the travel bloggers wrote about. To better immerse myself in the place, I played Balinese gamelan music on my computer. I pushed aside the bad sanitation and terrorist threats and instead planted on my forebrain the image of Loy playing in the jungle with her new Balinese and European friends, ooh-ing and aah-ing over the harmless glossy bugs that glided by on the Balinese breezes.

I pictured quiet walks alongside the green fertile rice paddies with Victor's hand in mine. I saw us making love in a bamboo bed, a cooling fan turning lazily above us.

I saw Victor teaching a roomful of inquisitive interesting children from around the world, all eager to soak up his brilliance.

Yes, I filled my glass with Bali juice and I drank eagerly.

Victor helped his school hire a new seventh grade teacher for the following year. Through Craigslist we found a family to rent our house. We canceled our utilities and had our mail forwarded to my mother. When it came time to choosing what to take and what to store, I fell apart. Do I bring all my photographs? How many books will I read in the course of a year? I doubted that I'd find any organic, non-GMO, politically correct, child-nurturing, fair trade bug repellent or sunscreen, so I bought enough to get us through to the Second Coming.

"Lisa, don't you have more important things to worry about than how many pairs of pants to bring?" Victor said. "I doubt you'll be wearing more than shorts and a T-shirt every day. Remember, it's really hot in Bali."

He was right—how hot, exactly?—I had bigger fish to stress over. I knew Loy would need a shot or two to keep her from catching some unpronounceable disease, so I clicked on the State Department's website about *Requirements for Vaccine-Preventable Diseases.* When it opened, I tried to look away from the computer screen, but it was like trying to avert your eyes from a car wreck when you're on the interstate going ten miles an hour.

The list was unnervingly long. Because we were so entrenched in the local alternative/homeopathic/naturopathic healing culture, we hadn't been in a hurry to give Loy all the prescribed childhood immunizations. We figured we'd space them out; wait until she got older. Of course, she got the polio vaccine and, because Victor was exposed to so many children in school, the whooping cough shot was absolutely necessary. We were aware of the risks we took choosing not to vaccinate her, but she was a healthy kid living in a first-world country. In her entire six years, Loy had only ever swallowed one ibuprofen pill.

The shot that came close to stalling me on the Road to Bali was the Japanese Encephalitis (JE) vaccine which the State Department "recommended if you plan to visit farming areas..."

Visit? We planned to *live* on farmland.

Apparently there is no cure for JE and if you get bit by a carrier mosquito, you have a good chance of dying. But, if you're lucky enough not to die from it, you will most assuredly be left with permanent brain damage.

And those at the highest risk?

Children less than fifteen years of age. Check.

Who live in or near rice paddies. Yup.

Close by pigs and/or wild birds (vectors). Ditto.

During rainy season. That's half the year in Bali.

After reading no fewer than seventeen websites describing the ups and downs, the percentages, the adverse affects, and the death rates, we decided to err on the side of paranoia and get it. But there was a hitch: the vaccine had to be administered in three separate doses, spaced out in 0, 7, and 21 days, and while most bad reactions—hives at one end of the spectrum, instant death at the other— come *not* after you're given the first dose, but after you get the second or third shot, we'd planned to be in the middle of a thirty-hour plane ride to Bali after the second dose.

I called my Ob/Gyn friend, Lela. We'd gone to college together and she'd done me the honor of catching Loy on her way out my cervix. She was my go-to for all things medical and vagina-related.

"What happens if we're in the air and one of us gets hives or can't breathe or..." I wailed into the phone.

"Buy an EpiPen. But, you'll have to remember to show it to the TSA agents so they know you're not trying to hijack the plane with it."

"*It* being ... ?"

"A big needle with epinephrine. If Loy gets a bad reaction, you just have to jab it into her thigh."

A thousand non-insurance-reimbursable dollars later, our immune system overflowed with anti-venom. We ended up getting them all: Typhoid. MMR. Hep A and Hep B.

We also bought tons of Tamiflu just in case there was an epidemic of H_5N_1 or H_1N_1.

We stopped short at the rabies shot, because I'd read that Bali was a rabies-free island, or at least it was trying to be.

Speaking of which: how were we going to get Rex to Bali?

"I'm not going," I said to Victor's back as he was bending over, filling a box with Loy's winter clothes.

"Why not this time?" he said without bothering to look up. Okay; so maybe I'd thrown out more than a few lame excuses why we shouldn't move to Bali. The time for us to leave was fast approaching and I was getting cold feet.

I suddenly started loving the incensual smell of my writing studio. I began to appreciate the looming oak outside Loy's bedroom that scratched at her window's glass when the wind blew, and the murmuring sound of the creek when the rains filled it, and the violet lilac bushes that lined our house. With a renewed sense of wonder, I followed the daily flitting of the pair of blue-like-the-sky bluebirds that lived in the crooked birdhouse Loy built at Home Depot last year. I had already begun to miss the way-cool food co-op where I'd run into no fewer than ten people I knew, and the deep and supportive teachers at Wild Mountain yoga studio, and my generous friends Andrea and Elisa and Lori and Marina and—

"Lisa! What now?"

"Bali won't let animals in from a country that still has rabies. Unless you're a diplomat."

"Lisa," he said, twisting out the tension from his back. "It's too late to change our minds."

"But—"

"Please let me pack. You're smart. Go figure it out."

I wrote to the Consulate General Republic of Indonesia and begged them to give either Victor or Rex diplomatic status. They were kind, but, not-surprisingly, they refused my request. Finally, in a last-ditch fit of desperation I turned to the shady *international* transport companies, the ones the online pet forums warn you never to use. After exchanging many partially decipherable emails with Wati at Groovy Pet Transport of Indonesia, she and I hatched a plan to get Rex into Bali. I printed out the itinerary and ran outside to interrupt Victor and Loy's tetherball match.

"Hey, so I figured out how we're going to be able to bring Rex with us," I said, launching into our cat's travel plans. First, we'd put him on a flight from Sacramento to Amsterdam, where he'd be met by a "representative" who would wait with him during an eight-hour layover in a nice lounge. From there he'd fly alone to Kuala Lumpur where he'd be put in quarantine for up to fourteen days.

"Would his room be air-conditioned?" I'd written.

"No, Miss," Wati replied. "Only ceiling fan."

While in the gulag in Kuala Lumpur, Rex's records would be purged and he'd be given new false identification and medical papers, mutating him into a Malaysian cat, born and bred. Then, if he was still alive after his two weeks in prison, he and his new papers would be flown to Jakarta, because Bali does not allow any animals—even the pets of diplomats—to land on their island by air. From Jakarta, he'd get to enjoy a 25-hour car ride to Bali with his own personal driver, who would hand him off to us at the airport, where we'd have to be waiting for him.

I looked up from the paper. Both Victor and Loy were staring at me. I didn't need to add that it would cost $8,000 to smuggle Rex into Bali. There was no way our fifteen-year-old cat would survive the trip. As sad as it made me, we'd have to let Ellen, Loy's godmother, look after him.

Ten days to go and my enthusiasm peaked and sagged, looking very much like a read-out from someone's EKG. I got a bit melancholy as I emailed our new Skype names to our friends and family and warned them not to bother sending us real mail because it'd never reach us. I floated on air when our Seattle friends Marci and Renee said they'd enroll their two daughters at Green School once we settled in and lived there for a year. Then I heard from my doctor friend, Lela, and

her husband Tim, who said that they'd visited Ubud back in the early
90s and remember loving it so much that they, too, planned to move
down with their son next year. Within two more days, a half-dozen
more friends emailed or called, promising that if they could somehow
swing it, they'd move to Bali, too!

Five days before leaving I had no idea why we were choosing to
run away from all that was good and familiar.

But it was too late.

Or was it? We didn't have to go. No one could make us. Victor
could get his old job back. Loy wouldn't have to make new friends
or be forced to wear sunscreen 365 days a year. I'd move my desk
so it faced a different view and write my new book as I stared at our
huge oak.

Two days before our departure Victor got an email from Johnny,
the teacher from New Zealand, who'd already moved to Bali with his
wife Phillipa, their daughter Emily, and son Elliott. He sent it to the
new teachers:

> Dear All,
>
> As we have sat here amongst the palm trees over the last few languid
> evenings listening not only to the distant rush of the river, the chirrup-
> ing of crickets and the gentle thrumming of kites overhead, but also to
> the chatter of builders, the tapping of hammers and the buzz of dusty
> grinders, we have discussed the fact it might be a good idea to let you
> know what to expect ... But where to begin? Perhaps the best place
> is by mentioning a few things to prepare for when you get here both
> physically and mentally.
>
> On the whole, the feeling that takes precedence is of being a part
> of something quite extraordinary, with an emphasis on the extra. You
> don't tend to feel overwhelmed at any point but just part of the busy
> flow. There are frustrations—but much like life anywhere really.
>
> It is very exciting watching one's house being constructed and fin-
> ished with its hairy coat and waxy bamboo floors. It is very frustrating
> when you want to express how you feel about where your shower is

going but the house designer is too busy to hear. It is invigorating to stand gazing into the enormous space of the classroom and imagine the children moving through their day. It is disturbing to watch toadstools growing out of the earthen floor, no doubt from the secret-ingredient—elephant-dung—that was used in its production. It is marvelous to sit down in the sunset to another feast prepared by one's own cook while sipping a cool Bintang. It is humbling to carry the family's night soil bucket to the hu-manure compost (but also faintly rewarding to be in charge of such a simple procedure ... don't ask me why). It is fantastic to go shopping in Ubud and bring home chocolate moose [sic] cake for less than $2 a glorious slice. It is irritating to know that while you've come with good intentions to eat like the locals you find that eating rice three meals a day really is taking things to the extreme. It is fun to be a part of the busy office, sharing conversation over a pre-cooked lunch in a banana leaf. It is annoying to get back to where you are staying to find no hot water in the house and then half way through the shower for the power to go off leaving you stranded in the darkness ...

Certainly, nothing is perfect but it makes for a different sort of day everyday! What we have all chosen to be involved in is no small thing. This is a huge complex with a huge vision. There will be many challenges for us on a personal level, on a collegial level, on a philosophical level and on a plain old get-your-hands-dirty physical level. However, the rewards are numerous and the memories will be a glorious, colorful book that we may all be able to look back on and smile. I am looking forward especially to pizza evenings and taking my class for walks along the precarious, bright green rice paddies.

We can't wait to see you all here.

We'll have a list of information waiting for you on where to get things—including the chocolate moose cake.

We'll also have a smile.

And some insect repellent.

Best wishes from the faculty ghetto.

Johnny

What did he mean by no hot water?

"Victor. What if we're making a huge mistake?" I said as we watched the Bekins Moving and Storage truck slowly back down our driveway.

"Well, if we are, it's too late now." He kissed me on the cheek and skipped off to see what Loy was doing—images of cheap chocolate *moose* cake bouncing around his head like a kangaroo gone mad.

I wanted to run back into the house and unpack the case of Tom's toothpaste. I wanted to not be afraid that my child would be bitten by an insect that could potentially kill her. I wanted to wear wool sweaters instead of tank tops in December.

With a questioning whine on the tip of my tongue I ran upstairs where I found the two of them huddled together against the wall of Loy's empty room, reading a book from a still-unsealed box that was coming with us to Bali.

I wondered how they could be so calm in the face of such momentous change. I wanted to say something like, "Victor. Ellen is going to let Rex die, I just know it. Bali is so far away. What if Loy gets sick while we're there? I think we should rethink this. I think we should just stay here and play it safe," but I didn't.

Instead I joined them on the floor where we took turns reading *Owl Moon* out loud. It's about a little girl who ventures out into a moon-filled night with her father in search of owls. After Loy read, she passed the book to me. On my page the little girl is holding tightly to her father's hand, silently wondering what might be hiding in the dark forest. When I got to the last line, I smiled.

When you go owling
you have to be brave.

Exactly.

Part 2:
Please Don't Smoke the Bamboo

A S THE AIRPLANE DROPPED FROM THE SKY I STARED OUT the streaky window and saw the jagged coastline, the palm trees, the turquoise water, and the white sands of Bali.

"Mommy, let me look, too," Loy said as she leaned past me.

"How does it look?" Victor asked.

"Like paradise," I replied, grinning. Tired as I was from flying, I felt electrified by the sudden swarm of emotions—fear, joy, hope, curiosity, relief—coursing through me. There was no turning back now.

We'd moved to Bali.

After the chaos of customs, where Victor had to prove that he was a schoolteacher (*guru*) and not a book peddler hoping to make a buck selling the many copies of *Holes* he'd brought along, we walked outside and were accosted by a hot blast of breezeless air and a mob of drivers. We'd flown some thirty hours across the world and were surprised, if not a little bummed, that no one from Green School was there to greet us other than Gusti, a driver who worked for the school. He held up a sign with the name VICTOR PRUSSACK printed on it.

Gusti and Victor and another guy named Wayan jammed our seven boxes of worldly goods into a large van. Gusti drove them up to the campus for safe-keeping, and Wayan drove Victor, Loy, and me, and our two suitcases filled with clothes and toiletries and money, to the Kori Ubud Resort, Spa & Restaurant. This was where we intended to hole up for three days to get over the jet lag that was already weighing down on us with such ponderous force, we didn't even have the energy to jump into the swimming pool we passed on our way to our hotel room.

Instead we stripped off our clothes, turned the air-conditioner to HIGH, and collapsed into bed.

Six hours later we woke up and found Bali outside our door.

Bali.

Beautiful, warm, flower-scented Bali. Exactly as I'd wanted it to look.

As we made our way toward the open-aired restaurant for our first Balinese meal, I was giddy. I stopped to make small talk with a white couple lounging by the pool. Like the newest member of a secret society, I wanted to meet other people brilliant and daring enough to come to this magical place known as Bali.

"Hi. Where are you from?" I asked.

"Germany. We are here for our honeymoon," the skinny young man replied as he looked at his sunburnt bride beside him.

"Congratulations," Victor said.

"Why do we have to eat?" yelled Loy, who could care less about honeymooners. "I'm not hungry. I want to go swimming now." She stared at the pool as if it were hypnotically beckoning her. "*Loy, come swim. It's so good here in the water. Loy, you must swim . . . Loy . . .*"

"Come on, Loy. You've got to eat. Then I promise we'll go swimming," Victor said, taking her hand.

After filling our bellies from a *rijsttafel* buffet ("rice table"—derived from the Dutch colonists who ruled Indonesia from 1908 to 1949), we unpacked our bathing suits, smeared suntan lotion on our skin, and settled in for three days of family R&R before Victor was to begin his new job helping to open an innovative international school in the jungle.

The next afternoon as we three lounged in the shade of a palm tree listening to the exotically unfamiliar songs of Balinese birds, and chatting with a honeymooning couple from Sweden, Johnny showed up for a surprise visit with his wife and two children. They came bearing gifts: three slices of the famous chocolate moose (mousse) cake, as well as some news.

"Daddy, will we get this cake every day?" Loy asked through a mouthful of creamy chocolate.

"Nah, there's nothin' up at the school," remarked seven-year-old Elliott, as he hoisted himself then his sister, Emily, out of the pool. "You gotta drive to get anything good."

I glanced at Phillipa, Johnny's blonde-haired, adorably cherubic wife. She shrugged and then smirked. "I guess, yeah," she said in her thick New Zealand accent. "We're mostly in the middle of nowhere; nothing like down here in Ubud."

"Uh-huh," I said, suddenly noticing the many hundreds of welts on her children's legs. "Phillipa," I began, careful not to insult the woman who was soon to be my neighbor, "what's—"

"Call me Pip."

"Pip, what's going on with their legs? Are they allergic to something?"

Phillipa pulled Emily into her lap and wrapped the five-year-old in a hotel towel. "Those? They're bug bites they won't stop scratching," she said rather jauntily. "I have some naturopathic cream for the itch, but Em and Ells aren't too keen on using it, are you, Emily?" She stroked her blonde child's wet hair from her forehead. "Just wait till you move up to campus; Loy's legs will look like this in no time."

"What?" I looked at Victor, but he and Johnny were talking school. I watched Loy stand up to jump into the water and I stared for a moment at her perfectly creamy legs. "Don't you use bug stuff? I mean, that's a lot of bites, Pip."

She laughed. I already adored her, even though at the moment I was seriously questioning her mothering skills. "Of course, I do. I use the local stuff—it's all natural. It's pretty good, but..." Emily unwrapped the towel and ran off to join Loy in their mermaid tea party. Phillipa sat up. "Lisa, you folks haven't been up to see your house yet, have you?"

"*Tidak.*" No.

"Oooh, you're already speaking Bahasa. Good for you."

"Pip, what am I going to see there that I'm not seeing here?" I saw a few bugs buzzing around in the air, a swatch or two skimming the surface of the pool, but nothing resembling the swarms I imagined it would take to cause those pocked legs.

"Well, for one thing, here," she waved her arms all around the hotel grounds, "they spray nasty poison every night to kill the bugs. Don't look so surprised; they do it while you're sleeping. And second—Ells, leave those girls to their game, please. Thank you—here, you're sleeping indoors, with windows and screens. We have no screens, or windows for that matter, up at school. I mean, sure, there's mosquito netting on the beds, but they're kids. They're outside playing all day, and it's really muddy, so there's lots of bugs."

"Muddy?" I quietly gave thanks that we were inoculated against Japanese Encephalitis and typhoid, but what about all the *other* diseases?

"Sure, it's muddy, Lisa, it's a bloody construction zone. You know that, right?" Phillipa looked over at Johnny. He and Victor were too absorbed to hear her, but she lowered her voice to a small dot. "Honestly, it's more, more, ah, well, the place is less ready than we expected, yeah. Like there's no hot water, and—"

"There's still no hot water?"

"No. I mean they're trying to figure it out, but, Lisa, really, you'll be fine. We'll all be fine. It's a grand idea, this school, yes? And now that your family is here, too, it'll be even better!" With that she smiled a mother's smile that promised everything will be all right.

Of course, it would be all right! I mean, we'd rented our house to another family and given Rex to Ellen and moved so far away that the very notion that it would be anything but didn't compute for me. Not then, no. I loved Bali and Pip and the smells of sunshine-toasted flower petals. I would learn to love rice in all its forms. I would be okay with Loy having bug bites adorning her legs. I wouldn't let any of what Pip was saying distract or deter me from the adventure we were about to embark on. I'd made us come here. I found the website. I wrote the cover letter. I pushed Victor into flying to Bali to check it out. And I agreed to move here.

I took a deep breath and smiled at Phillipa. From this moment on, I would not see Bali as anything but what I'd dreamed it would be: paradise. And my husband and daughter and I were going to get lost in paradise, muddy or not. For the time being, though, I would enjoy being a tourist like the transitory honeymooners around us. I leaned back and admired the clean concrete surrounding the pool, the bug-less air, the nice man walking over to us with a tray of tropical drinks. "At least I have another two days of this before we move into our house," I said, wanting more than anything to match Phillipa's optimism, wanting her to like me for being the sort of supportive wife that she obviously was.

"What do you mean? Victor, didn't Brad tell you about your house?"

Victor and Johnny turned their attention to their wives, their glass-is-half-full-wives. "I thought Brad's on vacation for another week," Victor said. "I haven't spoken to him in a while, why?"

Johnny answered for Phillipa. "I thought you knew your house isn't ready. Most of them aren't." Some of them, he told us, were merely posts in the ground. Some were bamboo shells. The other three-bedroom designated for us was supposedly on the verge of being finished, but as of now only two teacher houses were even close to habitable: the three-bedroom hut that Johnny and Phillipa had snagged, and a one-bedroom spot that we were welcome to move into until ours was done.

The news that we had no real home of our own was less than great, sure, but ultimately it didn't matter, because we were in Bali; beauteous balmy Bali. And so, after saying "so long— see you in a few" to Johnny and family, we went wild, filling the remaining days of our vacation with all that Ubud—the universe's center of grooviness—could offer. We walked miles, exploring the many shops and museums; ate new and delicious food; and then lounged some more around the chemical-laden garden in the overpriced hotel, slowly letting our body clocks reset themselves to GMT+7.

We didn't dwell on our move up to the school. We didn't fret. We didn't get anxious. We didn't for a moment think about the three of us and our acres of toys and clothes and books crammed into two rooms.

We didn't start any of that until we checked out of the Kori Ubud Resort and got a taxi up to Green School.

The one-bedroom hut they were offering us was super cute, actually. It was an A-frame made of bamboo. It had a small living room with a table built into the floor, surrounded by pillows, maharaja-style. It had a workable kitchen and a huge bathroom with a rain shower the diameter of a wok overhanging a black stone floor. Up a narrow spiral staircase there was a loft bedroom with a few bookshelves. I was so taken by the novelty of the place that it took me several minutes before I noticed the layer of bugs on the floors, walls, pillows, and table; some alive, plenty dead.

"Why are there so many bugs, and why are they so big?" I asked Meliana, one of Green School's marketing assistants who'd been assigned to help get us settled.

"See the floor here," she said, pointing down. "It's too close to the ground. It's not such a good design." She had to shout over the din from the sanders and hammers and saws just outside the hut.

"Oh," I said. I looked at Victor who was opening and closing the few cabinets in the kitchen, surveying the cooking pots and the tiny stove.

"Victor. Come here."

"What?"

"Do you see that the floor is *on* the ground and that there's no barrier between inside and outside?"

"Yeah?"

"Do you see those ants strolling in and out as if they owned the place?"

"Yeah."

"This house needs to be raised up so it's not on the floor," Meliana added.

"And that would be happening when?" I asked with maybe a little too much sarcastic salt in my voice.

"Look, it's like camping, right?" Victor said. "And it'll only be for about two weeks. Let's go see what's going on with our house so we can get a better sense."

We walked out the bamboo front door onto a lava-rock path set in among the deep dark mud, which wound around piles of sawed-off bamboo planks, half-formed hunks of bamboo, discarded bamboo shards and scraps, and mounds of bamboo sawdust. Scattered over the ground were chunks of cement and rebar with sharp edges.

After I cried out, "Be careful! No, Loy, don't walk over there!" Victor picked her up and carried her over to where our house stood. We peered up from the ground into the bamboo carcass. Inside were no fewer than a dozen sweat-soaked Javanese men and women shaping grinding fastening forcing tightening—all those verb-rich activities that are required for building a house.

A few folks looked down at our clean white faces.

"*Selamat siang*!"—Good afternoon—I yelled, puffed with self-delight over the freshly memorized greeting.

A thousand smiles and "*siang*'s" were flung back at us.

"What do you think?" Victor asked hopefully.

I surveyed the large kitchen area, the half-finished staircase, the rounded walls and door jambs—all bamboo. "It's awesome—it'll be great," I replied, seriously grateful to see that the floor was a full three feet off the ground.

As we turned to leave, Loy tripped on a piece of PVC piping and fell knees-first into the mud.

"Forget the ants; there's no way in hell I'm letting Loy live around here," came Victor's voice of reason next to me. "It's a freakin' construction zone! I don't know what they were thinking," he said, pulling Loy up.

"Thank you," I whispered. Then I waved goodbye to the workers, saying, "Please build me a nice safe house," even though I knew they didn't understand me, before running to catch up with Victor.

Many phone calls and texts later, we were handed off to Jared, an American expat who specialized in finding people what they needed, be it drugs, the best tattoo artist in town, a cheap motor scooter, or a short-term house rental.

"You guys are gonna totally love this place." Jared's sunglasses glistened against the glare coming through the windshield as he zoomed us along narrow country roads. "The house has never been lived in. I mean, man, it was like finished last week!"

"Who owns it again?" Victor asked from the back seat.

"Some rich Belgian dude, I think. Or maybe he's Swiss. Anyway, he was gonna live here but for some reason he can't yet, so he wants to, you know, rent it out. Your school's totally paying for it, and you don't even want to know what it's costing. Shit. Oh, shit, I'm sorry, man. Sorry, Lori."

"It's Loy," I corrected for the 5,983rd time since naming our child after the ultra-sophisticated 1940s movie star Myrna Loy, believing the name would be both unique and super easy to remember.

We pulled into a short driveway behind someone else's truck and got out. The house was your basic, Southern California, stucco-looking box, but the front walls were glass and it was surrounded by a man-made stream.

"Check this out," Jared said, as we walked over a tiny bridge. "Real fish in there. Pretty awesome, right?"

Loy stayed outside to watch the fish while we went in. We found four workmen in the kitchen installing a stove.

"I thought the place was finished," Victor said.

"Yeah. Wow. Me, too." Jared went over to the workers and started speaking Bahasa with them while we went to scout out the rest of the place. Upstairs we found three bedrooms with three bare mattresses, but no sheets or blankets. And no mosquito nets. There was no furniture anywhere else except for a slender stone bench in the living room. It looked out toward the fake creek.

I waved to Loy who waved back. I regretted not spraying her with bug spray and thought to go out to the car to get it; but I had a feeling things were going to heat up between Victor and Jared, and I didn't want to miss any of it.

"There's no bedding or sheets, Jared," Victor pointed out when Jared came to tell us that the kitchen should for sure be done by tomorrow. "No pillows or towels. No mosquito nets, either."

"Uh."

"And I'm guessing there are no pots or pans or plates or any kitchen stuff, right?"

"I'm thinking I didn't see any, no." Jared played with his key ring and bobbed his head a few times to his own silent beat. "But hey! We can get all that, yeah? We'll just shoot over to Delta Dewata and get it there."

I was too hot to even contemplate buying furnishings for an entire house. Wait, was there even a refrigerator in the kitchen?

I knew Victor would be having none of that. "Jared," he said slowly and patiently, which meant he was losing his patience, "let me get a few things straight."

"Sure."

"Is there Internet here?"

I could tell where he was going, my boy Victor. I sat down on the bench and waited for it to play out.

"Not that I'm aware of, no." A screechy sound like a heavy metal object being dragged across a floor came from the kitchen. Jared nervously looked behind him, then scratched the side of his thick black hair. A dragon tattoo ran the full length of his right arm.

"How far are we from Ubud, Jared?"

"It's nothing. We're like, what, about a five, ten-minute drive."

"But we don't have a car. How far on foot?"

"Oh, wow. You wouldn't want to walk it. People drive crazy around here. It'd be pretty dangerous to walk it."

"Then if Loy and I wanted to hang out in town while Victor was working I'd have to take a taxi there and back, right?" I asked.

Victor didn't let Jared answer that one—he had his own agenda to deal with. "We're not talking about you going shopping or getting massages, sweetie. We're talking about my job. How am I supposed to get up to Green School every day? It's a half hour from here. Will I have to take a taxi back and forth every day?"

"No, hey, it's no prob. Brad said the school would send a car down to get you guys and take you up to work."

Victor looked at me. Loy and I had no intention of going up to campus every day. Victor would be working full-time getting the school ready to open. What would we do there, other than get in Victor's way? "I'm not going up to school with him," I stated.

More key jangling, only now Jared's right leg joined in. "No, I didn't mean *you,*" Jared replied. "The other people who are gonna be living here. Another teacher and her husband are going to be staying here, too."

"WHAT?" Victor.

"WHAT?" Me.

"Mommy, you have to come see this long line of poop coming out of a fish's butt." Loy.

Exasperated, we asked Jared to drop us off in Ubud at Pizza Bagus (Pizza Good), so we could eat lunch, throw our options out on the table and figure out what to do next. The house on campus was out. We weren't sure how comfortable it'd be to live with another family in an unfurnished house patrolled by fish out in the middle of the Bali boondocks.

"We should find a place here in town," I said through a mouthful of super-tasty onion pizza. "That way at least Loy and I could get around without a car."

"And we could eat here every day!" Loy added. Two tables over from us six European tourists were eating and smoking. They managed to make holding a slice of pizza in one hand and a cigarette in the other look almost fashionable. For a moment, I wished I still smoked, the mingled smells of cooked dough and burning tobacco taking me back to times gone by … backpacking alone in Europe … hanging out in bars in Paris … lighting up after sex …

"Loy, finish your pizza. We've got to get out of this place," I said, remembering that I needed to protect my six-year-old's lungs from deadly second-hand smoke.

Were we bad parents for moving Loy to a country where it was legal to puff away anywhere and everywhere? Did I dare bring this up to Victor now, I wondered.

I thought better of it and went to pee instead.

On the way back from the bathroom I spotted a glossy brochure for the Bali Putra "Bungallow," just across the street.

"Look at this," I said, handing it to Victor. "We can stay in a gallows!"

Seeing that word on the cover was just too funny not to at least check out, for at Bali Putra, we'd be "welcomed friendly by our staff and you can see beauty panorama such as rice: terrace, many trees, if the weather is clear you can see the beauty sunrice and quite place so good for take a rest."

We wandered across the street, where we were "welcomed friendly" by Putu, the head room clerk. (Most first-born babies in Bali are named either Putu for girls or Wayan for boys.) We told her that we needed to rent a place for a minimum of two weeks and possibly for as long as two months. She walked us down a narrow path alongside a rice paddy to a small, simply furnished two-story brick house. It had a workable kitchen, complete with glasses and plates and pots and pans; a great bathroom with a tub; a queen bed downstairs, and a king bed upstairs, where, from the balcony we could indeed see the sun and the rice.

Breakfast was included in the price of $25 a day.

"Can you find us another mosquito net for the downstairs bed?" I asked after noticing the large holes in the window screens.

"*Ya*. This no problem," Putu replied. "But you pay for it, okay?"

"Yes!" I exclaimed quickly, because for me, the place was supremely perfect.

For Victor, though, it was a huge inconvenience not being able to live on campus as he'd been led to believe. He wrote a letter to the Director:

Hi Brad,

The house you found for us off campus won't work. Living on campus is my family's desire. For this to happen, we need more than just a completed house. I have spoken with other faculty members and this is the list we've come up with:

1) Piped hot water.

2) Reliable and non-overly noisy electricity [the large generator they used was situated smack dab in the middle of the community].

3) Safety (not walking through and living amidst a construction zone).

4) All major construction completed (finish work can be expected, but the noise can be intolerable when it is 12 hours a day).

5) Stop allowing motorized access through the housing road. Guards are allowing people, even at night, to drive their motorbikes through campus.

Until then, we will be living at Bali Putra across from Pizza Bagus. The rate is 250,000 a night (for long-term), just over $800/month. This includes housekeeping and a basic kitchen with hot plate and small fridge. Internet access is across the street.

Again, our goal is to be living on campus. It will be best for us as well as for the school. A productive faculty is the goal.

Thanks.

Victor

At Bali Putra we settled into a nice easy pattern. After Victor went off to work in the morning Loy and I often hung out with Putu up at the front desk, swapping English and Bahasa Indonesian phrases like recipes at a supper club. She was our go-to girl for all things Ubud. She told us which hotel pool was the best to sneak into. Which drivers charged what prices. Where to shop for pillows for our new house on campus. Who made the best black sticky rice pudding. She replaced our phone minutes when ours ran low. And she gave us the best exchange rate around for our dollars (1 US dollar equaled about 10,000 IDR—Indonesian rupiah).

Loy and I would then grab our swimming gear and head to some fancy hotel where we'd swim and read and race from one end of the pool to the other. Sometimes we'd share a watermelon juice or mango smoothie and bowl of soupy noodles for lunch. While Loy dove for the rupiah coins I tossed into the pool over and over, I'd chat with any English-speaking tourists willing to talk to me. It was like being on vacation every day, but not really, since the most fun member of the family—the one who did cannonballs until there was no water left in the pool—was busy getting an environmentally focused international school ready for its students.

On our walks home, Loy would come up with some pretty convincing reasons why we needed to stop at Pizza Bagus for an ice-cream cone.

"It's so hot, Mommy."

"You just swam for three hours."

"I'm sweating and I need to bring my core temprature down."

"It's temperature. And I'll turn on the AC in the room when we get back."

"If I don't eat something cold right now, I might not make it home alive."

Three weeks into living in Bali, she broke out in a sand-papery rash that started on her cheeks then spread over her torso, then legs, feet, and hands. It was ghastly red and patchy dry. I remembered the welty rash that Elliott and Emily had on their legs from bites, but I knew Loy couldn't have gotten bit that many times.

I compared her rash to no fewer than a hundred online images of rashes, confirming that it wasn't dengue fever. I learned that the only rash to be afraid of is the one that doesn't blanch; meaning when you press the rash it's supposed to turn white, then when you take pressure off the skin, the redness returns. If the redness stays when the rash is compressed, it means you are bleeding under the skin. And you are most likely dying. And you should fly to Singapore pronto, but it will probably be too late because a non-blanching rash is a terrible thing.

Every morning when Loy woke up I'd scan her whole body, pressing, pushing, poking her ever-spreading rash with my thumb, my forefinger, my palm. She'd look up worried, asking, "Is it blanching, Mama?" me knowing how emotionally maiming it was to scare your six-year-old like that, but still I pressed on.

Victor seemed casual and unconcerned about her health. "She's fine, sweetie. She has no fever. No headache. She's not complaining. She'll be fine. It's nothing. Please try not to be so paranoid."

I emailed Doctor Lela in California, and asked if she thought maybe Loy could be reacting to one of the fifty-seven immunizations she got, and, if so, what should we do. I had Victor take a photo of Loy's rash-streaked belly and attach a jpeg.

Lela wrote back and said the rash looked like something you'd see with a streptococcus infection. Taking no chances, Putu hired us a driver named Agung to take us to the International SOS Medical Clinic in the village of Kuta, about an hour south of Ubud.

On the way to the hospital I could tell Agung was a sullen type. He had no interest in letting me practice my Bahasa on him. After a few fruitless attempts at friendly banter I closed my phrasebook and held tight to Loy as Agung, like all drivers in Bali, assaulted the road in front of him.

Let me point out that the idea of safety is relative. Yes, I can be irrational when it comes to Loy, but putting her in a car in Bali felt a little like giving her a box of broken glass to play with and hoping for the best. None of the cars had seat belts, or if they did, they didn't work.

Driving in Bali could feel like being a rider in the chariot race scene in *Ben Hur*. Victor or I would sit in the back seat and hold onto Loy because drivers often had to stop short to avoid hitting a battalion of motorcyclists and motor-scooterists, half of whom suddenly decided to swerve into the middle of the road, because *they're* trying not to plunge into a three-foot-deep pool of muddy rain water, or crash into any of the shoulder-hugging stray dogs or running children or men pushing saté carts or long colorful lines of women strolling to temple while balancing enormous baskets of offerings on their heads.

Agung drove with the abandon of a man who had one toe planted in the spirit world. I kept one hand on Loy and opened my phrase book with another. *Pelan.* Would he please *pelan*—slow—I asked. He grunted and slowed, but still I held tight.

He leaned against the car in the clinic parking lot, smoking cigarettes, while Loy and I waited over an hour for someone to swab her throat. When I asked how long before we'd know the results—was this the standard five-minute test, or the longer 24-hour test—I was told we'd hear back in five to seven days.

I called Victor to tell him the non-news. He said as long as I was going to pass through Denpasar, the huge capital city of Bali, I should stop at one of the hundreds of "electronics malls" and buy new speakers for my recently silenced laptop. I handed my phone to Agung while Victor put Meliana the marketing girl on his phone to direct Agung to the supposedly best spot to score a cheap pair.

"I want to go home and go swimming," Loy whined when she found out we were going to make one more quick stop.

"We can skip it," I said, "but would you rather watch Tom and Jerry movies with sound or without?"

"Yeah. Okay."

Agung followed along with us when we went into the five-story, open-aired concrete blight they called a mall. It was more of a souk-like maze, with hundreds of small tables manned by two or three people, their wares spread out in front of them.

I just needed some speakers that had a USB plug. How hard could that be?

"*Selamat sore*," I said to the first table. Good afternoon. Then I said, "Stereo," which is the same in every language, simultaneously putting my hand to my ear as if listening.

"Weosnughushinso…" the shopkeeper gurgled, to which I replied, "*Saya tidak mengerti*." I don't understand. And I added, "Please get your cigarette out of my daughter's face," but he didn't get that one.

I grabbed Loy's hand and yanked her down the crowded, heat-stifled, smoke-filled corridor, wishing I'd find a Radio Shack around the next corner. Agung was no help. He stood next to me as I rummaged through the electronics on table after table trying to unearth speaker-like components. At every table there was someone holding a cigarette at precisely Loy's height.

"GET THAT FUCKING CIGARETTE AWAY FROM HER FACE. DO YOU NOT SEE THAT YOU ARE ABOUT TO BURN HER?"

Okay so I got hot and frustrated and first-world ugly, but Loy looked pale and sickly, overcome and out-of-place. I realized I should have waited another day or two before dragging her out to this dreadful mall in this merciless heat.

Agung stared at me with such horror that I wondered if I'd inadvertently insulted his personal God. "I go to car. You come later," he said and sped off.

"Wait. You can speak English? Then why aren't you helping me?" I shouted at his departing back. "Arrrggh! How hard is it to find a pair of fucking speakers!" I directed my rhetorical question to the two guys in the corner who were eyeing the crazy American woman and the small rashy child whose hand she was crushing.

"Speaker, *ya*! You come," one of them said, waving me over.

Oh blessed be. I bought a pair of small, round, silver-colored computer speakers for $16, thanking the men who sold them to me with much profusion, even though they blew their smoke in Loy's face as I paid.

I found Agung sitting in the car in the parking garage, *his* stereo speakers blasting. When we got in he didn't bother to turn the volume down, and I didn't ask him to. He started the engine, put the car in REVERSE, looked in the rear-view mirror, put the car back in PARK, and turned off the engine.

"*Apa?*" I asked. What?

Without making eye contact he flicked his thumb over his shoulder, inviting me to check out what was behind us. I turned around and saw a car parked perpendicular to our car, blocking us in.

"*Apa?*" I repeated. What now?

Agung shrugged his shoulders and turned the stereo up even louder.

Try to imagine the heat in that car. Or the feeling of your child's sweaty head as it slumps against your chest. Then when you hear your cell phone ring, gingerly touch Agung's shoulder and mime PLEASE LOWER THE VOLUME with an apologetic smile.

Then feel free to shriek a stream of heat-triggered imprecations at your innocent husband who was phoning up to see how the speaker shopping was going.

Fifteen minutes later the driver of the blocking car appeared and we were on our way, Loy asleep in my lap.

Thirty minutes from our mosquito-less, air-conditioned room at Bali Putra, Loy sat up and declared that she had "to poo."

"Can you wait, sweetie?"

"No, Mommy. I have to go now. My belly hurts."

"Agung," I began. "Loy…" That's it: invoke the child. Balinese love children and would never want to see them harmed. "Loy needs … (flipping pages) … *kamar mandi*." She needs a bathroom.

"*Di mana?*"

Where? I looked out the window at the busy streets, shops, people, motorcycles, burning garbage piles, featureless buildings. I scanned the signs, looking for one that advertised *restoran* (restaurant). There! A Chinese restaurant. "*Ini!*" I shouted, not sure if I was saying "here" or "this," but figuring he'd pull into the parking lot, which thankfully, he did.

As soon as we got inside and smelled the stir-fry-scented air, Loy said, "I'm hungry. Can we have lunch here?"

Sure, why not. We were shown to a table and given menus. I told Agung that he should order himself a drink while he waited, but when we returned to the table a few minutes later, he had nothing in front of him. I opened a menu and pointed to the list of beverages and flapped my hands around gesturing for him to CHOOSE ONE.

He ordered a bizarre pink and green drink that looked like slabs of gelatin and avocado over crushed ice. Loy saw it and wanted one, too, but I convinced her to settle for a fizzy lime juice.

I asked him what he wanted to eat, making it clear that I was paying and he could order ANYTHING, but what did he order?

Nasi goreng.

Fried rice. The national dish of Indonesia. Agung, like most Indonesians, probably ate it six times a week. I tried to get him to order the shrimp egg rolls or the kung pao chicken. I again made it clear that I was paying, but he wouldn't change his mind. I shrugged, then ordered sweet-and-sour chicken for Loy and a spicy pork dish with greens for me.

The food was pretty good, too.

When the check came I noticed a discrepancy—the pork dish I ordered was supposed to be $10, but they charged me $15. I asked our waitress if she could please bring me the *daftar* (menu), and when I pointed to the dish I ordered, she said, "*Tidak*," and turned the page and pointed to a chef's special pork dish that I had 100 percent NOT ordered.

"This is wrong," I said to a person who spoke no English.

She smiled, said something directly to Agung, then walked away. I assumed she was going to get a manager or to ask someone to help out, but she strolled back over to the front of the empty restaurant and stood next to the other waitresses.

After a minute or two of waiting for something to happen, Agung stood up and walked out, without a word.

Then Loy stressed that she really wanted to go back home.

I paid the extra money and got in the car and we drove in silence back to Ubud, whereupon Agung dropped me and Loy off ACROSS THE STREET from Bali Putra. I was opening the door to get out when he turned in his seat, handed me another driver's card, and said, "You no call me no more. Here. You want driver, you call my friend, Made. *Selamat jalan.*"

I had been fired by my driver.

Working up at Green School was a mixed bag for Victor. He loved the camaraderie with the other teachers and the excitement of creating a new *green* curriculum … but he didn't love the state in which he found the school. He'd expected there to be more in place in the administration building. Instead, he found a leaking roof, nowhere to sit, no computers or laptops, and no direction on who should do what. By the time the driver dropped him back at Bali Putra at the end of the day, he was sapped, but still full of optimism that this jungle experiment was going to change the face of education as we knew it.

Soon after Victor started work, master teacher Carol and her husband Richard arrived in Bali from England. Since their hut was still in construction mode, they were taken to The House In The Middle Of Nowhere, the one that that Jared had tried to unload on us. By then it'd been furnished, but Carol and Richard wanted none of it. Like us, they thought they would be too isolated out there with no car and no Internet access.

They tried to rent a *bungallow* at Bali Putra, but tourist season was in full swing and every room in Ubud was full up. They had no choice but to live with the fishes in the fake creek.

While Carol was up at the school for those beginning weeks, Richard would take a taxi into Ubud and hang across the street at Pizza Bagus, using their wireless connection. Loy and I shared a sausage and onion pizza with him a couple times. After work, Victor and Carol would be driven back to Ubud and we five would sit on the shady patio of bungallow #2 drinking cocktails and munching cheese and crackers. Carol and Victor would talk shop and Richard would show Loy card and magic tricks.

"Pick one, Loy. Go on."

In my slightly buzzed and languorous state, I was only half-listening to Carol complaining about the state of affairs up at Green School.

"Victor, they don't have a bloody computer for me to use."

"I know. Brad should have had one here for you. I am glad I brought my own."

"And what about those chairs? Do they expect us to work eight hours a day whilst sitting on a log?"

"I think they do. Yes."

Victor felt a lot of the same frustrations that Carol did; but he knew going in that opening a new school was going to be difficult, which is why he made us move to Bali two months before school started.

With no computer to use, Carol was more or less useless. "Richard and I should have gone on holiday for a few weeks instead of coming early," she said, pacing around our small grass lawn. "You know, my contract doesn't even begin for another two weeks. I came out of the goodness of my heart."

"We all did," Victor replied.

"Yes. I get that. We all arrived early because we thought they'd be ready for us. Bad enough the houses aren't ready."

"You can say that again," I said, commiserating with her feeling of unsettledness.

"But the fact that the office staff isn't ready either, well…"

"Carol, you need to relax," Richard said, pulling a 50 rupiah coin out of Loy's ear.

"Richard. Do not tell me to relax. I am fifty-five years old. Do you have any idea how it feels to be treated like this? To be made to sit on a tree stump all day with millions of bugs flying about you?"

"Can't say that I do, love."

"And what about what Brad said to me this morning, about my lowering the group's morale?"

Victor swirled the melting ice around in his glass. I could see that he wanted to move on from the negative. "Why would he say that?" my polite and sympathetic husband asked.

"He heard that I told Dawn that since Richard had a job offer in Singapore, we'd most likely be moving there next year."

"And?"

"He went mad on me, Victor. He said he expected all of us to commit for *three* years and telling Dawn otherwise was terrible for morale because we're—what'd he say—'we're a community of committed people.' I said, 'Well, then maybe you should have given me more than a one-year contract,' but he kept banging on like some strict headmaster talking to a naughty kid about how we had a moral commitment and—oh, never mind."

She stopped pacing, sat down on a wrought-iron patio chair and turned to watch the man in the rice paddy next door yell at the birds. All day long the shirtless Balinese rice farmer paced up and down his small field holding his arms out, cursing at the birds as they swooped to snatch the green shoots.

"He's a very false man, don't you think?" Carol said, referring not to the hollering farmer but to Brad. "I mean, what he tells parents when they ring up or he takes them on those tours ... he can't even answer their questions about curriculum. Are we teaching Waldorf or are we teaching International Baccalaureate?"

"I know. I wish I knew what to tell parents, but honestly, who gives a shit?"

"What?" Carol asked before I could. "What do you mean?"

"Come on, Carol, you and I and Johnny and Dawn and every other teacher are here in Bali for the same reason—because we think Green School is a great idea. And all of us, supposedly, know how to teach."

"Yes. Presumably."

"So all that matters in the big picture is we're going to give the kids an incredible year, regardless of what curriculum they choose. If they get out of our way and *let* us teach, that is."

"Yes, I see your point, Victor, but still, it seems to me that Brad and the Hardys are not as forthcoming … or, to put it bluntly, I feel they're being dishonest about what the parents are signing on for."

"Maybe they are, Carol. But we'll soon see, won't we?" Victor said, not yet knowing how prescient a person Carol truly was.

Mere days after that conversation, Victor returned home to Ubud without Carol, looking more weary than ever. "What is it, sweetie?" I asked while keeping an eye on Loy who had just trapped a rather nefarious-looking bug under a glass.

"Carol quit."

"What? I thought she was just threatening to." Now Loy was on her knees peering into the glass.

"So, you know how I got paid, right? I made a deal with Brad that I'd get paid for helping get the school off the ground."

"Uh-huh."

"I guess Carol never made that deal; she just assumed she'd get paid for coming early." Loy pulled the glass up, then ran as far from the bug as she could get.

"I would have assumed the same thing. Loy, it's not moving," I said. "You can come back."

"Me too, but no. She didn't get paid. And when she asked Ted why not, he had the gall to say that no one ever saw her do any work."

"What? That's ridiculous. She was up there every day."

"I know, but …" Before Loy could continue harassing the red bug, Victor slid it off the patio with the side of his shoe. "Thing is, she wasn't actually *able* to do anything. I mean, she tried to work on the curriculum, but she had no computer to use and nothing is in place."

"What do you mean?"

"There's still no consensus on the curriculum, so we can't even order books yet," he said exasperated. "Or … look: it doesn't matter what she did or didn't do. No one should be treated like that."

The next morning Victor asked to meet with Brad and the Hardys to tell them what had happened with Carol was inappropriate and destructive. If it reflected how teachers were going to be treated in the future, he'd have to think twice about staying. Lots of agreeable nods and promises later, the Carol matter went away, and teacher Sam was quickly found to replace her.

Sam had just finished a teaching stint in Beirut and was, according to Victor, one of those itinerant teachers, the sort you find working all over the world. They like teaching but love traveling around the globe even more. As Victor put it, "They're teachers willing to do anything but don't do anything well. They get hired because they're smart enough and adaptable enough and usually funny enough, but all that hides the fact they're mediocre teachers. Sam doesn't have a tenth the experience Carol had. So much for me getting to learn from a master educator."

Two days after Green School lost Carol the master educator, Victor found Seni the master housekeeper, soon to become the fourth member of our family. Victor had been working up in Green School's administration building when Seni came in to apply to be a *pembantu* (maid). After she was given an application to fill out she waited for someone, anyone, to talk to her, but the staff in the office ignored her. Victor came to her rescue, asking her about her work background, how it was she knew some English, and when she'd be available to start.

That night, in the middle of a tropical downpour, the three of us were running back to Bali Putra from dinner when suddenly a motorbike swerved right up onto the sidewalk in front of us.

"*Pak* Victor! I recognize you from the road and I come to see you!" a soaking wet Seni squealed into the warm wet wind. She offered to throw Loy on the bike and drive her the few blocks back to Bali Putra, but—seeing how she liked to spontaneously beach her bike onto sidewalks—we graciously declined. But I did agree, given how friendly and helpful she was, to interview her as soon as possible.

The next morning, while sitting together in the shade of our patio, Seni told me her former employers were a Japanese family with two children who left Bali a few months ago. "I say you, *Ibu* Lisa, I love those children so much. They love me, too. We are hugging all day. I cook for them good food, everything they love. I make them fat!" Seni was herself an affably plump woman, with dark smooth skin and eyes and teeth as white as the rice that grew in the field not twenty feet from where we sat. With her imperishable smile and belly-born laughter that echoed off the clouds, she could have been the love child of Oprah Winfrey and Dom DeLuise.

While we were chatting, our kitchen boy, Wayan, appeared with our all-inclusive breakfast: some toast, jam and citrus-y honey for me, and for Loy, an order of *dadar unti*, a thick crepe stuffed with ultra-sweetened coconut. I asked Seni if she wanted a piece of toast or a cup of tea. She seemed surprised.

"I no eat your food, *Ibu*." I would soon find out that not one of her former employers had ever offered her food—not even food *she* cooked for them.

"I can't finish this. Please share it with me." I handed her a piece of toast and continued on before she could protest. "Are you married?"

"*Ya*. His name Ketut [name given to fourth-born males or females]. He so good to me; he no smoke or drink. He no gamble or fight chickens. He no beat me."

I tried not to appear grieved by her appreciation for having such a righteous spouse.

"Does Ketut work?" I asked through a thin smile.

"He used to make sculpture but no more because his boss, he very mean. He promise he pay him but he steal the money. He bad man."

"So what does he do all day?"

"Oh. He watch television. He sometimes drives car for tourist people."

"Huh. Do you have any children?"

"*Ya*, of course. *Tiga laki-laki.*"

Three boys.

"Then Ketut takes care of them while you work?"

"My husband, he good man, but he not so good for being daddy. His mommy, she is good for my boys. They with her when I'm no there."

"Why do you want to work for us?"

"Oh, *Ibu*. You and *Pak* Victor, you so nice. I see him in the school office when I come there. Nobody talk to me. Nobody care. But *Pak* Victor. He smile. He care. I LOVE him. I LOVE you, *Ibu*. I LOVE your little girl, Loy," she said smiling at Loy who had her mouth full of *dadar unti*. "I will cook for her, yes? I feed her. I feed you and *Pak* Victor, too. *Ya*?"

"Of course!" I replied without a moment's hesitation.

I told her that as soon as the workers from PT Bambu—Green School's construction facility—finished building our house on campus, I would love her to come be our housekeeper/cook/nanny. Her starting salary was supposed to be $70/month for working eight hours a day, six days a week. I asked Ted, the business manager, if it'd be okay to pay her a couple shekels more, say $80/month. My radical display of generosity was rejected on the grounds that it would upset the delicate balance of the local economy and cause the other lowly paid workers to revolt. I knew we'd pay her $100/month regardless, because there was no doubt in my mind that Seni would be worth more than her weight in gold.

When the news arrived—*six* weeks later—that our hut at Green School would be ready for vacancy in a few days, I texted Seni. Then, finding out that the school would be providing us nothing but basic furniture and a $600 housing allowance, Victor, Loy, and I went on a Balinese shopping spree, buying all the goods we didn't think to cart along with us from California.

We found smooth white cotton sheets in one shop, brightly colored lightweight quilts in another. We bought bath towels, beach towels, and hand towels. Napkins, silverware, and glasses. A toaster, coffee maker, two reading lamps, and two floor lamps. After we found an awesome wooden Balinese dish drain we knew couldn't settle for cheap MADE IN CHINA dishware; not with there being so many talented artisans all over Ubud.

We strolled the galleries and chatted with the potters, eventually choosing to buy everything we needed from Tamin, a Chinese-Indonesian ceramicist who threw pretty, earthy-green pottery imprinted with delicate leaves. We bought eight large soup bowls, eight small soup bowls, eight salad plates, eight dinner plates, three huge serving bowls, two large platters, innumerous tea mugs, an assortment of tiny bowls, a teapot, a vase, and a water pitcher. All those pieces—plus the many candlesticks and incense holders Tamin pushed into Loy's hands every time we visited his studio—came to a whopping $150, give or take. Back in the states the same artisanal craftwork would have cost thousands.

Victor couldn't wait to move. He'd grown desperately tired of his commute and looked forward to walking to his classroom once school started. Me? I would have loved to have stayed put in *bungallow* #2 for the rest of our stint in Bali. It was with a heavy heart that I said *ciao bella* to rooms with windows; see ya later to air-conditioning; and *selamat tinggal* to the hustle and flow and food and fun of downtown Ubud. I also had to bid *adieu* to our good friend, Putu. When I looked at her face while she tallied the numbers of our final bill I knew something was up.

"Putu. What's wrong?" I asked. "Why so sad?"

"*Ibu* Lisa, please. My boyfriend, Wayan, he loose his job with German family. He do security for them."

"And?"

"Maybe you get Wayan job at *Pak* Victor's school?"

"Why doesn't he become a driver?" One who will drive me to the hospital and back if I need him to, safely, slowly, and without crushing my soul with his antipathy.

"He have only scooter."

"I see," I said with a weary sigh. Putu had taken such good care of us. Even if she had been the one to find Agung for us, she'd never charged us for that new mosquito net, and she always made sure we got our breakfast served first every morning. I heard myself utter, "*Tidak apa apa*" (no problem). I said it any time I thought there might be a problem.

I talked about poor unemployed Wayan to Victor, who gently nudged Director Brad, who asked another Putu, who was Green School's office and HR administrator, to offer him the job raising and lowering the big bamboo security pole at the south entrance to the school.

I looked forward to being reminded of the first real friend I made in Bali whenever I came and went.

The saying goes that when one door closes, another opens. And if that door happens to be anywhere on the Green School campus, you can be sure it is a bamboo door. At Green School virtually *everything* was made out of bamboo: the desks, chairs, floors, walls, doors, bar stools, bed frames, curtain rods, staircases, banisters, and bookshelves. Even the ceiling fans, kitchen countertops, cupboards, bathroom vanity, couch frames, coffee table, dining table and clothing wardrobes were constructed out of bamboo. We also had a compost toilet made of bamboo, the contents of which were to be covered by, yes, bamboo sawdust.

Who would have guessed that bamboo could be good for anything other than a panda's lunch?

A few elements were not bamboo. The exterior wall of our bathroom was a huge sheet of thick canvas. Another gargantuan piece of the same white fabric draped from the apex of the pointed roof, down over our open living room/dining room space, providing shelter from the daily rains, as well as shade from the tenacious sun.

Our roof was covered with a long thick grass called *alang alang*. Our kitchen and bathroom sinks were fashioned from a luxuriously handsome dark obsidian stone.

The house was magnificent. An architectural spectacle. Balinese, yet anti-Balinese. Like nothing we'd ever seen before, like nothing we'd ever see again. It was a masterpiece of elegant design and accomplishment. A work of art.

A mold magnet.

"Holy shit. Victor, look at this."

Victor stopped arranging his recently arrived shipment of textbooks on the bookcase upstairs and looked over the bamboo balcony that fronted the large landing at the top of the staircase.

"Why are you holding that barstool upside down?"

"Can you not see this from there?" I said pointing at the black growth. "That's mold."

"Mold?"

"Yeah, and guess what—I bet it's growing on more than just the barstools."

"I don't get it," he said, as I ran upstairs to check the bedrooms. "Brad said they treat the bamboo so insects won't eat it and it won't mold."

I came out of Loy's room. "Well, they must have forgotten to treat our furniture because our wardrobe and everything in Loy's room has mold growing on it," I said on the verge of tears.

Victor stopped stacking books and emailed Putu in administration. She sent over Tineke, the facilities manager, to assess the situation. Tineke guessed that maybe PT Bambu hadn't aged the bamboo quite long enough because, yes, much of our furniture was indeed covered with dark green mold.

"Can we have new chairs and shelves and tables and—"

"Yes, but they must be built, and at the moment we are still building the school and the rest of the teacher houses, so it will be not very soon." A short stern Javanese woman, Tineke wore thick glasses and seemed a bit beaten down. I tried to relax her by offering her something to drink, but she said she was far too busy for such things. "I will request that this furniture is removed soon. Good day."

"She's right about them still building the school," Victor yelled over the balcony without bothering to stand up. "It's because of me they're still building desks."

"Am I crazy or is the first day of school in like ten days?"

"Yes, it is, but I never told you that Aldo designed all the desks with sharp corners, because he liked the look of triangular desks." Aldo Landwehr was John Hardy's creative director. When Victor saw the desks, he sent them all back to PT Bambu and asked to have them replaced with square desks with rounded edges.

"Why?" Aldo had protested. "Squares are so square."

"If a kid falls and hits his head on the corner of a pointed desk," my husband had responded, "what do you think is going to happen?"

"Well, good for you that you made them change the desks." I pushed under the mosquito net covering our living room couch to do an Internet search on local furniture companies. "Do you care if I go buy some new stuff for our house?"

"Be my guest, sweetie. Just don't ask me to come along."

"No worries. I know how busy you are."

"No, you don't, but that's okay."

I stopped typing. "What are you talking about? I totally—"

"No, Lisa, you don't. You have no idea how it's been, and school hasn't even started yet." I couldn't see him at this point, but I knew he'd be rubbing his face up and down with his hands—what he did when he was stressed. "It's really hot and I'm already wiped. This school is not ready to open, but there's nothing I can do about it."

A shock of guilt coursed through me. Me. The one who suggested we move to Bali.

"What can I do to help?" I asked. "Seni starts work tomorrow. Loy can hang with Pip and the kids. I can live without barstools and wardrobes for a few days."

"No, sweetie. I appreciate it. I do. Just let me do my thing, okay?"

"Really? Are you sure there's nothing I can—"

"Maybe you could be a little more supportive and a little less grouchy. And not complain so much."

Before I could respond he dropped to his knees and continued stacking books.

He was right. I'd not realized until we arrived in Bali how much I coveted comfort, quiet, and privacy. Now I had none of those things. All I'd done since our move into the bamboo castle was gripe about what was wrong, from the constant noise to the lack of hot water to the litany of small annoyances that had been eating at me. I'd been so self-absorbed and negative that I'd all but ignored how my attitude could be affecting my family.

So much for being grateful for what I had.

I vowed then and there to focus not on what I'd given up, but on what was being offered. To stop seeing the imperfections of the trees and start reveling in the uniqueness of the forest, even if it was a bamboo forest.

The ants arrived two days later. All three of us were in Loy's bed, tucked safely under the mosquito net that draped down from four bamboo rods, reading aloud from *James and the Giant Peach*, when Loy pointed toward the top of the net. "There's a bunch of bugs up there."

Bugs were such a normal part of life in our open-aired hut that neither Victor nor I bothered to follow her finger's trajectory. Instead Victor kept reading and I kept listening.

Loy interrupted with, "Hello? Are you guys not seeing what I'm seeing?" We looked up. I screamed. Victor jumped out of the bed and grabbed one of Loy's flip-flops. I grabbed the other. Loy took shelter in our room as Victor and I fought off the army that had laid siege to her bedroom.

When the ant assault happened again the following night, Victor called Putu, who called Richard the engineer who built the school, who passed it off to Aldo who designed the school, who emailed Tineke, who sent over Gede, one of the many gardeners who worked on campus, who sprayed Loy's bedroom with NEEM, a non-toxic herb purportedly able to ward off ants.

Sadly, it didn't work.

But I didn't complain. Instead, Victor and I took turns squashing the invasion of ants in her bedroom each night while Loy showered (in cold water) and brushed her teeth. By the time she got under her cool sheets with the fan turning above her to keep her relatively comfortable all night, her floor would be littered with dead ants, a few strays escaping back to wherever it was they came from. Ever the trooper and insect enthusiast, Loy didn't seem to mind. As long as she knew they couldn't get under her net, she felt safe, and would be asleep as soon as the lights were out. I felt okay about it, too.

Four days later, the smoke began.

John Hardy, our resident forward-thinking, hyper-creative, jeweler/private school founder thought it would be ingenious to heat water using bamboo sawdust. After all, there were piles of the stuff sitting on the ground at PT Bambu, just down the road. John asked Richard, the engineer, to please make it happen.

Swaggering, cigarette-sucking, foul-mouthed, English-born, Richard was a character right out of a Guy Ritchie movie. He'd been managing the construction of gas and oil fields on other islands in Indonesia when John Hardy headhunted him to Bali and gave him a budget of a couple million dollars to build Green School.

After his first meeting with John and Cynthia Hardy and their designers, Richard felt like he'd landed in an alternative universe, and knew pronto he'd have to learn a new argot—using terms like *sustainable*, *eco-friendly*, and *green*.

"The whole lot of them seemed to have been drawn to this spot by some unseen magical force on a mission to save the planet," he told us. "A kind of close encounters of the hippie kind."

Before accepting the job, he'd asked to see the drawings for the full-scale operation. They had none. They used bamboo models instead. Richard said he'd "smiled politely and suppressed the urge to say 'that's so fucking stupid.'"

Richard and his Indonesian wife and two children had been looking for a change in lifestyle, so he took the job and oversaw the construction of the school. Then one day, after a long ramble about the evils of heating water, John Hardy decided that instead of utilizing a traditional gas water-heating system, they'd build a sawdust-burning hot water heater which was, essentially, a copper coil inside a box of burning sawdust. The water passing through the coil would be heated by the burning sawdust and stored in an insulated holding tank until needed.

In theory, Richard related, it sounded quite feasible, but as soon as they started to build it, they could not do a thing right.

They had too many coils. Too tiny a pump. They made the box bigger and added more sawdust. Reduced the coils and extended the chimney and re-laid all the pipe to the teachers' housing. When it was finally finished, the water it spat out was limited and it ran cold because of the high demand. And most of the teachers hadn't moved in yet since their huts weren't ready. There was no way the bamboo sawdust water heater would accommodate a whole community of shower-taking, dish-washing humans.

And then there was the smoke. By the end of the first week that Victor and Loy and I were living in our new house, the smoke belching out of the thing blew back through our open window holes, located twenty yards away.

On Sunday night I looked in on Loy's sleeping figure, a swirl of noxious smog dancing around her head where palm sugar fairies were supposed to be. Even though I promised myself I would not complain, I had to say something to Victor.

He was in bed, working on his laptop. Since moving to Bali he'd stopped reading both novels and nonfiction before turning out the lights. Now he just worked. "Bad enough the ants come every night," I said slipping in beside him. "But the smoke? You don't think maybe we should just live with cold water and call it a day?"

He looked around our bedroom at the smoky air. "God, that's a lot of smoke. They can't even get this right. Bad enough we have to live with the smoke from the trash piles and the burning bodies in the cemetery next door. I'll call someone tomorrow. Promise." And then he kissed me goodnight. It was more of a peck than a kiss, but seeing as he was about to make the bamboo smoke go away, I cut him some slack and said nothing about his ever-waning interest in me. I knew he was distracted by the school. I was patient. Or, at least I was trying to be. It was the least I could do.

The next day Victor spoke at length to the heads of all the decision-making cadres who instructed Richard to deconstruct the heater and move it down the road inside the grounds of PT Bambu. Except that Richard got so fed up with John Hardy's never-ending quest for quixotic engineering feats that he quit before finishing the project.

But at least we had no smoke.

And, of course, no hot water.

And sometimes no water either, for that matter.

But I said nothing.

I said nothing because two days before school started Victor came home at lunchtime so enraged that I thought for sure our Bali dream would go by way of the bamboo smoker. "What's going on?" I asked.

He took a pitcher of cold water from the refrigerator and downed two glasses. Seni came downstairs before he could tell me what was up. "*Pak* Victor. You home! I make you some food, *ya*?"

"No, Seni, *suksma*. I ate already."

"Okay, then I go eat my lunch with Ayu," she said, referring to Johnny and Phillipa's *pembantu*.

"Yes, of course." I replied. I knew Victor would be relieved to have Seni out of the house for a little while.

"Victor, what is it?" I asked after she'd gone.

"School is starting Monday, right?" he asked rhetorically. "We're freaked out. All of us. We are not close to being ready to open so we met this morning—that's why I left so early—and we sort of voted on it as a group, you know, that we shouldn't open now but should postpone for a few months."

"Like for how long?"

"I don't know. Personally, I think we should wait six months, one semester, but I was open to other options."

"Of course."

"Anyway, we met with Brad and I spoke first." He went on to describe the scene with the whole lot of them sitting around the big central table in the admin building, the few desk fans barely blowing through the clouds of bugs circling above. Calmly and precisely, Victor listed off the school's most egregious problems, suggesting that the best thing would be for the Hardys to postpone opening for a few months.

Brad had not responded, and instead asked if anyone else had any issues. Victor waited for someone else to talk. Teacher Johnny, as well as Susan, the Kindergarten teacher, and Sinead, the pre-K teacher, made a few weak-kneed comments, but nobody else would look up, let alone speak.

Brad again asked if anyone had more to add. When the room fell silent, he'd appeared self-satisfied that he'd put out a small fire that might have gotten out of control. Before getting up to leave, he informed his faculty that if they were not happy, maybe they should consider finding another job elsewhere because there were a hundred people waiting in line to take their places.

"Why didn't anyone say anything?" I asked, stunned.

"They were afraid."

"Afraid of losing their jobs?"

"Afraid of Brad."

"Oh," I replied, not surprised by what Victor was telling me. I'd wanted to like Brad, I really did, given Victor's initial impression of him as someone who was super smart and profoundly supportive. When I met him back in early July I was surprised how stiff and cold he came off, and I'd mistakenly attributed his perfect posture, slow precise gait, and pen-light direct stare to his professed Buddhist spirituality. Now I knew better.

Victor leaned out over the bamboo railing that circled half the hut and stared at the large spider that had taken up residency on a banana tree outside our living room. I looked at its six-inch-long hairy legs, then looked away.

"I mean, let's be real here," Victor said, turning back to me. "He's the director. We're his teachers. What do you think he should have said?"

"That you, ah … That he will, ah…" I had not an inkling of how best to fill in that blank.

"He should have said, 'Look guys, we know you've all been busting your butts, and yeah, we can see there is still a lot to get ready, and sure we want what's best for the kids, so let's work together to make this a great school,' or … he should have acknowledged the fact that his teachers are 100 percent committed, but we need more help. Better direction. That we're … I don't know. He could have been supportive. Sympathetic. Something. Instead he threatened us."

I still didn't know what to say or do so I sat there.

"Oh, and you're going to love this—Dawn is leaving."

"What? One of the reasons we moved to Bali was because of Dawn. She's supposed to be the best teacher they hired!"

"I know. But she has a good excuse. She's got cancer."

I gulped. "Oh, no! What kind?"

"Breast. And there's no way she can get it treated here. I can't blame her, but it's bad news all around."

As bad as I felt for Dawn, I had my baby to worry about. "Who's going to teach Loy's class?" I asked.

"Andrea. She's from Arizona. She'll be here by the end of next week. I saw her resume, and I gotta say I don't have high expectations—not that I do for any of the replacement teachers. When Brad recruited me he said I'd be joining a team of teachers any one of whom you could build a school around. Rock stars. The replacements they're finding are not ones you build a premier international school around. I mean, they're showing up without acclimating. They'll have had no orientation, no training. It stinks for the kids."

At that moment, I saw Seni and Loy making their way through the muddy path toward our hut. Seni was holding her hand.

"I'm just hoping—oh hi, kiddo," Victor said, cutting his thoughts off before they veered too far into the unpleasant unknown.

"Hi, Daddy," Loy said before running up to her room, presumably to nurse her baby doll.

I sighed, grateful that someone was going to get what they needed, even it that someone was made of plastic.

Green School wasn't ready to open its bamboo doors, but one hundred children from around the globe showed up for their first day. It was on a hot Monday morning at the end of August. Victor, along with the other main teachers—and their Western and Indonesian co-teachers—stood in front of their classrooms with eager smiles on their faces, a fierce love of teaching in their hearts, and more than a hint of disquiet in their minds. Green School—the reason we moved to Bali—was in session.

It was a great first day—for the kids at least. They didn't seem to care about the bugs and the noise and the heat. They loved the muddy fields and the wall-less classrooms and the bamboo water fountains. For a ten-year-old kid from South Africa, Green School was heaven. The teachers, though electrified by the adventure of it and dedicated to the success of their students were, by Friday afternoon, exhausted and frustrated.

A few weeks into the semester I awoke, thinking it would be another typically atypical day. I had just tossed a scoopful of bamboo sawdust into the bamboo toilet when Loy yelled down through the slats in the bamboo ceiling above me.

"Mommy! Did you spray my clothes yet? I need to get ready for school."

"No, sweetie," I yelled back up through her bedroom floor. "I want to take a cold shower first. Make sure you stay inside the mosquito net till I'm done." Since moving to Bali I'd learned that while Japanese Encephalitis was virtually non-existent, it was quite common for locals to catch dengue fever—more poetically referred to as "break-bone fever." The vector that transmits dengue is the *Aedes* mosquito, known to be most active in the early morning.

"Just stay in your bed," I repeated upwards as I twisted the shower handle to ON.

After two seconds, I turned it back to OFF then to ON again.

"Victor," I said through the bamboo door, "the water's off again. Can you please call Putu or Kumar or someone in administration?"

"I already called. No one answered."

"Could you maybe call again or email—"

I heard a grunt, then the drop or deliberate hurling of a metal utensil into the sink, and then: "Lisa. Do you really have to take a shower right now?"

"Well, yeah, I'm really sweaty," I replied, the door a comforting barrier between us.

"I'm sorry, but you're going to have to stay sweaty. Brad wants me to come up with a report card template and I still have prep to do. I promise I'll let someone know when I get to class."

I wanted to wash the night's layer of salt off me and feel fresh. As I stood there, naked, sticky, frustrated, I tied my sarong around my waist. Exasperated, I untied and tied it again. No matter how many times Seni showed me the proper Balinese way to wrap the batiked skirt around my belly, it always took me three, sometimes four, tries before I could stop worrying about the sarong flapping open and exposing my underwear to the many Balinese and Javanese workers who surrounded our hut on a daily basis.

I came out of the bathroom in my crookedly tied sarong to find Victor sitting up on a bamboo stool with his laptop open on the kitchen counter.

Over his shoulder, I could see the partially drawn report card on his screen. I suppressed the urge to quote from our Skype conversation back in May when he was being interviewed here. Back when he'd said there was "so much that's still not in place," but he had "the sense that they mostly have their shit together." I wanted to ask him how he'd been so blind, but I'd asked him that question too many times already. His answer was always the same: he still believed in John Hardy's vision, and he still had faith that somehow Brad would come through and work with the management team to fix the pervasive disorganization running rampant. He still believed, ultimately, that everything would work out.

Victor and his persistent hopefulness. I loved him so much for seeing through to the light, even when someone throws a hood over his head.

Without a word, I stepped out onto our bamboo deck, spread out the arms and legs of Loy's tiny pink shirt and khaki pants, and saturated them with DEET-containing bug spray. I knew it was toxic, and I wasn't about to put that carcinogen/mutagen/teratogen directly onto Loy's skin, but I was going to use what I could to keep those bone-cracking bugs away from my delicious child.

I turned the shirt and pants over and doused the other sides, then whipped them up and down, so they'd dry faster. When Katy, the school's fifty-something academic support specialist, waved at me from her living room couch, I waved the pink shirt back at her.

"Morning, Katy!"

"Good morning, Lisa!"

"You don't have any water, do you?"

"Nope. I think those guys are moving the line again or something." She pointed at the four Javanese men digging a hole by the now-defunct bamboo sawdust water heater. "Bummer, huh?"

"Yeah. Bummer." I touched the pants to see if they were dry.

"Hey, I hope I didn't play my DVD too loud last night."

Of course, you did. We live ten feet apart and neither of our huts have walls. You watched Enchanted *for the third time.* "No, no. All I heard were the bugs," I politely lied before going upstairs.

I found Loy lounging on her net-protected bed, a book propped open against her raised knees. "Hi, baby," I said leaning in to give her a kiss, a tickle, and her clothing.

"Hi, Mommy. A bat just flew by my bed."

I looked up and out into the jungle surrounding our hut. "I don't think so," I said while considering what else might have flown by. "I'm pretty sure bats are only nocturnal."

"That means nighttime, right? What's the word for daytime birds?"

"Diurnal. Now get dressed. Daddy is leaving soon."

After delivering the prophylactic ensemble, I came downstairs to drink the cup of tea Victor had made for me. For fourteen years, he'd made my morning tea, whether we lived in a blue house on a hill in the Sierra Nevadas or in a mold-coated, ant-infested bamboo hut in Bali.

"How's it going?" I asked, wiping a mob of ants off the honey jar.

"Fine. I'm just really busy."

"Shouldn't they have had report cards figured out by now? I mean, it's almost October."

"Uh-huh." He stood up, pulled his watch out of his front pocket and looked at the time. It was an action that reminded me of my grandfather, who'd pull his silver pocket watch out of his slacks a hundred times a day and check it quickly, before sliding it down the silk pocket liner with a whispery hiss. Back in California Victor never took his watch off, but here in hot soggy Bali, sweat pooled under the leather band and gave him a heat rash, so he carried it instead of wearing it.

As I twisted the honey cap back on, my hands got sticky. I went over to the sink but stopped mid-reach. "Damn. I can't even rinse my hands off."

"Use a piece of ice."

"Good idea, thanks," I replied. I was still a little mad at him for not getting the water turned on. Petty yes, but after many weeks of living like this, a missing shower seemed ominously close to that one last straw. I grabbed an ice cube, rubbed it between my sticky fingers until I had cold wet sticky fingers. "Actually, not such a good idea," I said as I tried to scrape the goo off with a dish towel.

"Oh well, I tried."

I looked at him to see if he was either teasing me or being mean and I noticed how smooth his face looked.

"How did you manage to shave?" I asked.

"I got up two hours ago when there was water, but you know what, I have a job to go to. What are your plans for the day? Are you going to do some writing today?"

Before I could throw out some excuse about how it was all but impossible to get inspired in this hot noisy place, Loy came bounding down the bamboo stairs. "Baby, you can't brush your teeth," I said as she walked into the bathroom. "There's no water."

"Oh, yay," she said.

"Come here and let me put bug stuff on you."

"No, I want to eat my breakfast."

"Let her eat some cereal first."

"Excuse me?" I had the tube in my hand, waiting to be squeezed. "You don't get bit by mosquitoes, but they swarm her so please don't tell me what to do."

"Fine. Whatever. Do what you want. You're going to— "

I thought he might finish his accusation, but he answered his cell phone instead.

"I can't. I have the kids down at the river at 8:30," he said into the outdated Nokia. I listened while smearing Mosi-guard, a non-toxic, anti-critter crème all over Loy's exposed dermis.

"No. Yes. Okay, fine I will, but I want it known that I think it's a really bad call on the administration's part."

He pushed the red button and flung the phone across the counter, much like I imagined he did with the spoon just minutes earlier. He closed his eyes and put his hands together on top of his head.

"What?" I asked, trying to snap him out of his deep thought mode. A truck filled with workers rumbled by on the dirt road just outside the hut.

"Yeah, Daddy. What?" Loy said through a mouthful of wildly expensive granola imported from Australia.

"An English-language Chinese newspaper is coming to do a story about the school. I'd planned to have the kids down at the river learning about currents at eight-thirty, but no, that's when the reporter and photographer want to show up and of course they want pictures of the kids in my classroom."

"Gotta sell the school first, right?" It'd been like that ever since we landed: anything to get media attention. John Hardy was hoping to recruit more children wanting to pay the $10,000-a-year tuition to attend his one-of-a-kind, all-bamboo institution. Whenever any newsperson or potential parent wanted a tour, everyone had to drop what they were doing and put on a show. While all the teachers had open-aired classrooms constructed out of bamboo, Victor's 7th/8th-grade classroom had the one and only ridiculously useless canvas BUBBLE. If it got too hot to teach (which was more or less *always*), Victor was supposed to inflate the bubble with the feeble air-conditioning unit attached to it and teach inside it. He never did because the material smelled bad and the air inside never got remotely cool, let alone conditioned. With the entire class assembled inside, it felt a lot like teaching in a tent. "I'd rather sweat all day than breathe that air," he remarked the first and last time he tried to teach a lesson on Indonesian politics in there. "The kids got it right when they said it smelled like wet dog mixed with burning pencil erasers."

But whenever the media came a callin', the edict came down from above: RAISE THE BUBBLE!

"I just don't get it." He closed his laptop harder than usual. "This place..."

"What?" I asked. "This place what?"

"They want us to teach sustainability, but there's nothing sustainable in the way they treat us. We're like guinea pigs in a bad experiment. They made me so many promises and still haven't come through. This hut isn't ready. There's no hot water; hell, now there's no water. The kids don't have computers to work on, but I have a bubble that does nothing. At some point, they're going to have to face the fact that..."

What? They're going to have to face the fact that all the teachers (and their spouses) are being pushed too close to the edge and some are about to fall over? Or that some might actually jump off?

I held my tongue and waited for him to say something, but he started packing up his laptop in silence. I kissed Loy's mouth, told her to have the best day ever and when I turned to say goodbye to Victor, I saw the sadness on his face. I wanted to tell him that he needed to face the facts: we hated it here. Victor hated the falseness of the school. He wanted to teach kids and not have to deal with what was turning out to be yet another example of Western exploitation. I hated the heat. I hated being inundated by construction noise and smoke from burning trash and burning bodies from the cemetery next door. Loy hated it because her parents were cranky all the time.

I knew we should go back to California, but I couldn't say that out loud. I didn't need to remind Victor that we'd be better off leaving this place. He knew it. The sinister-looking red and yellow bug crawling up the kitchen wall knew it. The gecko hovering over the bookcase in the corner knew it. That mosquito flying by Loy's hand knew it—

"Loy, there's a mosquito on your arm!" I yelled, diving for it as it bit into my supposedly mosquito-proofed child. She quickly slapped it flat. Before I could say a word she looked at it, narrowing her eyes into child-made magnifying glasses.

"You guys," she said, "it's a dengue fever mosquito." She handed the remains to me. Sure enough it had the black and white body, the telltale markings of the dreaded *Aedes aegypti*.

"Oh, my God!" I shouted, already visualizing the deadly venom racing through her bloodstream.

"Lisa. Stop it."

"I can't fucking believe this." I threw the dead bug on the floor and slammed my hand on the counter. Out of the corner of my eye I saw Sam, the 5th/6th grade teacher who'd replaced Carol, heading down the path toward school. I was certain he'd heard every word I'd yelled as he passed by our hut. Unintentional eavesdropping was a way of life on campus.

"Lisa," Victor said in a calm even voice. "I said stop."

"What am I supposed to stop? You want me to stop worrying that in five days she might get a fever of 105 degrees and break out in a rash all over her entire body? Or that she'll develop a skull-crushing headache and her body will feel like all her bones are breaking?" I could feel my brain turning black.

"Lisa, please."

"You want me to shut up?" I came closer and moved my face right next to his. "Do you also want me to *not* freak out that just maybe she'll get the kind of dengue that turns into hemorrhagic fever which is almost always fatal to children?"

"Mommy? What are you saying to Daddy?"

"Nothing, Loy. Mommy's saying nothing." He zipped his backpack closed and lowered his voice. "Lisa, you're scaring Loy, and that's not okay. Remember when she got that rash back in July that turned out to be nothing? You said you'd try not to be so paranoid all the time."

I held my hands on my hips, conveniently grabbing hold of my slowly slipping sarong. "This is different," I said as I backed away from him and stared at my daughter's bitten arm.

"No, it's not. The odds of her getting dengue are pretty small and you know it."

"I know the odds are small, but there's still a chance!" A crack of thunder blasted overhead.

"There's also a chance I get hit by lightning, or by one of the cars and trucks that blast by here every day, or the goddamn bubble collapses on me and I suffocate! Christ, Lisa. You know this is not the time or place to be fighting." Just as he finished his sentence a torrential rain started. Victor reached over the front door gate and grabbed two umbrellas. "I have to go teach. Loy has to go to school. And you know how fun it is to teach when I'm soaked all day? No, you wouldn't. You wouldn't—forget it. We shouldn't have to deal with this shit just as we're about to begin our day."

"Well, I don't want to deal with this shit, either." I tried not to be nasty, but I kept falling further into the darkness.

"*You* don't have to deal with this shit," he retorted in an ever-rising octave.

"Since when don't I deal with shit? I don't deal with shit all day? The rain and the noise and the mold and the—"

"No, you don't. You get to escape it. You get to go for a walk when you want, when it's not raining, and come home and drink iced coconut juice, and write when you feel like writing. You go into town and get massaged and take yourself out for lunch in air-conditioned restaurants while I sweat all day in a classroom and eat steamed fish mush in banana leaves." He took Loy's hand in his. "I'm sorry you hate it here so much and I'm sorry that it wasn't what we thought it was going to be but like it or not, we're here."

I should have just shut up and waved goodbye to them. Instead I started in with, "Yeah, well, we shouldn't have to—"

"Just wait a minute!" Now he was really pissed. "*You* were the one who wanted me to apply. You remember helping me write that letter? Do you? That was you. It's too late now to change your mind. We're committed, okay? I made a commitment when I signed that contract."

Inexplicably I did it again. "But you didn't sign on to living in a half-built hut with—"

"Screw what I signed on to. If I commit to something or *someone*, I stay committed, no matter how bad it is."

I was about to shout the perfect response, when he added, "I'm still married to you, aren't I? Come on, Loy. Let's go."

That was the meanest thing he'd said to me in fourteen years, and boy did it get me defensive. As they slid their feet into their flip-flops I tried to think of a few invectives I could fling in order to out-mean him. I was about to slam one across the bamboo floor when he walked over to me and beat me to the punch.

"Lisa," he said in a low bare voice. "You promised you'd try to make the best of it no matter what we found here, but all you do is tell us how much you're suffering. And now you're trying to make us suffer along with you."

"But I'm honestly trying to—"

"Shut up and let me finish. Listen. It's your choice. Either you give in, change and help make this okay for all of us," he said, slinging his backpack over his shoulders, "or *you* go back to California."

It felt like he'd punched me in the chest. I could almost feel my lungs closing down. A surreal feeling—a thrust of emotion that marked a shift in my entire world—washed over me. At that tick of time I wanted more than anything to go home. But there in front of me were my husband and child, which meant I was home.

When did *home* become so unfamiliar and terrifying?

"You want me to go?"

He looked at me. Behind him Loy opened her umbrella. I wanted to tell her it was bad luck to open an umbrella in the house, but I'd already placed too many burdens on her tiny shoulders for one day.

"You really want me to go?" I repeated, as if by asking it again it'd make him take it back.

"Where's Mommy's going?" Loy asked, twirling her pink umbrella with all the innocence of a dengue-free six-year-old.

"At this point," he said reaching out to take hold of our daughter, "it sounds like a pretty good idea to me, because what's going on here is fucked and I'm done with it. I gotta go to work. Have a nice day."

"Bye, Mommy."

"Bye, Loy."

The moment after they walked off down the lava rock path into the rain, I regretted everything I'd said and done. Why did I have to push him? Why couldn't I be happy where I was, happy to be by his side here in a place people call paradise? This was Victor's dream; he genuinely wanted to make the world a better place. I should do all I could to support him.

I said, "I'm such an idiot sometimes" out loud, but there was no one around to hear me. Other than Katy over there buttering her toast, and Mr. Gecko over there in the corner basking in the sun.

I retied my sarong with my sticky hands and gazed up at the tree growing through the middle of our hut. I looked at the insidious mold spreading up the sides of the bamboo dining-room chairs and the bamboo walls and the bamboo bookcase and the—I looked at the laptop that lay open inside the mosquito net. I should email Victor. Tell him he's right and I need to grow up. Or maybe I should tell him he's right and I will leave for California as soon as I can buy a ticket out of this nightmare.

California. Crisp clean safe California.

Of course, I'd take Loy with me.

Where would we live? What would I do for money?

Had my husband said his life would be better if I went away? Fourteen years? Just like that? Gone?

The rain stopped as quickly as it had begun. I had to get out of the hut, had to go somewhere else before I started throwing random objects at the stray dog that just peed on my front stoop. Before I started searching Expedia for airfares.

I needed to go for a walk. A meditative walk through the jungle where I could gather what was left of me.

Where I could cool off.

While I changed out of my sarong and into a pair of shorts that could not unravel, I pictured Victor telling me to go back to California. His angry words stung me as I slathered my skin with Mosi-guard, then put on my hat and sunglasses and opened the gate. I walked down the lava-rock path with my head down. I had no interest in engaging in the per usual friendly give-and-take with the Javanese workers who cleaned the mud off the lava rock paths after heavy rains.

"*Selamat pagi.* [Good morning]," I couldn't help but utter as I passed by.

Before we arrived in Bali we tried to learn some Bahasa niceties, the three of us on our thirty-hour journey across sixteen time zones, flipping through the *Lonely Planet* pocket phrasebook, quizzing each other. "How do you say, 'How are you?'"

"*Apa* ... ah, I don't remember." That was me.

"*Apa kabar?*" Loy.

"How about 'Yes'?"

I jumped on that one. "*Ya.*"

"And 'no' is *tidak.*" Victor.

"Right, Daddy. Now how would you say that you're fine?"

"*Di mana?*"

"No, Mommy. That's how you ask where something is. Sheesh. You say *baik* if you're fine."

"What about 'My name is...'" Victor asked his two girls.

"*Nama saya* Loy."

Okay, it wasn't a contest, but after an hour I'd thrown the book at Victor, turned around, and put on my headphones. Loy's brain could obviously hold more newly acquired information because she was six, not forty-seven, as I was. Plus, I was going through peri-menopause, and had twice experimented with hallucinogenic drugs.

"*Pagi!*" the crouching dirt-soaked group replied. I could feel their stunned eyes on me as I passed by, affronted, I am sure, by my uncharacteristically impolite silence. They mumbled a few words that I could not translate in the slightest; for all I knew they were more relieved than I to skip over the badinage for a day.

The only place to take a walk near the campus without getting run over by motorcycles was along the trails bordering the *subak*, the miles and miles of irrigation canals that watered Bali's multitudinous rice paddies. Before I could get to the closest one, I first had to wend and wind my way through the village of *Sibang Kaja*.

I followed the road down past the administration hut until I came to the long, thick bamboo pole that ran across the entryway—the school's absurd attempt at security.

"*Pagi.*" I waved to Wayan, Putu's boyfriend.

"*Ibu* Lisa! *Selamat pagi, Ibu* Lisa! You are good? *Baik*?" Wayan said, all but festooning me with a garland of flowers and showering me with confetti because I helped get him his job.

No, Wayan, nothing about my morning so far can be construed as good.

"*Ya, baik, baik. Suksma,*" I added, thanking him for asking after my welfare before moving on toward PT Bambu, the factory down the street where all the structures and furniture for the huts and classrooms got built. No one had yet to come out and say as much, but it was obvious that part of the reason John Hardy opened the school was to use it as his living, breathing bamboo showroom; a way to show off the amazing things one could do with bamboo. He and his designers hoped that the rich expatriates who moved to Bali to enroll their kids at Green School would buy the high-priced furnishings for their compounds. That would make for a highly sustainable enterprise—for some folks, anyway.

I could hear the annoying mewl of the bamboo sanders behind the towering bamboo gates and held my breath as I walked by. I'd read that bamboo contains silica and breathing in too much of its dust can cause silicosis, which is a lot like asbestosis. I kept my distance, picturing the hundreds of workers behind the gates breathing in the bamboo dust as their ragged dust masks hung uselessly from their sweating faces.

I saw Kumar, the new general manager of both the school and the factory, talking to a pair of Balinese workers, his lovely Indian head slowly pendulating back and forth on his neck like a metronome. He glanced over at me with a pained smile. He was a robust man, about six feet tall, with narrow eyes set deep in a flawless face. I'd always thought of Indian men as being slight, and Kumar was slight, but only in the way he moved, not in his body. You couldn't hear him when he walked into a room. You could hardly hear him when he spoke. Yet he wielded considerable power on campus. The teachers and their families were recently instructed to take any of their concerns to him.

Kumar had moved to Bali soon after Ted the business manager quit, and after Richard, the only certified engineer on campus, left over his disagreement with John Hardy about how to get hot water to the teachers' huts. Kumar no longer had an expert around to assure him the buildings on campus wouldn't come crashing down. Days after he arrived, the ceiling fan in Loy's classroom dislodged at high speed and spun down to the floor, thankfully failing to decapitate any of the first and second graders. After a worker found a faulty attachment, Kumar ordered that all ceiling fans—in every hut and every classroom—be removed, fitted with a safety bar, and replaced. I, for one, had applauded his cautious overkill.

On top of that fiasco there was this week's discovery of a thick crack in the eight-foot-high mud retaining wall surrounding the third-grade classroom. There was also the issue of what to do about that water-logged, root-protruding, very tall tree growing less than ten feet from the Kindergarten hut. And the poisonous snake found under the desk of an eighth grader. And the fact that no permanent school nurse had been hired. And only yesterday a fifth grader came screaming by me as I brought Loy her lunch, his eyes on fire because he and a friend were horsing around and he fell into one of the jalapeño bushes growing next to his classroom.

No wonder Kumar's smile looked so pained.

I tried not to catch his eye, but—dammit—he saw me and waved me over.

"Good morning, Miss Lisa. You are well?" he asked after shooing away the two workers as if they were annoying flies.

"Hi. Um..." It was impossible to speak while holding my breath.

"I am apologizing for the water having to be off. I hope you have not been too inconvenienced."

"Well, I would really like to take a shower." I almost oscillated my head. "When do you think it will be fixed?"

"The men, the ones I have fixing it, we are trying a new method in the factory," he said, gesturing behind him.

I nodded, trying not to breathe in too much of the dusty air.

"Other than the water situation, are there other complaints or worries that you wish to speak with me about?"

Before I could say something like, "Oh, Mister, do I ever! Do you have an hour to kill?" he pulled his ringing cell phone out of his black uncreased slacks. I subtly unstuck my T-shirt from my chest, noticing that Kumar's white cotton shirt looked downright billowy. Standing there with this large dry man under a meltingly hot Balinese sun became too much for me, and I had to move on. I smiled, pointed my thumb in that "gotta go over there" direction, and fled.

I circled around the factory, heading east, and held my breath again. When John Hardy went looking for a location for the school, he found cheap land across from a cemetery, which saved him a couple hundred million rupiah. In the Balinese Hindu tradition, a person who dies is buried; but only until the family of the deceased can afford to dig up what's left of the corpse, and burn the remains atop a funeral pyre. It can often take years to save enough money for the death dowry since the cremation ceremony is as extravagant as a Hollywood wedding, complete with weeks of preparation, bounteous food, music, and the making of much merriment.

And ashes.

And starving dogs that try to snatch the burning bones.

Okay, it's a little different than a Hollywood wedding.

Living across the street from a cemetery was like being a vegan at a never-ending pig roast. As I passed by the open cement temple area, I looked to the sky for a sign of funereal smoke, but the villagers and their dead relatives were quiet.

I lowered my head and saw John Hardy careening down the road on his bicycle. I looked at the ground, hoping he wouldn't see me because having to listen to one of his bombastic soliloquies about the greatness of bamboo or the evils of power companies or the quickly disappearing Balinese culture, was the last thing I wanted to do.

John Hardy may have created an international name for himself sculpting highly desirable upscale jewelry inspired by peace and love and nature and harmony, but he came off as an uncouth, patronizing boor in person. He had great ideas, but the way he expressed himself made it impossible to be within ten feet of him when he opened his mouth, particularly when he ranted about the Balinese people. He wanted to keep Bali "Balinese," in a demented reverse-colonialist kind of way, almost taking it personally that the Balinese culture was sinking under the weight of western-style media and technology. He relegated all Balinese behavior into two categories: Good Bali and Bad Bali. Aspiring to own a television or car and not dressing in traditional clothing was Bad Bali. Washing clothes by hand or praying daily to the gods—Good Bali.

Opening a private school where only twenty percent of the students were Balinese—under which heading would that fall?

And now he was heading straight for me. I hoped he'd fail to recognize me as the wife of one of his teachers, as he'd done countless times before. My heart sank as he approached and the squeal of his brakes got louder. But he was only stopping to answer his cell phone. I walked past him and his tight spandex shorts as he yelled at whoever was on the other end.

For at least twenty feet I kept my eyes fixed downward, making it hard to ignore the heaps of garbage clogging the drainage ditch that ran alongside the road, a river of scummy water pushing past pink and blue and green plastic bags, cigarettes, candy wrappers. A pregnant dog with more mange than fur ran out from an alleyway to yark at me—my term for the Balinese dogs' shrill cross between a yap and a bark.

"Yark! Yark!" she warned, expecting me to kick her or something worse, because most Balinese people hate dogs. They believe that past sinners get reincarnated as street dogs, and the only reason Balinese people suffer the presence of dogs is because they also believe these former murderers and thieves are malevolent enough to ward off even scarier demons.

I crossed quickly to the other side of the street, whereupon a straggle of village children whose parents probably couldn't afford to send them to school (public school in Bali costs $15/month) came screaming out of their family compound to chase the dog away.

I said *"pagi"* to the children who were both awed and spooked by my use of their language. One little girl, beautiful in her green sundress, bare feet, and dirty knees, yelled, "Hello!" and scampered off to join her friends. I continued on my way, holding my breath every time a motorbike with its suffocating two-stroke engine smoked by.

I turned at the corner of the main road that went to all points south, whereupon the stuff of Balinese village life percolated up through my ears and eyes and nose. *Sibang Kaja* is not by any stretch of one's imagination a tourist village. There are no shadow puppet shows or souvenir shops peddling Balinese arts and crafts. No pizza joints or cafes selling yoga-wear. You will not find stores filled with sunglasses or stone carvings in a village located thirty minutes from the trendy tourist town of Ubud, or ninety minutes from Bali's famous beaches.

What you'll find instead is some basic commerce and a few street vendors hawking their specialty foods out of tiny metal stands, the steam or smoke spreading the air with the scent of meat and spice. There was the *babi guling* (roasted pig) man next to the *bakso* (meatballs) guy. Across the street was the saté man, long sticks of some fat-spewing mammal sizzling across the coals. This is not the picture your travel agent paints for you when she coaxes you and your betrothed into spending your honeymoon here. This is just a typical Balinese village where people burn their garbage out on the broken sidewalks, and men sit around chewing the fat, literally.

I ran across the main street to avoid getting sideswiped by a family of four on a single motorbike. I watched it speed off, shaking my head with parental outrage when I saw the small baby perched between the driver's legs wearing no helmet. No one on the bike wore one.

Then I remembered Loy's bug bite and felt a burn of fear across my chest. I replayed the fight I had with Victor; him telling me to leave, and the heat spread from my chest to my back, my face, my eyes. The fear crawled deep inside me. Sickened me. The fear and stress and sweat and noise. I swallowed hard, trying to pull into my mouth the sweet taste of love, the true and deep friendship that Victor and I had always known, but all I could taste was bitter smoke from the smoldering piles of trash surrounding me.

Where the hell was I, and what was I supposed to do now?

I stopped walking and leaned against the side of a building, resting my cheek against the cool cement. I wiped the salty, sweaty wetness from my face and dried my hand on the front of my shirt. I might have stayed propped up there all day with my tear-filled eyes closed, listening to the yarking dogs and crowing cocks; but I needed to decide if I had it in me to stay in Bali and keep my marriage from disintegrating. The only place to think clearly was in the jungle, the blessedly quiet, smoke-free Balinese jungle.

I turned off the blacktop, down the dirt lane on the right, past the building with the blue sign that read CAT OVEN (paint-drying garage). I adjusted my baseball cap on my sweat-soaked head. I glanced to my left and waved to the man standing next to his burning pile of GodKnowsWhat, then proceeded past the aged, topless lady raking around in her cassava field, her long sagging breasts swaying back and forth, almost touching the top edge of a once colorful sarong. In a fit of futile habit, I waved, but she didn't wave back. She never waved back.

I skirted a pair of small dogs, narrowing my eyes so I couldn't focus on either of them. I was too afraid of what I might see. One step … two … "Go! Shoo!" I yelled, keeping my gaze to the left. "Why are you following me? Do you—" Darn. I looked. One of them was a puppy with ribs so distinct I could have picked him up sideways like a small pocketbook. I had nothing to offer him. I should have grabbed that last piece of toast off the counter for the strays, especially since I knew that by the time I got back home the ants would have had their way with it.

I held my breath and flew by the entire length of a chicken tent packed with thousands of newborn chicks warming themselves under grow-lights. The Indonesian news had recently reported a major Avian Flu outbreak and warned people to steer clear of chickens. Hadn't we ordered Loy to hold her breath whenever she walked anywhere near a chicken? Had I just breathed in any chicken ether? Did I have enough Tamiflu back at the hut?

At the end of the lane I stepped in something squishy and green but didn't bother with any CSI: Bali-style forensics as I scraped it off against a rock. I didn't want to know what it'd been or where'd it been or who it might have been a part of. When I reached the edge of the jungle, I was briefly attacked by a swarm of something out of an entomologist's wet dream. To be on the safe side, I wiped a travel-handy Buzz Away Extreme Towelette all over me, and headed into the thick.

Before long I got to the Coconut Challenge, the 100-yard-long row of coconut palm trees bulging with plump fruit. I didn't know if it was an urban legend, but I'd heard lots of Balinese people have been killed by plummeting coconuts. I wasn't about to take any chances.

Ready. I made sure my sneakers were tied.

Set. I pulled my hair-tie tight.

Go. With a hand on my head—as if that would keep me from sustaining a serious brain injury from a large weight falling more than fifty feet—I tore down the path, stopping when the trees ran out, to double over and catch my breath.

At this point in my walk I usually took out a plastic bag that I'd stashed in a pocket so I could pick as many frangipani as I could find. Seni's mother-in-law sold the flowers for pennies per kilo: a little pocket change for the old woman who watched Seni's boys while she worked for us.

But today I picked no flowers. I just walked. And thought and sweated and cursed Bali and apologized to Victor and called myself nasty names and swatted mosquitoes and fretted about Loy's bite and scratched at three welts on my arm and readjusted my underwear and thought some more. I thought about what it'd be like to live without Victor. I fantasized the beginning, middle, and end to the story where Loy and I sneak off in the middle of the night and we fly back to California and Victor hates me so much he never speaks to me again.

I passed by Cuma, the old farmer who had muscles like Jack LaLanne, hacking at a tree with his machete. I said hello in Balinese. He returned the hello in English (he used to be a teacher), and went back to hacking.

I came around a bend and saw a naked mother bathing her young child in the canal. The woman was stunning; her dark hair floating freely in the water like an oil slick. I knew she'd be embarrassed if I acknowledged her so I pretended she was invisible and fixed my eyes on the dirt path.

I wondered if Victor and Loy would be happier if I were invisible. Gone.

What if I left? Went back to a solitary existence in California. Again, I tried to picture a life without them, the two bookends to my reality, and I almost toppled over like so many dog-eared books on a wobbly shelf.

What a sick mind. What kind of parent wonders if her child would be better off without her? I thought about disappearing entirely and for a few moments I imagined throwing myself, Ophelia-like, into the waterway. I needed purging. I had to rid myself of this unhappiness I had roiling around inside me—the blaming, the anger, the discontent. I wanted more than anything to again be the third member of that spirited threesome we used to be.

How was I to find my way there again?

I heard the sound of an engine and looked up, surprised to see someone coming down the pathway, on a motorcycle, no less. I'd walked this trail at least a dozen times and rarely saw another person. Certainly not one on a motorcycle.

The driver was a young man—twenty-something, and there was something about the look on his face that made me uncomfortable. He didn't have that lazy, contented expression most Balinese men have. This guy had a sort of sultry sneer you'd see on a barfly in Los Angeles, angling for a new fish to hook onto his tanned arm.

He pulled up next to me and cut the engine. I almost expected a "Hey, babe, whatcha doing out here all by yourself?" to fall from his mouth.

He had a gun slung over his shoulder "*Selamat pagi,*" I said nervously. Obviously, he'd been hunting. Hunting what? What was in that large bumpy bag tied onto the seat behind him? He asked me something—I think he wanted to know if I was Australian—and then he pushed back in his seat and the bag jiggled and out fell an arm. A monkey's arm.

He had a bag of dead monkeys.

My tongue's tip felt around for *why*. I mean, Hindus revered monkeys. Surely there had to be a reason why this man would shoot—

"*Makan?*" I asked, putting my hand to my mouth as if I were eating. Did he shoot the monkeys to eat them?

He said, "*tidak*," then he spoke so quickly that I understood no part of his supposed explanation. I could make out no reasonable reason for shooting monkeys out of their trees.

The man with the gun waited for me to reply, but all I could do was stand there staring at the bag of formerly playful, adorable, innocent monkeys. I willed him to drive off so I wouldn't have to see that arm anymore, that small hairy arm. A few seconds ticked off. He waited for me to say something. I waited for him to shoot me, too, because maybe he'd just broken the law and thought I'd turn him in. In fact, I should ask his name so if he did let me go I could go to the police and have him arrested.

"His name was Wayan, Officer."

"Wayan? Okay, since the Balinese naming system basically uses only four names per gender, that narrows it down to about a quarter of all Balinese males. What did he look like?"

"Uh, brown hair. Brown eyes. Dark skin."

"Well, *that's* certainly helpful."

I did a quick scan of his bike, looking for some unique detail, a license plate, something. There was nothing.

He unslung his gun and—he *was* going to kill me. I could yell loudly; maybe Cuma or the naked mother would hear me. What was the word for HELP—and then he put it on his other shoulder and zoomed off before I remembered "*BANTUAN!*"

Bantuan. Help.

I stood in the middle of the path and waited for my heart to stop palpitating. What should I do? Who should I tell? Where should I go now?

Nothing.

No one.

Nowhere.

There was not a bit of anything I could do. I was in Bali, halfway around the world from my blue house on the hill.

I ran, trying to fix on the smell of the frangipani, the sound of the moving water beside me, the high-pitched babel of insects, the shifting lashes of the wind on palm fronds, the faraway yark of a dog . . . but all I could see was that arm. That little bitty arm.

When I came upon the last open meadow where I usually turned around I heard a screech and looked up. There, in the trees, I saw monkeys. Blessedly live monkeys. Lots of them swinging, eating, playing, roughhousing. Did they know that some of their relatives had just been murdered? Is this how they grieved? No sitting shiva for these primates, no.

I watched them for a long time. I wanted their joyous chatter to expel the gruesome images from my mind, but I couldn't escape the arm. I looked at my cell phone. I wanted to call Victor and tell him to leave his classroom and come out here now so we could stand together, holding hands, and watch the monkeys play.

When I turned around I saw a large male monkey in the center of the path staring at me.

He seemed angry. How anthropomorphically lame of me to think that.

But honestly. That look on his face. He looked mad.

I spoke to him in my best lulling mommy voice: "Hi there, big guy. Did someone in your family die this morning? Do you see I don't have a gun? Look, here are my two hands. No gun. It wasn't me. I don't know why that horrible man shot your friends. It made me sad, too. Really sad. I—"

And suddenly that enormous monkey charged down the path toward me, yowling this horrific KRAAAAAAAA!!!! bark and baring his three-inch-long, razor sharp fangs. As he got up close, he lunged at my ankle. I felt the slash of his teeth as they ripped into my flesh, saw the blood spurt out, emptying my femoral artery in a matter of seconds.

I screamed half a lung through my throat then fell to my knees in a quavering whimpering mass.

… Only the thing is … he didn't bite me. He never touched me.

He just wanted to scare me. Teach me a lesson. Make it clear that he'd had enough of us gun-toting humans and we'd better go crawl back into that bamboo hole of ours and STAY OUT, because he's mad as hell and he's not going to take it anymore.

I caught my breath and slowly stood up, grateful for my totally intact left leg. I looked around for monkey man and saw him sitting in the field twenty feet away, his angry back facing me, a breeze rustling his fur. He couldn't even look at me, I so sickened him. The other monkeys stared in hostile silence from their perches in the trees above me. I kept my eyes fixed on that back as I calmly, quietly, tiptoed down the path until I could no longer see him.

I took off running so blindingly fast, that I completely forgot to put a protective hand on my head as I raced back through the coconut trees.

I ran to Victor's classroom without stopping—dodging old ladies, hurdling chickens, bounding through piles of decomposing offal as if they were merely crunchy leaves on an autumn day. By the time I came up behind my best friend in the whole world and grabbed his arm I'm sure I smelled like carrion.

"What the—Lisa? What happened?" Victor asked, his eyes taking in my flaming red face.

"A monkey," I said heaving my hot breath in and out, "charged me … tried to … he almost bit me. His teeth. Jesus, his teeth … this close to my leg … would have ripped…" I sat down and started shaking.

"Wicked!" came the voice of an auditorially keen adolescent.

Sara, Victor's co-teacher, appeared by Victor's side. "A monkey charged you?"

"No, well, it did, but it didn't bite me, or actually touch me, but ... oh God, it was so scary."

Victor twisted open his water bottle and handed it to me. I drank down half of it in one gulp, my mouth anticipating some of the crushed ice he'd filled it with this morning, but there wasn't even a sliver left. How long ago had it been that he'd stood by the freezer, getting both himself and Loy ready for school, before I began screaming at him because of a mosquito? I wiped off the lukewarm water that had dripped onto my chin and looked at Victor's face for some reasonable sign of everlasting love. I saw none.

When he placed his hand gently on my shoulder I almost wept with relief, but I didn't want to make a scene. Well, actually, I did want to make a scene. I wanted to scream and yell and rage out the fear and disgust I felt about the dead monkeys, our injured marriage, the sheer improbability of the moment; the absurdity that was me sitting on a bamboo chair in Bali, sweat pouring off my shaking body, the smell of burnt shit coming off the bottom of my shoes.

Yes, I could have easily made a scene, but I knew Victor would not want me to embarrass him in front of the kids. Instead, I reached up and put my hand on top of his and tried to show him with my eyes how sad and hurt and vulnerable I felt, but he took his hand away. The morning's trauma was still obviously wearing a hole in his heart. I could almost smell the estrangement between us.

"Just relax. Tell me what happened. Did the—Justin, cut it out," Victor said, raising his eyebrow. I watched Justin the middle-schooler look up at Victor's face then immediately cease tapping his pen on another kid's head. I think I could count on two fingers how many times I've seen or heard Victor raise his voice to a child. It was all about respect with Mister Victor—treat children the way you want to be treated. Had it been me in charge I would have walked over, grabbed the Bic out of the kid's fist and snapped it in half.

"Everybody! If you want to hear my wife's story about getting charged by a monkey, feel free to close your books and come join us."

My wife's? Okay, so I was still his wife, at least for now.

They crowded around me, Victor and Sara and their students, and listened as I told them what had happened, in hyperbolically enhanced, exhaustive detail. At times I had to shout to be heard: how did Victor teach with all that noise/song/laughter coming from the wall-less 3rd/4th-grade classroom only a few feet away?

"So? What was in his bag?"

Oh yeah, I was the one talking. "And he had this super scary look on his face and I knew something was wrong." And then I got to the part about the bag of dead monkeys and the kids went ballistic.

"Oh no! I have two monkey stuffies at home."

"*Mengerikan!*" (Terrible)

"Sounds like a proper nutter to me."

"We should hunt the dude down and shoot *him*!"

"Yeah! We should!" I shouted probably a little too eagerly for Teacher Victor's taste.

I moved from the dead monkeys to the killer monkey part, reaching down every few seconds to touch my left ankle to be sure it really was bloodless.

"How creepy."

"Ohmigod. I am SO never going to walk in the jungle again."

I drank in their water and their attention and their abundant awe and felt much better by the time I finished sharing my harrowing account. I could have sat there all day, basking under that sympathetic spotlight, but Aldo appeared and tapped Victor on the shoulder.

"Hey, Victor, I'm sorry to interrupt but—oh hi, Lisa—we've got a Japanese tour group coming through in about twenty minutes. I want to get the bubble up again, and get you and the kids inside it, okay?"

That was a rhetorical question, of course. Even if Master Teacher Victor had said, "Well, Aldo, you can see my wife is in the middle of telling us how she almost got slaughtered by a rogue monkey, so I'd rather you didn't," he'd go ahead and pump it up anyway. Aldo needed to be certain the visiting news people or investor or prospective parent would exclaim, "Ahhh," while taking lots of photographs of the cool kids learning algebra inside the bubble in the outside school made of bamboo.

"Okay, sure. Sara, can you get them going on music while he inflates the thing?"

"Of course, Victor. Anything you need. Bye, Lisa. Glad you made it out alive," Sara said, patting me on the back.

Anything you need? Sara was a thirty-year-old, very blond, very pretty teacher from Toronto who looked far too clean and dry for someone who'd been teaching middle-schoolers all morning.

Victor took my arm and led me over to the path. "We aren't going to fight like that anymore, you know," he said.

"I know." Over his shoulder, I watched Sara pick up a guitar and start strumming. The kids grabbed assorted instruments and gathered around her.

"Loy was really upset. I had to spend the whole walk to school calming her down."

"She was? I didn't think she even realized what we were fighting about."

He shook his head in what I gauged was disgust.

"What?" I asked.

"How did you not see it on her face when she said goodbye? What the hell is wrong with you?"

"It's because of this place, I mean, I don't know; I was too busy freaking out about the bite, and also, well, she still has you and I know she loves you more than she loves me and—fuck, I don't know. I'm such a bad mother."

"You're a great mother. And guess what? That kid loves you more than anything in the world. But God, you say the stupidest things. I mean, Lisa, it's like I don't even know who you are anymore."

"Yeah," I said. I did say a lot of stupid things. "But what about us? Are we okay? Do you still think I should—" I bit my lower lip and pulled up a sweat-soaked sock instead of saying it out loud. Saying it would have made it too real.

"No, Lisa. We're definitely not okay. I don't think we've been okay for a while now."

"But what should I do? I mean I want to—"

"For one thing, you can figure out how to be happier."

"Happier?"

"Yeah. You're a total downer, you know."

"But it's because of Bali. It's nothing like we thought it'd be." I could see that Aldo was just about finished.

"No, it's not, but like I've said a hundred times, Loy and I will make the best of a bad situation. You have to decide if you can do that, too, because if you can't, then maybe … maybe we need to reevaluate."

What did that mean, *reevaluate*? Before I could choose whether to get defensive or contrite, he said, "Look. I can't talk about this right now. I've got a class to teach," before he turned around and walked back to his bubble.

Stunned, I lowered my head like a bad dog and made for our hut, the one place in all of Bali that offered me the least amount of solace. I had nowhere else to go.

I'd wanted more than anything to talk to Victor that night about *us*, but we didn't. Nor did we talk the night after that or even after that. Because most days after school ended, Victor and the other teachers were required to meet with Director Brad for hours on the shaded *bale* (a large platform with a cushy surface) next to the administration building, to try to smooth out the hundred and one bumps that lay before them on the lava rock road to Green School perfection.

They *still* had no idea—given that most of the school was a giant construction site—where the kids could hang out and play ball or Frisbee after they'd finished eating their lunches. They needed to figure out what to do about all the classroom materials that either disappeared or got soaked through every night. Katy, the education specialist who lived next door to us, tried to guide the staff through identifying and evaluating the numerous special needs kids who were enrolled. No one could agree on the best way to integrate the children who spoke no English. And even though back in May, Brad had promised Victor that founder John Hardy would not be involved in what the teachers taught, Hardy continued to vacillate between what curriculum he ultimately wanted the school to be known for. Would it be Rudolf Steiner's Waldorf? Alan Wagstaff's Seven Springs? International Baccalaureate? Or the still half-defined "green" thing?

Over the course of the next week, Victor came home more depleted than I'd ever seen him, eating a quick Seni-cooked meal with Loy and me before working for a few hours on his computer. He then fell asleep, turning off his light before I could ask him if maybe we should talk about what was going on between us. He stopped kissing me altogether.

By the end of the second week, post-fight. we began to coexist in our wall-less hut, letting the sounds of bugs fill in the silence between us. We went on with our lives, gliding past the fight and the suggestion that I go back to California as if it were an ugly piece of artwork on the corner shelf. It was always there, but neither of us wanted to look at it.

I began to hate myself as much as I hated our living situation in Bali. I stopped jogging through the shady jungle because I was too afraid of wild monkeys. I stopped going up to campus to volunteer in Loy's classroom. I tried to work on my new novel while wearing the possible dissolution of my marriage on my back like a heavy shawl. I needed a backstory for my main character beyond the fact that he wouldn't be able to smell. As for his love interest, I hadn't a clue. Writing a love story when one's own love life is being challenged to a duel makes for some rather large holes in a story line.

Just before lunch one Thursday, I was trying to write. Victor's sad face, his smoldering anger, and the tortuous irresolution hanging over us kept nudging my distractible mind. I needed to narrow the gap between me and my husband. I closed my computer and slid on my flip-flops. Though I was afraid to confront him because of what he might say, I knew I had to tell him again that I loved him and Loy. I had to push past his silence and convince him that I could be a better wife and mother. And that even if he insisted, I wouldn't run away from Bali.

I ran out the gate and started toward campus, but I saw John Hardy standing next to the tank where everyone emptied their compost toilet buckets. He had his right hand up to his mouth so I knew he was busy talking into his tiny Dictaphone. What was he saying? Would we all receive an email tonight admonishing us for creating too much body waste?

I quickly did an about-face and walked the other way. I was just passing by our neighbor Sinead's hut when I heard a crash followed by a screechy yelp. At first I thought maybe someone had shot a stray dog with a poisoned dart (perfectly legal in Bali), but soon realized the cry had come from Sinead's bathroom.

I went around to her front gate and saw her crawling on all-fours toward her bedroom, a towel barely staying wrapped around her body.

"Sinead? What happened?" I asked, taking one of her arms and helping get her up.

She limped forward, slumping onto the bamboo bed in her downstairs bedroom. With an "Ow. Ow. Ow," she slowly turned her body so she could face me. She pushed herself up on her elbows and declared, "I went to take a shower and of course there was no water again. I was getting out when one of the bloody planks on the floor broke. My foot went right through to the ground!"

I looked past the bathroom door and, sure enough, I could see a long bamboo floor pole sticking straight up at the ceiling.

"I fell hard. I really smacked my lower back, Lisa."

"Dang."

"Fuck is more bloody like it." This, from the school's thirty-three-year-old pre-K teacher.

"We've got to get some ice on your back right away, Sinead," I said.

"Yeah, good idea. Oh, shite! I used it all up for drinks last night."

The *Irish* pre-K teacher. Sinead had only just moved into the finished hut next door to us, but since word got around pretty quickly in our tiny bamboo community, I already knew a lot about her.

She was born in Ireland but raised in the Middle East. She'd taught in Singapore and some other place in Indonesia and spoke a couple of languages. I knew she was engaged to a Muslim man who lived in Singapore and was in the middle of converting to Islam. And I heard through Victor that the little kids loved her.

"We have ice! I'll be right back," I said maybe a tad too eagerly, grateful as I was for suddenly having something important to do, at least for the moment, because all I had to do here in Bali was write a book.

Yet most days I spent huddled inside the mosquito net trying not to watch the mold creep up the walls of the house … trying not to get bit by death-inducing mosquitoes … trying to sound cheerful when I Skyped my mother … trying to download last week's *Project Runway* without effectively slowing the bandwidth of the entire campus … trying to teach Seni how to cook Mexican food … and … most importantly, trying to figure out how to fix my quite-possibly-irrevocably-damned marriage.

I clambered up our steps and made for the freezer. Seni was nowhere to be seen so, thankfully, I wouldn't have to choose which of the ten ways we wanted our rice cooked for dinner that night. I cracked an ice tray into a dish towel and went back to Sinead's.

She had by this time managed to wrap a sarong around her waist and put on a black tank top. She was smoking a cigarette. "Oooh, you are so good to me." She leaned sideways and I shoved the ice pack between her and the pillow.

"Okay." I looked at her cell phone lying on the bed and noted the time. "You've gotta ice for twenty minutes," I pronounced with the cocky confidence of a back-injured pro, because when I was thirteen years old I said, "for sure, dude" to Rusty, the way cute older brother of my girlfriend Beth, when he asked me if I wanted to blow off his little sister's birthday party and go smoke a doobie. We jumped into his VW van and when he swerved around a corner showing off at forty-something miles an hour, the passenger door flew open, and I, the un-seatbelted passenger, twisted sideways and shot out backwards—my (then) tiny teenaged butt and lower back taking all the impact.

"Will you stay and keep me company, please?" Sinead asked.

"Of course, I will." *Because you see, if I stay here with you while you ice your back, I won't have to be in my hut thinking about whether or not my husband hates me. Instead of writing a book, I will sit on your bed and talk to you, get to know you a little more. That way I won't have to think about ME, or why I pushed Victor and Loy into moving 8,000 miles away to Bali.*

"I'm yours for the day," I said, and asked if she'd called Brad to let him know what had gone *down*, pun intended.

"*Ya*. Har-har. I told him I probably wouldn't be able to teach tomorrow morning. He sounded insanely upset that I fell and said Kumar was coming by to check on me. Why d'you suppose the big cheese is getting involved?"

"Duh. You fell on school grounds. Kumar must be freaking."

I wondered if he'd want to rebuild all our shower floors.

"Go on," Sinead remarked. "Why would Kumar care?"

"He and Hardy are both going to care about you getting hurt on campus. They're liable for you. Plus, if you can't work for a couple days or even weeks, they'll have to pay workman's comp, or disability, or whatever it's called in Bali," I said.

Sinead laughed. "Workman's comp? You mean like accident insurance? We don't have that here. This is Indoneeeeesia, baby," she said, the "baby" sounding more like *bay-bay*, a mottled mix of Irish lass and Australian drunk. "It's teach at your own risk in this country."

Did Victor know about that? Would we not be covered if anything awful happened to one of us? Loy hadn't yet developed a rash from that dengue mosquito bite, but—"Really?"

Sinead took a drag of her cigarette then rearranged the sarong around her body. "Oh, yeah. I mean I taught in Jakarta. I know all about this stuff. He probably wants to make sure I don't go yapping about how dangerous this place is for the kiddies. *Ya*, that's it." She flicked her ash into a bottle cap (no bamboo ashtrays), exhaled, and smiled.

I had no interest in dwelling on how dangerous this place was for kiddies. I didn't want to think about how treacherous it was for the adults, either, for that matter. "It's been twenty minutes. Here, move." I pulled the wet towel out from her back a little too hard, and Sinead winced in a way I recognized from my pre-yoga days. "Wow. You really are hurting. You have any ibuprofen?"

"No, I have paracetamol."

"That won't do anything for the swelling. I have plenty."

"You're lovely for taking care of me, you know."

"Yes. I know." A little ice, a few pills and you'll be good to go. Me? What's it going to take to fix me?

When I got back to Sinead's with the pills, I found Kumar standing by her bedside, taking in the gravity of the situation. "I have made for Miss Sinead an appointment at Doctor Bobbi's later today," he said quietly to me. "Lisa, I am wondering if perhaps you will accompany her."

"Yes. Of course." An outing off campus sounded great. Any place but my own hut sounded great. Besides, the car would probably be air-conditioned. I'd be able to bring my body temperature down by a few degrees during the drive.

Kumar smiled and moved into the bathroom, where two Balinese men were attempting to extricate the back-maiming bamboo pole from the shower floor with machetes. A lot of Balinese men carry machetes, because in Bali a man's machete is an important tool. In fact, the Balinese celebrate their machetes during the holiday known as *Tumpek Landep*, where families make offerings and pray that their metal objects stay sharp. The holiday used to be mostly about steel weapons—machetes, daggers, swords—but there hasn't been a need for such weaponry since the mass killings of 1965. (Tens of thousands of Balinese were hacked to death by other Balinese because they were suspected of being Communists or sympathizing with them. According to Geoffrey Robinson's *The Dark Side of Paradise: Political Violence in Bali*, the Indonesian military coup that spilled into Bali in December 1965 was beyond ferocious; some 80,000 people—five percent of the island's population—were massacred. The violence was so widespread, it was said that rivers ran red with the blood. As military leader Sarwo Edhy said, "In Java we had to egg the people on to kill Communists. In Bali we had to restrain them, make sure they didn't go too far.")

Not that I have anything against sharp tools. A few days ago, a young coconut fell from a tree and landed in the dirt next to our house. Seni yelled out the kitchen window hole to one of the men working on the hut next door, and he came running over. I looked up from my laptop in time to see the guy drop down, pull a machete out of a string loop tied to his pants, hack off the top third and hand the coconut to Seni. She scooped out the soft white flesh and put it in a pitcher, then poured in the coconut's clear water. She squeezed half a dozen limes into it then stirred in some melted palm sugar and added ice.

"Here, Lisa," she said, pushing a glass through the mosquito net. "Good healthy drink for you." It looked like pasty rice milk and tasted bland, like a watery milkshake, but I liked it and was glad for the machete.

I handed Sinead the pills and she washed them down with a glass of milk.

"How do you feel?" I asked.

"Crappy. Like someone smacked me with a stick. It's really throbbing."

"We should ice you again. I'll go get some more."

Sinead grabbed my wrist. "No, don't leave me here alone with him," she whispered. "He's scary."

"No, he's not," I whispered back. I stood up and went into the bathroom to check out the floor proceedings.

The two workers were standing in the corner staring at the hole in the floor. Kumar had the piece of broken bamboo in his left hand. "Now," he said into his cell phone while staring directly at the two young men, their machetes hanging uselessly at their sides. "I want you to send to me now a man who can fix this broken place. Yes." He held the pole out in front of him, inspecting it, turning it, rubbing the surface with his thumb. "Then take him from that project. Do I sound like I should care about that? I would like someone here in five minutes. Yes. I am happy you are understanding me. Yes. Goodbye."

Okay, so maybe Kumar was a little scary.

And a little sexy, now that you mention it.

"Ladies. I am apologizing for the intrusion, but these men cannot be the ones to fix the problem with the floor. I have another man with better tools to make it stronger, and so it will not break again, okay?" The head-moving again. "He will come here shortly."

"*Ya*, sure, thanks." Sinead looked almost meek.

Kumar reached into his pocket and pulled out a wad of Indonesia rupiah. Of course, in Bali that could mean he had about $14 on him. "Here. I will be paying for the appointment with Doctor Bobbi. And now I must go."

He said something to the two workers who were at this point cowering behind him. They put on their flip-flops at the front gate and ran off. "As I have already stated, if you need anything from me, you are to phone or text me directly. Let us hope the doctor will make you completely healthy again. We need you back teaching the children very soon, yes?"

Before Sinead could respond, he opened the latch and walked out, stopping for a moment to light a cigarette.

"Did you not just hear what he said?" she asked.

"I did. What part?"

"Not what he said, exactly. It was how he said it. It was that 'we need you back teaching, *yes*?' part. The way he said it, it was so, so creepy-like, like if I didn't get back to work soon, they'd..."

"They'd fire you? What are you saying?" I was still guiltily ruminating on the idea that my husband's Indian boss was hot, in a non-sweaty kind of way. That anger in his eyes when he looked at those guys … his calm yet intense power … his dry shirt—

"Lisa. He sounded really threatening. Hand me those cigs, would you please?"

"Nah. You're just being paranoid." Actually, he *had* sounded a little threatening, and why hadn't he uttered a single word of apology?

A cicada-type creature as big as a Bosc pear flew into the bedroom and hovered for a few seconds before attaching itself to the top of Sinead's folded-back mosquito net. After a redoubtable chorus of high-pitched "Ewww's," Sinead said, "Hey, can you go get that ice for me now, please?"

Seni was cutting up a papaya the size of a rugby ball when I got home. She did that for me because she knew it was my all-time favorite snack. After she chunked it, she doused it with about four limes' worth of juice, then stuck the bowl in the freezer. When there's ninety-seven percent humidity, eating it is like a being a five-year-old again, sucking a sweet red ice pop on a hot summer's day; only better, because there is no high fructose corn syrup in papayas.

"Wow, that is so pretty," I remarked as I watched Seni move her knife around the fruit like a woman who knows both fruit and knives oh so well.

"Ya, *manis* [sweet]. *Ya.* Here, you taste," she said holding out a piece toward my mouth, her hand dripping juice all over the counter. "See if it's enough sweet for you."

I liked Seni. I did. It had been nothing but great having her around keeping hut. From the first day she came to work for us, she'd been bringing joy into our lives. Of course, we paid her those big bucks for doing more than putting smiles on our faces.

Seni's tasks included: (1) Clean the house. (2) Put up the mosquito nets in the morning, and take them down at dusk. (3) Make the beds. (4) Sweep up the dead ants from Loy's room. (5) Scrape off the gecko and bat poo from the floors and walls. (6) Keep up the supply of excrement-smothering bamboo sawdust for the compost toilet.

(7) Bleach the mold/mildew that grew back every week on the chairs and tables and beds and shelves and shower and—well, pretty much the whole house. Seni could have, if we let her, spent her entire day scrubbing dark green spores off bamboo, but we learned to co-exist with it, in much the same way one puts up with their next-door-neighbor's accumulating junk heap, or dog that barks all night. But I hated it. Seeing it. Not seeing it. Just knowing it was out there, lurking, growing, exponentially replicating itself.

(8) Wash the ever-present mud/clay/dog and/or chicken shit off our shoes. Seni liked to perform shoe ablution in the Ayung River that ran through the campus next to us. It gave her an excuse to go down and hang out with the local women, who were often there scrubbing their laundry. And brushing their teeth. And peeing. And pooing. And bathing. And fishing.

Before Seni landed her previous job fattening up the Japanese children, she spent two years squatting and digging up sand from the river bed twelve hours a day—balancing her full bucket on her head then lugging it to some nearby construction site, where she'd be paid the rupiah equivalent of pennies per bucket. Washing our dirty sneakers must have seemed altogether luxurious in comparison.

(9) Put away our laundry when it arrived back from the laundry family. They motor-scooted around the teachers' housing once a week, picking up bags of dirty clothes and zooming back a few days later; everything clean and ironed. We paid them about twelve dollars for this service.

If they washed our clothes in the river I didn't want to know about it.

(10) Do some of our grocery shopping (for the local market stuff like fresh blocks of tempeh, enormous bags of rice, and coconut oil).

We didn't have her shop at the main emporium-like store in Ubud for the dearly priced imported cheeses and cookies and western foods we craved now and then, or for the organic fruits and veggies that miraculously got delivered weekly from a local farm.

(11) Bring Loy her lunch when I didn't want to. Her classroom was about a fifteen-minute walk away. Sometimes it gave me a great excuse to not write and instead go check on her, but usually I sent Seni. (12) Fetch Loy home from school if Victor was too busy to walk her home, which was most days. (13) And prepare for us delectable Balinese food.

But eating food from her hand? *Tidak* thank you. To Seni, germs were an abstract concept. The first time Seni cleaned our house I caught her using the bathroom sponge on the breakfast dishes. I was so proud of myself, the way I kept it together, didn't bite my bent index finger in a show of shock the way my grandmother and mother would have.

"Seni," I had said slowly, trying to control my voice. "You just wiped the toilet with that sponge. Please use a different one for the kitchen."

"Why I do that, *Ibu*?"

I gingerly removed the soapy sponge from her hand and threw it onto the bathroom floor. "Because, well, because it's disgusting, that's why."

"What mean *disgusting*?"

"I mean that it's gross. Unhealthy." Since it'd been our first day together I hadn't wanted to scare her away with my neuroses. I was living in *her* world view now, not mine. I had to respect that.

I'd already gleaned, in that depthless, new-to-town, gringo sort of way, that for the Balinese there is a fluid connection between the secular, religious, and supernatural worlds and that if the spirits are not happy, we earthly beings could pay the price. The Balinese did all they could to maintain a balance between the body/corporeal part of the universe and the spirit/life force part. Illnesses emanated not from germs, but from an imbalance of some kind—forgetting to make appropriate offerings; building a house in a sacred location (like next to a cemetery); forgoing one of the thousands of ceremonies they celebrate. From Seni's standpoint, it made perfectly reasonable sense to use one sponge on the whole house. If we were going to get sick, it'd be because of some bad deed, not some bad seed.

I'd asked Seni to humor me and to please, in the future use:

The BLUE sponge for the toilet.

The RED sponge for the bathroom sink.

The YELLOW sponge for kitchen dishes.

One sponge for the whole house? I could hear my mother's mother—who wore rubber gloves like a second skin—turning over in her grave. Although I'm certain the salad spinner incident would have killed her. Just before the semester started, a very tall family from Australia came to check out the school to see if it was the right fit for their daughter. They liked what they saw. They particularly liked *Pak* Victor, who would be their daughter's teacher. Before flying back to Australia, the mother asked, "Is there anything you forgot to bring with you that you can't find in Bali? Anything at all you need that we can bring back from home?"

Before Victor could be his usual unselfish self and say, "No, thank you," I subtly pushed him aside and replied, "Yes! We forgot to bring our salad spinner. If it's not too much trouble, it'd be wonderful if you could buy us one."

And they did. A lovely red plastic salad spinner that I used every single day to wash the organic dirt from the arugula and baby spinach and mixed greens that came in our weekly delivery. When I came home one day and found a RAW CHICKEN SOAKING IN THE SALAD SPINNER, it was almost too much to bear. I came close to firing Seni on the spot.

But I didn't. I loved Seni. I loved her stories and her devotion to the three of us, and the way she whooped like a reality-show host out the window hole as she did the dishes with the YELLOW sponge, calling to anyone who passed by and asking them *"Apa kabar?"* (How are you?), and would they like a glass of her cold, freshly squeezed limeade?

Which is why, after two seconds of hesitation, I ate the papaya. Because at that moment, with her hand filled with the piece of sweet dripping fruit, I really needed someone to offer me more than I had.

I picked at a bug bite scab on my ankle as I sat on a rusty wrought-iron bench, watching Doctor Bobbi insert thin stainless steel needles into Sinead's back and legs. It had taken over an hour of slow driving through villages and hillsides, then snaking down a long, rutted road between two egret-mottled rice paddies for our hired driver to get us to the tiny, open-aired shack where Doctor Bobbi (Roberta) Aqua—a hardy, loquacious, fifty-something American expat—practiced alternative healing.

I knew Doctor Bobbi wasn't going to completely heal Sinead's back; I knew from experience that any back injury would need plenty of time for a full recovery. I also knew that some Qi-redirecting needles, and an hour of relaxing background music couldn't hurt. Besides, I was happy to be there lounging in the inadequate but fragrant shade of a frangipani tree.

Lulled by the sounds of the meditative CD, I closed my eyes and did a quick scan of our time since arriving on the island of Bali. Instantly my thoughts began jingling around my brain like coins, the cold, tinny clattering drowning the velvety wash of strumming harps. Victor. Loy. Wife. Mother. Stay. Go. The ants. The mold. The smoke. The school's empty promises. Kumar's face as he'd handed over the money.

I needed to figure out why Victor and I had come to this impasse. I refused to believe that he wanted to stay in Bali without me.

Why did I have such a hard time seeing the beauty in the moment the way I used to? What had changed me into such an unsettled person?

When I opened my eyes, I saw Sinead being helped off the table. Maybe on the car ride home I'd share some of my worries with her, get an objective hearing. I needed feedback from a girlfriend. I hadn't written a word about my woes to my close friends back home. Nor had I shared more than a shade of darkness with my mother in San Diego.

"Victor is getting more and more frustrated with the school," I had said when we spoke recently, "but we're still on this crazy journey together. It's all good!" It'd kill her to think Victor and I were considering separating; she'd barely survived the news of her daughter and granddaughter moving to a time zone that you had to use a calculator to figure out.

I had no one to talk about Victor with except Victor, and he didn't want to be in the same room as me, much less talk.

But in the car ride home, Sinead wanted to tell me what it was like growing up in Bahrain. "I'd say it was pretty odd," she said from the back seat where she was stretched out on her side. "We lived in a compound..."

I stared straight ahead listening to her go on about miles of sand, oil conglomerates, women in head scarves. Without asking permission from our driver, I turned up the AC and tried for the third time to change the direction of the vents, but they kept dropping to one side, the black plastic inserts dusty and broken.

We drove by about a hundred women walking along the side of the road on their way to temple, their heads topped with tall baskets of fruit and flowers and cakes and other spiritually appropriate offerings. It was that same image one sees in every brochure and every website of Bali. I regarded the prismatic procession for a moment then turned my attention back to Sinead who had just made some remark about the beauty of Hindu rituals.

"You converted to Islam, right?" I asked.

"I'm in the midst, *ya*." She fished a cigarette out of her green canvas satchel. "I met this lovely man, you see, in Singapore. He's Muslim, obviously. And well, we dated, and fell in love really fast, and we knew that if we wanted to get married I'd have to—" Our driver answered his ringing cell phone and spoke so loudly that Sinead stopped talking, turned onto her back, and puffed. After he switched it off, he smiled at me and offered up a weak *"maaf"* (sorry).

"Tidak apa apa," I replied, the aphorism gliding off my tongue easily now that I used it twenty or more times a day.

We passed a slow-moving pickup, two enormous pigs crammed into its bed. I tried not to meet their eyes as we went by, because I knew where they were headed. *Babi guling* (spit-roasted pig stuffed with chilies, turmeric, garlic and ginger) is the most popular dish in Bali. At restaurant *Ibu* Oka, one of the trendier spots, they typically kill about six pigs a day. I was sure those pigs wished everyone in Bali, not just Sinead, would convert to Islam.

I continued nodding my head at all the right parts and thought how lucky I was that I didn't have to convert to marry Victor. No meetings with his God's spokesperson behind closed doors. No special school. We'd only had to deal with finding a really good jazz band.

Sinead had to take classes, learn about confessions and ablutions, specific prayers, how to give alms, and about fasting during Ramadan and making the pilgrimage to Mecca. When she stopped talking I stared out the window. I figured she was done.

"And *ya*, I was going to fully convert, but I still had problems with all those rules. I went through periods of praying and not praying, not drinking alcohol and drinking alcohol. Then a few months ago, I starting getting waves of doubt. Like I'd made a mistake."

"Oh? About converting?"

"About converting—" she stabbed out her cigarette in the overflowing ashtray behind the driver's seat—"and about getting married."

"Whoa." I turned on my side so I could face her fully. "And now where are you?"

"I told my fiance that I needed some time to think."

"And that's what you're doing here in Bali—thinking?"

"*Ya.* I took this job so I could get away from the intensity of Islam for a little while. Get some perspective. Hang around with a couple million Hindus." She laughed.

I saw my chance and jumped in. "It's hard when your partner, or, lover, wants you to change, isn't it?"

"For sure."

"Victor and I—we ... he thinks I'm being too negative about this place and thinks I should, you know, change." I couldn't quite get my mouth to say *leave*.

"Change how? This place stinks."

"It does. I mean, it does?—you think so?"

"It's such a bloody joke, this school. It's Hardy's big bamboo wet dream."

I started laughing so hard that the driver swerved to the right and almost hit a dog.

"You know what some of the teachers call Hardy?"

"What?" I asked. We were back on campus, jerking slowly over the lava rocks so the driver could get Sinead as close to her hut as possible.

"Colonel Kurtz. You know, from *Apocalypse Now*?"

"That is so perfect for him! But I didn't know; I mean, Victor never told me."

Victor used to tell me everything. What happened to us? He'd been my best friend since the very first day we met.

January 5, 1994.

It all began when my college friend, Karen, called to tell me about Louis, the single high-school physics teacher who lived next door to her. "He sounds great," I'd replied, "but I live in Seattle and he lives in California. No, thank you."

Three months later she called again and said, "Louis' older brother, Victor, is here visiting from Seattle. He teaches middle-school. He's not as cute as Louis, but he's super nice, and really funny."

"And?"

"Should I tell him about you?"

"Sure. Why not?" I was thirty-three years old. The last guy I dated threw up out the car window while he was driving me home from a party.

At the beginning of January, Victor called. We talked for three hours on the telephone. He was, as Karen professed, funny. And honest. And smart. Two days later we met at the 211 Club on 2nd Avenue. He was shorter and more balding than he'd sounded on the phone—if that's possible—but he had earnest eyes that sparkled when he smiled. His hair, what there was of it, was a deep red, and he had a darker red, sexy goatee on his chin.

I could tell immediately that he was not the sort of man who would ever throw up out a car window.

While playing pool and drinking beer, we fell into an easy banter, as if we'd never hung up the telephone. He was who he was, he said, because he grew up in New York City, but spent every summer camping or backpacking in the Adirondacks or Canada or the low green salty hills of Maine.

"I really like Seattle, but ultimately," he said after shooting the red ball into a pocket, "I won't stay in the city. I need to live in a place where I can pee off my back deck."

"What. You can't do that in Queen Anne?"

"No. I'd hit the apartment below mine. Let's get out of here."

Over a pitcher of *Hefeweizen* at the Belltown Tavern, he informed me that a few months ago he got arrested after getting caught climbing the Tacoma Narrows Bridge.

I sat up straighter in the booth. "Why were you climbing a bridge?"

"I met this AP photographer at a party. He travels around the world taking pictures from the tops of bridges. He asked me if I wanted to go with him."

"And if your friends jumped off a cliff, you'd jump too?"

He laughed. "No, it was pretty safe. We used harnesses and were clipped in the whole way. The climb was pretty straightforward. It was amazing at the top."

"Yeah?"

"Yeah. Here, have some of mine." He poured half of his beer into my empty glass. We were already an item. "We would have gotten away with it if some schmuck hadn't been looking through binoculars. It was four-thirty in the morning."

"What happened?"

"I guess he thought we were suicides and called the cops. We're there, waiting for the sun to rise, and suddenly there are four police cars, a fire truck, and an ambulance below us. Sirens were going off all over the place."

"And?"

"And they charged me with criminal trespass and reckless endangerment. Luckily, I got a good lawyer and ended up with a suspended sentence."

"What's that mean?"

"It's not on my record. Otherwise, I might have had to kiss my teaching career goodbye."

"And that would have been bad."

"That would have been more than bad. I love what I do. I love those kids."

I let him kiss me goodnight when he walked me to my car.

He left me a bouquet of dried lavender and homemade Indian food on my doorstep the next day.

The following week we went winter camping in eastern Washington's Methow Valley, him "kicking steps" into the deep snow so that I wouldn't have to work so hard to make it up the mountain behind him.

In honor of Chinese New Year he cooked me a Chinese dinner at my house: sautéed snow peas, Japanese eggplant, fried tofu, and clams with garlic and black bean sauce. As he watched me take an enormous bite of tofu he remarked, "I am so glad you're not a typical girl eater."

"What do you mean?"

"You know how lots of women eat like birds? The last woman I dated would take two bites and say she was full. I couldn't go out with her anymore."

In March we walked around Alki Beach together, holding hands. As we sat on a bench sipping hot chocolate and sharing a bag of take-out fish and chips, he confessed that he dreamed of being a stay-at-home father with a wife who supported the family.

"I thought you loved teaching."

"I do. But I want to raise my kid if I can. I want to be the one to teach him or her how to read and draw, and be there to play in the snow and—I want to have the tea parties."

On a Thursday in May, five months after our first date, I woke up and, rubbing my eyes, opened the shade and looked out my front window toward Puget Sound. My brain silently uttered, "What the heck?" because I saw Victor reading a book on the park bench across the street.

It was a weekday morning. Had he been fired?

He glanced up and waved for me to come outside. I put on a sweatshirt and went down the stairs to my front yard. "What's going on, Victor?" I asked when I saw the little café scene he'd created. There was a white-cloth-covered table and two chairs. On the table were two glasses of champagne, a ceramic pitcher of OJ, two teacups and saucers and a pot of coffee, a basket of homemade strawberry scones, a bowl of whipped cream, and a glass vase stuffed tight with long-stemmed red roses.

"Good morning," he said. "Come sit here." He led me over to an Adirondack chair and sat me down.

"This is a nice chair," I said, sliding comfortably backwards.

"Thanks. I made it myself."

"You did?"

"I did."

"Cool."

"I love you, you know."

"I love you, too."

He knelt down. "Wanna know why?"

"Because I live on the beach and make more money than you do?"

He laughed then took my hand. "Yeah, but also because you make me laugh every day. And because you're incredibly smart and sexy and really passionate about the things that are important to you. And there's no one in the world I'd rather go on adventures with than you."

I nodded—there was no one I'd rather go anywhere with than Victor.

"I want to spend every waking day of my life looking into your eyes."

I blushed inside and out, but remained quiet.

"Will you marry me?" he asked.

"Yes!" I screamed into the air. After I kissed him I grabbed a scone, dunked it into the whipped cream, and ran inside to call my family and friends so I could brag that my boyfriend had just proposed with the prettiest and biggest *chair* ever.

After getting Sinead settled back in her bed and making sure her *pembantu* Kadek (name given to second-born children) could take over, I ran home to see Loy and was surprised to find Victor there, too. The two of them were in the living room beneath the mosquito net, which was just large enough to cover our bamboo settee, a bamboo coffee table, and one bamboo lounge chair. Loy, wearing nothing but her underwear, was kneeling on the floor coloring in her *Kini Ku Tahu Bahasa Inggris* (Now I Know English!) coloring book and Victor was, as usual, tapping away on his laptop. He'd already changed out of his teaching clothes—a nice buttoned-down short-sleeved shirt and cotton trousers—into shorts and nothing more. He looked pissed off.

I stepped in between a gauzy opening and sat down on the couch.

"Move over. You're too close," Victor snapped.

"Mommy, stop. It's too hot," Loy whined after I leaned over and tried to kiss her hello.

"Gosh, it's so nice to be with my family," I said with a sad grin.

"Yeah, well, it's fucking hot, in case you haven't noticed, and I worked all day." We had by now lost the ability to censor ourselves when it came to commenting on the heat and humidity, as well as our dissonance, in front of Loy.

I wanted to ask him to go for a walk so we could talk about *us*. "How was your day?" I asked instead.

"It was great," Victor said with as much honesty as a snake oil salesman in a saloon full of drunk cowboys. He closed his computer and repositioned himself as far from me as the couch allowed. "Did you get hit by that monsoon this afternoon? We were playing ultimate Frisbee on the muddy field when it came out of nowhere. By the time we ran back to the classroom, all the kids' work had blown away."

Loy perked up at the thought of this Oz-like scenario. "What did you do, Daddy?"

"Instead of teaching, I had to spend the second half of my day picking through the jungle looking for their soaking wet papers."

For sure, I wanted the three of us to leave Bali *together*, and whenever I saw Victor inching ever closer toward total frustration and exhaustion, I couldn't stop the visions of DEPARTURE GATES from dancing, like neon fairies, in my head.

But I didn't want him to suffer. Every morning as I watched Victor leave for school, knowing he'd walk the half-mile to his classroom as slowly as possible because he didn't want his shirt to get soaked through with sweat before the kids showed up, I regretted ever opening that alumni magazine. He taught outside all day, his bamboo classroom barely throwing off enough shade to keep everyone cool. He played soccer or Frisbee with the kids on muddy fields during lunch. He often brought his class to the river below the school, holding his science lessons while standing in the slowly moving current. Then, after hours of after-school meetings with the teachers and administrators, he'd trudge back to our house, which was *also* open to the outside. Victor, more or less, worked, ate, and slept in an outdoor sauna 24/7.

What kept him and the other teachers going was knowing that every morning a hundred children would be waiting for them to fill their brains. Victor was devoted to those kids. Even though there was no place in his classroom to hang posters and pictures and maps and graphs; and the promised student laptops had yet to show up; and

Brad had yet to hire anyone to teach PE or music or drama, which meant the main-lesson teachers had to teach those classes, too. Victor would never dream of offering them less than one hundred percent of himself.

Even though he and his students spent their days having to shoo away many species of flying things. "You know what it's like to teach these kids a unit on Emerging Economies with them waving their hands around all day?" he asked me rhetorically one night. "I have to figure out who is asking questions and who's just swatting bugs."

For sure he was miserable. He knew it. I knew it.

But no one else did, because Victor was too classy a guy. For Victor to throw in the towel and call it quits, a whole lot more bad would have to go down either in his job, or in this hut.

When he finished his tale about the storm-ravaged papers, I wanted to reach out and hug him but I knew he'd repel me.

"I heard about Sinead's back. How is it?" Victor asked, wanting to move on from talking about his school day.

"*Ya*, Lisa, how Sinead? She no walk no more?" Seni echoed from behind the stove where she was frying up some oily assemblage. It took Seni all of four days of working for us to give up using the deferential *Ibu* and *Pak*. We preferred it that way.

"Not great," I said. "She can barely walk. You remember what I was like when my back went out? She's worse, for sure. I mean, she's definitely going to be out for a while."

"The parents aren't going to be happy."

"It's not like it was her fault. The freakin' floor broke!"

"*Ya*. Bamboo no so strong. Many mold," came the chorus from the kitchen. If anyone had a right to hate bamboo, it was Seni.

"I get it," Victor said, "but I know that a lot of the parents are pretty upset about her being out. Her co-teacher doesn't speak much English."

"Oh. I guess that's not so good. Considering the price they pay for tuition."

"I know. Anyway, maybe she'll be fine by Monday."

Today was Thursday. "No way. It'd be different if she taught older kids, but the little ones; she's gotta use her back—"

"You're right. When I teach I just stand in front of the classroom. I don't use my back or move around. In fact, I don't teach at all—the kids do all the teaching."

Loy looked up, a red crayon in her tiny hand. "You two stop fighting now!" she said.

"Sorry, pickle. We'll stop." He looked away from me, then got up and pushed through the mosquito net and walked over to see what Seni was cooking. "What's for dinner tonight?"

With one hand on her hip and another holding a wooden spoon, Seni stirred with a satisfied smile. "I make for you *nasi goreng ayam,* okay?"

"Chicken fried rice, Loy. Your fave," I said to the child who supposedly shared half my genetic makeup, although judging from her aversion to all things spicy, I had my doubts.

Seni made fried rice whenever she ran out of ideas for the week. One of her more uninspired dishes, to be sure, but as long as she made *sambal* (sauce) to go along with it, I was game. There are, if I am not mistaken, twenty types of *sambal* in Bali. They're all yummy beyond compare and deciding which one to have Seni make each day was like a porn addict trying to choose a video. There's the raw *sambal matah* with chilies, shallots, garlic, lime, shrimp paste and lemongrass. Add some tomato and palm sugar, cook it all together and you get *sambal tomat.* Sometimes Seni fried the shallots. Sometimes she added shredded coconut or she steamed the mush, or she added ginger.

For tonight's fried rice she had cooked a huge bowl of *sambal tomat.* It was already on the table safely residing inside a netted basket. We owned as many of those as we did water glasses.

I watched Seni scrape the food into a bowl, set it under another basket on the dining room table, and begin getting the house ready so she could go home. Leaving an hour or two earlier than the other *pembantu* in the teachers' neighborhood gave Seni a sense of power. She would often have dinner fully prepared by four so she could clock out early, after, of course, making her daily offerings to the spirits, taking down the mosquito nets in our bedrooms, and lighting three or four mosquito coils and placing them around the house.

While she quietly padded around the hut, Loy and I colored together. Victor sat up at the kitchen bar, doing schoolwork. He didn't get bit by mosquitoes: they hated his blood. He only sat or slept beneath a net to be near us. Whenever he had the chance to breathe unencumbered air he did.

Seni came downstairs. "I go now. All done," she beamed.

She waited for me at the gate to come say our traditional goodbye. I put down the orange crayon so I could go stand and face her. We both put our praying hands to our foreheads, closed our eyes, bowed toward one another and chanted in unison, *"Om shanti shanti shanti om"* (May peace be everywhere), and then off she scurried, zipping on a ratty winter coat for her long ride home on her motorcycle.

The fried chicken and vegetable rice tasted good, especially after Victor and I swaddled it with *sambal* and washed it down with a few Bintangs—Bali's answer to Budweiser. Just as we were finishing dinner a bat flew in, narrowly missing the fan blades.

Then the geckos started to sing. Which meant the sun would soon be setting.

I quickly made Loy get up and go brush her teeth and get ready for bed before the blood-sucking, disease-ridden mosquitoes clocked-in, their proboscises at the ready.

"Okaaay, Mommy. But who's killing the ants tonight?" she asked.

"Let me clean up a little and I'll go up," I said.

When I brought the dirty dishes over to the sink I saw that Victor had placed a red notebook on the counter with "COMPLAIN BOOK"

written on the cover. Underneath that it said: "Please fill all you complains and discomforts. We will have someone to pick them and revert
back to you ASAP."

"Oooh, look, Lucy," I said in my best Ricky Ricardo imitation. "A
complain book!"

Victor came over and tugged the book out of my hand. "No! You
are not allowed to even hold this book. Get away from it."

"What? I can't complain that we still don't have hot water?"

"No."

"Can I mention the five workers who showed up to work on the
house and just walked in without any kind of warning?"

"No."

"What about that it's a really sucky idea to turn off the power to the
entire campus at noon every day?"

No response to that one. My guess was that Victor would pen that
in when I had my head turned. Seriously, John Hardy randomly issued
an edict declaring that every day at exactly 12:00, all generators are to
be turned off. Silenced. So that lunches could be eaten in peace. Nice
enough idea if you wanted to only eat at noon, but most of the people in the administration office ate at their desks while they worked.
Teachers wanted to use the lunch hour for essential prep time, but
couldn't print a page.

"You're saying I can't write that we still have ants taking over Loy's
room every night?"

"No. Stop. You're like a fucking free-range whiner," Victor said.
"They know about that. And the workers. And the mold. Kumar
knows. That's why this book is here. Everyone is complaining about
everything all the time, and it's getting so he can't do anything but
respond to complaints."

"You mean *complains*."

"That's funny."

I saw what almost passed for a smirk on his face, and I felt that
warm rush that comes when you and a friend share a joke or funny

observation together. It'd been some time since I saw that look and wanted it to last so I threw out another bit of smart humor that I knew would keep him smiling.

"What about the floating poo in the—"

"No!" he suddenly yelled, making me lose the joke mid-stream. It fell to the ground like a juggled ball dropped mid-flight. "It's not like they don't know what's wrong. They all know. Just stop it."

If I didn't know Victor so well I would have thought he was about to hit me. "I'm stopping," I said and stepped away from the little red book.

"Jesus," he said, turning from me in disgust. "You promised me— remember—if the smoker got moved, you'd be happy. You'd stop complaining about everything else."

He was right: I really did make that promise. "Well, okay, yeah," I said. "I'll stop complaining."

"Good."

"Now, if you'll excuse me," I said to Victor's back, "I've got to go kill me some ants."

Just as I went to grab my flip-flops from the other side of the gate, who should I spy strutting down the path but the Great Decider himself, John Hardy. His large shoulders were back, his ample belly pronounced forward. "John's coming toward our hut," I said to Victor, my whisper scored with panic. "What should we do?"

"Did he see you?"

"No," I said, backing away from the threshold as fast as my feet could move.

"Quick!" Victor pulled me into the downstairs bedroom with him. He slowly closed the door and put his finger to his lips. I think we both held our breath as, a few seconds later, we heard the sound of flip-flops on our cement steps, then heavy breathing. He didn't open our gate or yell, "Hello, anyone home?" He just stood there, doing what, we had no idea. He started talking, either to himself or into his ever-present Dictaphone. He mumbled a few sentences then walked away. We waited until he circled around to the other side of the hut before opening the door.

The coast finally clear, I went back to the steps, put on my flip-flops, grabbed a pair of Victor's heavy-duty leather sandals, and climbed the stairs to Loy's bedroom.

To face THE ANTS.

Oecophylla smaragdina. Red weaver ants. Also known as green tree ants, the ants with the enormous mandibles. The species is known for having large colonies covering several trees. A few of those colonies lived in the coconut tree that grew up through the middle of our house and, for some strange reason, when they came out at night they—imagine 63,000,000,000,000 of them—invaded *only* Loy's bedroom. They'd been doing so for many weeks now, and the school had done virtually nothing to stop the pilgrimage. We had no choice but to adjust to the daily killing ritual.

I followed their long trail, starting as far up the tree as my vision allowed, then proceeding down the tree, across the bamboo wall separating our room from Loy's, crossing over the bamboo door lintel, down the bamboo door jamb, a long thin line of them traversing the bamboo floor, up over to the railing that surrounded her room—and kept her from falling down fifteen feet onto the dining room table should she accidentally walk the wrong way to the bathroom in the middle of the night—across the open bamboo shelves where she kept her clothing and toys, down to the floor again, then up the sides of her bed, then all over the mosquito net, up to the four-sided bamboo rod that held the net, on to the wall behind her bed, then up again to the ceiling and beyond . . . .

With the back of a shoe I bulldozed them off the doorway and furniture. Then I swatted them off the mosquito net, stamping, smooshing, and squashing the moving mass on the floor using my feet, Victor's sandals, and the vitriol that shot from of my mouth, respectively.

KRITCH!

SPLACK!

"DIE YOU FUCKERS, DIE!"

All disagreements between us aside, Victor decided to come to my aid. I yelled across the room, "Get the ones on the floor!" while I turned back to the mosquito net, prying off the ants still clinging for dear life. I had to use my fingers to get them to release their grips and I had to be fast, too, pinching them off and flicking them to the ground before they bit me.

Smashing, stomping, slamming our shoes again and again, my life partner and I trampled those ants into ant oblivion.

We both stared silently at the carcasses.

"Victor. I don't think I can do this anymore," I said, leaning back against a wall, depleted.

"You're right," he said, not looking me in the eye. "I don't think you should either."

"What are you—are you still saying I should go?"

Loy appeared at the door, a towel wrapped around half her tiny body. "Did you guys get them all?" she asked.

I'd let Victor answer that one.

"You know. This is ridiculous," he uttered angrily.

"I know. We need to talk it out. I can't keep living like this with you not—"

"That organic pesticide the guy sprayed did absolutely nothing. Nothing they've done has worked."

He wasn't talking about us, was he?

"What else can they do?" I asked, knowing full well that what needed to be done was to burn the hut to the ground.

"I'm sorry it won't look as pretty, but they're going to have to cut the tree down. I won't let them spray poison, or I don't know ... maybe that's ... come here, pickle," Victor said to Loy who was examining her dress-up clothes.

"Daddy," she said, holding out her blue-and-white satin and gauze princess dress to him. "Look. You forgot."

I went over, grabbed the dress from her and threw it on the ground. Then I knelt down and began to pick big, biting ants from the tangle of lovely white mesh that lined the midriff and wrists and collar, being careful not to pull off any of the silver sequins by mistake.

As usual, I slept little that night, tossing and turning between what had become nightly dreams strewn with images of ants crawling over my daughter's body. I would have liked to have talked to Victor about my insomnia-amplifying anxieties, but he was snoring away under Loy's mosquito net. He'd been sleeping with her often these days, using her fictional fear of ants as an excuse.

I had to pee. Darn. And I had to do it without turning on a light, because I made it a point not to smear bug juice on after my shower at night. Instead I would race upstairs, throwing my still-damp body into my bed, fastening every possible aperture in the mosquito net as quickly as possible. Then I was safe. Safe from the flying bats and blood-bound bugs that had no reason to stay out of my bedroom since it wasn't as if there were walls with signs posted: THIS IS THE INSIDE DAMMIT SO KEEP OUT!

I felt around for a seam and opened the net ever so slowly and ever so slightly. I slid my foot out, found bamboo ground, then walked to the top of the stairs, which resembled more a bamboo corkscrew than a staircase. There, in the pitchest of dark, I had to inch my toes across the run of each stair until I could feel the rise. I dropped my foot onto the next stair, my right hand out for balance, pawing at the bamboo wall with my left, hoping not to get pierced by any errant bamboo splinters. It was a slow process, and as I descended the narrow winding route I cursed Aldo the hut designer for the umpteenth time for not installing night lights.

As I continued my journey downstairs, I suddenly spotted the zigzagging light from a security guard's flashlight. John Hardy had recently hired a couple guys to supposedly make us westerners feel more safe and protected so far from home. Their presence on campus was absurd. They usually spent their days and nights talking to one another on their walkie-talkies, napping, smoking cigarettes, or tying and re-tying their sarongs.

I'd never ever before tonight seen or heard one of them guarding, let alone securing.

I froze halfway down the steps, thinking to hold my stance until he moved on past our house. But rather than shining the light around the perimeter to ward off those villains or ghosts, or whatever might lurk in a Balinese jungle in the middle of the night, the guard decided that maybe there were bad people *in* my house. He whisked his light around the couch, the coffee table, over the floor, up the stairs, his light creeping ever upwards until—BAM!—he shined that light right smack in the center of my girl parts.

He looked at me.

I looked at him.

Then I tried to remember the appropriate greeting for that time of night. Was it "*Selamat malam*" or "*Selamat sore*"? He coughed and ran off before I could choose.

When I told Victor and Loy the story of the peeping Wayan the next morning they both thought it was the funniest thing ever.

"Of course it happened to you, Mommy!" Loy said, accidentally spilling her cereal on the breakfast bar, which in California would not have raised calls of alarm, but here in Bali, where the cost of cereal is on par with cocaine, it's another matter.

"I almost broke my neck the other night, too," Victor said as I grabbed the yellow sponge to soak up the milk. "We need them to install an outlet under the stairs so we can get a cheap nightlight or something."

As long as I had the sponge in my hand I wiped a cluster of ants off the butter knife. Not the scary biting ants from Loy's room, no; these ants were tiny, red, benign buglets that come out the moment there's a bread crumb or cheese scrap available to steal. Every morning we woke to find torrents of them crawling all over the dirty dinner dishes we'd left piled in the sink for Seni to clean—the bowls and forks and glasses spattered with red dots. They were more a nuisance than a threat. I suffered their presence with grace and dignity.

"I thought we reached our electrical limit," I said, rinsing many dozens of them off the honey jar, "and we can't have any more plugs."

Wanting to greenwash his creation even further, Hardy had capped the number of electrical outlets in the teachers' huts. But it wasn't as if we had any use for the ones already installed. We had no stereo or television or blender or microwave. A plug behind the bookcase served no purpose.

"Oh, well. You can tell Aldo you want one there," Victor said, pointing to a spot next to the bottom stair. "Kumar is sending him over this morning to talk to you about the ants and the hooks for the bathroom. You can add it to the list of things we need taken care of."

"Oh, yay," I replied, eyeing the COMPLAIN BOOK on the table.

Victor got up and grabbed Loy's bag. "Let's go, Loy," he said. "Go kiss Mom."

As I kissed our child I saw an odd welt on her neck. "What's this? Victor, did you notice she had this spot when you were putting bug stuff on her?"

"I don't know," he said dismissively.

I raised her shirt and found two more spots above her hip. She had a rash.

I started counting back days in my head. "When did you tell me to go back to California?" I asked with increasing unrest.

"What? You want to talk about this now? Are you insane? I'm about to walk out the door and you're—"

"When did she get bit by that fucking mosquito?" I screamed.

"Christ. I don't know. Is that what you're—? Lisa. She doesn't have dengue fever. Come on, Loy. I've got to get to class."

"Mommy, when are you going to California?"

Ignoring my sure-to-be-emotionally-scarred child's query, I threw myself inside the mosquito net and fired up Google. "Please give me one minute."

They stopped at the front gate. I typed DENGUE FEVER RASH and clicked IMAGES; 24,101 pictures started to download. I glanced up. Loy was looking up at Victor, waiting for him to tell her what to do. Victor had his head cocked to the side. He stared at me with a mix of frustration, despair, and revulsion. I could almost hear his teeth grinding together.

No two rashes were alike. There were long red smeary ones. Big red welts with white dots in the middle. Grey clustery splotchy ones. I wanted to call her over so I could compare her skin to the skin of the dying man in one of the photographs; but Victor was unlatching the gate, so that he could, I surmised, put an even greater distance between us.

"She has no fever, Lisa," he said, adjusting his heavy pack. "Loy, how's your head feel?"

"Fine. Why?"

"She has no headache. And she got bit weeks ago. You're overreacting."

I had to let this go, or he would make *me* go. "You're right," I said standing up, but keeping the page open. "I'm sure it's just a heat rash." I walked over to them and while surreptitiously giving the welt one last feel, I said, "I'm sorry I panicked."

"Thank you for apologizing."

"You're welcome. Hey, maybe tomorrow we can go for a walk and—"

"Probably not. I have to work all weekend."

"You do?" When were we going to talk, make a decision, draw out all the possible scenarios?

When were we going to decide if we should stay married?

"Parent-teacher conferences are coming up, and there's absolutely nothing in place for them. I need to at least get some of the forms started."

I wanted to say, "So much for all that quality time Brad promised we'd have together," but that sounded too complain-like. Instead I leaned my mouth toward his mouth, but he turned away. "Can we still have *cumi-cumi* tonight?" I asked through the haze of his burning rejection.

"Of course. It's the highlight of my week. See ya."

Fried squid, a highlight? Really?

After I read about every possible symptom of dengue fever and convinced myself that Loy had exhibited not a single one—no diarrhea, no red eyes, no achy bones—I retied my sarong and ran over to Sinead's hut to check on her before meeting up with Aldo.

I shouted, "Hello there!" from her front gate.

"Come in!" she yelled back.

And why did we both need to shout to be heard? Not because it was raining, or because a gamelan orchestra was loudly playing along with a cremation at the cemetery next door. The deafening noise that drowned out our voices came from the procession of motorbikes and flatbed trucks driving to the school, loaded with workers and their mountains of bamboo poles and tools. When those convoys passed by—tens of times per day—the ground rumbled, the air filled with the grey stench of exhaust, the dust flew.

I found Sinead in bed, leaning against her headboard with her laptop open. I wondered why it was so hot in her room. The ceiling fan above the bed was going at full speed, but the air below it didn't move. How surreal it was to see the blades spinning but not feel the whoosh of the molecules. It was like we were in a photo—inanimate.

"*Selamat pagi,*" I said, offering her a big smile.

"Hi there," she said, not returning it.

I sat down. "What?"

"I just got the most lovely and considerate email from Brad, informing me that he hopes I will be back in the classroom on Monday."

"What'd he say?"

"You know, his usual passive aggressive new-agey crap. Oh, we feel so bad for you, Sinead—boo-hoo-hoo—and the kids adore you so much it'd be such a shame not to have you back soon, but *of course* we need to provide consistency..." She closed her laptop and grabbed a cigarette.

"What will you tell him?"

"Hopefully, I won't have to deal with him and maybe just Kumar. Actually, I have no idea who makes the decisions anymore. Brad's got everyone going in one direction and Hardy has us going in the opposite. It's gotten to the point that sometimes Brad can't even look us in the eye because he knows we know that Hardy's got his hand stuck up his ass."

I laughed but instantly grew more confused by Green School's ever-changing organizational chart. "Enough about Brad," I said. "How does your back feel? Did you sleep?"

"No, it was impossible. Every time I move, all the muscles around that one spot feel like they're on fire."

"Acupuncture can do that sometimes. It might actually be a good sign that your muscles responded to the treatment." I remembered being in such agony after getting acupuncture once that I spent hours lying immobile on the floor plotting my lawsuit. I would destroy that *Doctor* Chens's life. I would make it so no other person would have to endure his charlatan practices. I would tear his professional life limb from—

I felt astonishingly better a day later. Not healed, but the deep, flare-gun pain had settled down into more of a sizzle.

"Bollocks." She reached over and snubbed out her cig.

"No. Really. The day after you get anything intense like that, your body is going to react. Didn't Doctor Bobbi warn you?"

"No. I dunno. Maybe she did and I didn't listen. I wasn't exactly in the best place to take direction, yeah?"

It was Friday. She still had three whole days. "Did Kadek take care of you last night?" (Some of the single teachers—like those who didn't give a rat's ass about sponge differentiation—shared one *pembantu*. Kadek also worked for Sam and for Katy.)

"*Ya*, she did. She made me a really good *soto ayam*." Chicken soup, Balinese style. No matter what culture, what longitude, latitude, altitude or attitude, a good chicken soup is the best thing for what ails you.

"With or without home-made potato chips?"

"Of course *with*, dahling. I'm not paying her all those rupiah for nothing," Sinead said, lapsing back into her old bright self again. Even *talking* about Balinese chicken soup not only soothes the soul, it takes it out to dinner, slathers it with honeyed adulations, walks it home, and French-kisses it good-night.

That's because Balinese chicken soup is decidedly more suave than Jewish chicken soup (apologies to centuries of female ancestors). The soup of my measley/mumpy/streppy childhood was pretty basic. You had your chicken. And your soup. A couple of sapped carrots might make an appearance, along with an egg noodle or two.

Soto ayam is traditionally served with a smorgasbord's worth of accompaniments, such as rice noodles, shredded cabbage, *sambal*, thinly sliced fried potatoes, hard-boiled eggs, fried shallots, green onions, limes, and bean sprouts, all piled into one huge bowl of steaming, salty, chicken-morseled broth. "Seni makes it super tasty, too."

"Does she add coconut milk, like Kadek does?" Sinead asked, a little too competitively.

"No. Bummer. We should have a *soto ayam* cook-off!" I said, picturing Seni and all the other wondrous *pembantu*, chopping, dicing, frying together. Sort of like a Balinese Top Chef.

"Did she make you ice?" I asked.

"For the soup? What do you mean?"

"No doofus. For your back." I was too hot to sit there on the bed so I got up to check. The kitchen was a mess, the dishes in Sinead's sink covered in red ants. I passed my palm over a pile and they scattered like baby chicks. Then they went back into a pile again. I considered rinsing them down the drain, but I opened the freezer instead.

"Here," I said, coming back and handing her a hand-towel filled with clear fresh ice.

"How often am I supposed to ice?"

"A lot. If you hurt, you ice."

Outside Sinead's bedroom we heard one of the school's marketing employees leading a tour group. "This house here is a two-bedroom design. Our pre-K teacher lives in this one. She is from the Ireland."

"That's not true. I'm from the Singapore," Sinead whispered.

"It's so beautiful," a tour member with a non-specific European accent, declared. "What's it like to live here?"

"The teachers, they love living in these houses," the tour leader misinformed them. "This is a big reason we can attract many good teachers. They come from many places in the world and want to be here. They are very happy because the houses are so pretty."

Sinead rolled her eyes. "Jesus Christ. It's bad enough they built these crap huts, but do they really have to show them off to strangers like they're the Taj Mahal?"

I hated the tours. They made me feel like I lived in the Biosphere: like I was part of a living experiment. Whenever I passed a tour group I felt like standing behind the tour guide, wildly waving my arms and yelling, "No! Don't believe anything she says. We all hate living here. It sucks! The rooms are hot and there's no privacy and the roofs leak and the ants swarm and there's no hot water and the mold is like the

BLOB from the 1958 sci-fi film … it's everywhere … it smothers all it touches!"

During the first week of school I'd been busy getting Loy ready for school, encasing her skin in bug repellent, when a tour group stopped by our front gate. I looked at them. They looked at the tree growing up through the middle of the roof.

"Do you mind?" I'd asked, standing up, my hand on my hip to show my utter contempt for the intrusion. The guide seemed not to hear me.

"This is a three-bedroom hut. Our seven/eight teacher lives here. He is from California." Beside her a young white couple looked around as if I, a harried mother in a crookedly tied sarong trying to get her six-year-old ready for school, wasn't actually there, ten feet away. I put my greasy hand on Loy's shoulder and pulled her with me to the front gate.

"Please go away. This is a private home." I kept my teeth pressed together so that I wouldn't lose my temper.

The three strangers looked at me as if I were a gorilla in a zoo, one that had unexpectedly pushed her face up to the glass and given them the finger. "Come this way," the tour chick said, "I now show you the compost area."

I'd told Victor about the tour barging in on me and Loy, and it made him furious. He emailed John Hardy and said he didn't want any more tours coming around. Hardy apologized for the imposition but said that he needed prospective families to be able to see the whole campus.

"I told him he has to at least let you know beforehand," Victor had said, acquiescing to the ego-maniacal jeweler who had brought us to this place.

"What, so that I can tidy up, or retie my sarong, or—"

"No, so that you can leave. Apparently, word got back that you weren't very friendly the last time people came to visit."

"I think they heard you," I said to Sinead.

"Like I care."

"You don't want to get fired, remember?" I reminded her. The last thing she needed to do was piss off Kumar. The man who signed the paychecks.

She sighed. "*Ya*, you're right. I need to be a little less rude, at least till I find out what they plan to do to me if I'm not ready to teach on Monday."

I looked at my phone: I still had some time. Should I tell her about me and Victor and our slowly crumbling marriage? Or should I wait until I knew I could trust her not to tell any of the other teachers that I might leave or that I was trying to get Victor to leave or—"What's the whole Ramadan thing about?" I asked, deciding I wasn't ready to share.

"What do you want to know about it?"

"I don't know. You mentioned it being one of the things you have to learn about before becoming a Muslim. Why do they fast? For cleansing?"

"No. No. This ain't no hippie dippie fasting." She lit a cigarette. "Muslims fast because they want to be reminded of what it feels like to have nothing. Fasting makes you mindful of sacrifice and humility."

If I were to be without Victor for a day or week … it would feel like I had nothing. What would I sacrifice to make our love a constant whole again? "What, and then get to eat after you realize how humble you are and how much you've sacrificed?"

"The breaking of the fast is really fun. Everyone sits around at a huge table with all this food laid out before you. You sit quietly, thinking about the last few moments of the day, being thankful to have made it through another day, another fast, and then the sound of the prayer call comes, '*Allah Akbar,*' God is Great, and then you take your first sip of water."

"Then you dig in."

"We usually start with a date."

"Why a date?"

"The prophet, Muhammad, always broke his fast with dates, so it's tradition to do that."

"Mmm-hmm."

"Honestly," Sinead continued, "my stomach would shrink so much during Ramadan that my appetite bordered on the non-existent. Soup was about all I could stomach, and then later I'd eat fruit and maybe some vegetables. It turned out to be a very good weight loss program. But then I'd gain it all back during *Eid-ul-Fitr*."

"What's that? They celebrate that here, don't they?" By now I'd lounged backwards onto the bottom portion of her bed and directed my question at her feet, which, incidentally, were quite nice. Not that I have a weird foot fetish or anything but feet can tell you a lot about a person. Clean feet are good. Sinead's feet were clean and kempt and curvy. I reached out and started massaging one because foot massages—known in alternative medicine circles as *reflexology*—can stimulate healing throughout the body. The foot's various pressure points connect to distinctive points in the body, so where you push determines what you fix. My massage therapist Ellen (Loy's godmother who was supposedly taking really good care of Rex the cat) had avoided certain areas of my feet while massaging big round pregnant me because she didn't want to send me into early labor. Since Sinead wasn't pregnant I just pressed indiscriminately; pushing, smoothing, bending, and squeezing, hoping I'd serendipitously fix her back along the way.

Sinead "mmm'd," and went on to answer my question about *Eid-ul-Fitr*, which I could have sworn I saw on the list of school holidays. "*Ya*, for sure, they celebrate it here because Indonesia has the highest number of Muslims in the world, mind you, and it's a huge holiday for them. It's the celebration that ends Ramadan. It's like, it's almost like Christmas. Everyone visits their relatives and at each house there's massive amounts of food. Lots of sweets. All the children and anyone who isn't married get little decorated envelopes with money inside. Which—ooh, now do the other foot—is a really good reason not to get married, no?"

"So it's really more like Hanukah than Christmas," I said, attempting to make a joke, but given Sinead's contextual goulash—Irish/

Middle Eastern/Southeast Asian—and the quizzical look on her face, I figured I had to spell it out.

I poured some of her coconut oil from the bedside table onto her other foot and started in: "If you're Jewish and *not* married you get extra special attention, not that you want it. Jews give money for everything. Bar Mitzvahs. Weddings. Circumcisions. At Hanukah, the older folks always hide money and the kids have to go find it. Wait, sorry, that's Passover." How had I muddled that? I tried to grab hold of my ancestral rituals, but they were like a slippery carp swimming in my grandmother's bathtub, awaiting its gefilte-fish fate. "Never mind," I said, both embarrassed by and indifferent to my spotty religious knowledge, blaming the brain-spasming heat on my lapse. "More importantly, we get time off on *Eid-ul-Fitr*, right?"

"Yup. In a couple weeks we get a Tuesday, Wednesday and Thursday off."

Days off. Days not here. Victor and I needed a getaway to stir our love again. If I could just hold on, hold us together for a few more weeks. "I wonder where we should go," I said, daydreaming about being gone from this place. Then it occurred to me: "Hello! Then this is Ramadan! Aren't you supposed to be fasting right now?"

Sinead threw her head back and laughed from her belly. "Damn. You outed me, girl! I am totally in trouble. I really did try, but it's hard to go it alone, and then when I hurt my back—"

"Just give me some money and I won't tell all your Muslim friends."

Now she looked sad. "*Ya*. I've been a complete liar. I'm sure I don't much deserve to be Muslim."

I couldn't speak to that. If I had a penny for every Jew who felt less than Jew-worthy I'd be able to buy my own country.

More to the point, I had to figure out where we'd go for those three gloriously empty days. The beach? The mountains? Maybe we could we take off Friday, too, and make it a six-day getaway; head to Thailand for some authentic Pad Thai, or fly to Vietnam—

"It sucks that the holiday is going to be mid-week. Brad sent out an email that teachers have to be back on campus on Friday for an afternoon meeting."

Oh well. I substituted visions of tom yum soup and beef panang with white sand and cold clear chlorinated pool water.

I had to go meet Aldo. "Is Kadek coming back today to feed you?" I asked as I got up.

"No. I'm all alone for dinner tonight. Poor, lonely, pitiful me."

"*Tidak apa apa*, babe. We'll feed you. Should we bring the food here or can you make it to our house?"

"Is Seni making *cumi-cumi* tonight?"

"Do geckos poo on the floor? It's Friday, isn't it?" There was only one thing that announced Friday in the teachers' hood and that was Seni frying up some seriously scrumptious cephalopod. That and a few Bintangs, and Bali can be a beautiful thing.

The "tradition" started before Victor and I had our big blowout fight. His co-teacher, Sara, had been over at the house dealing with curriculum changes yet again (they'd tried out a unit on river ecology, but the local village kids kept jumping into the river and stealing the current markers). The two of them were drinking coffee, chatting. Loy and I were stretched out in the downstairs bedroom reading *The Secret Garden*, coveting the stark wintry enclosure that Mary had stumbled upon, wishing that we, too, could be there in our woolen coats, playing with Dickon's animal friends.

Seni had called out to us, "Everyone, come here. You try *cumi-cumi* now while is hot." We came into the kitchen and huddled over the counter, each of us grabbing a hot crunchy squid circle from the plate, dipping it in some fresh tomato *sambal* then stuffing it in our mouths.

Oh my god.

At the time, I wondered how much more money we'd have to pay her to be able to eat *cumi-cumi* every night. Of course, we couldn't do that unless we wanted to die of heart disease at a relatively young age, considering the copious amount of coconut oil Seni used for frying.

Victor had whipped up a non-spicy bowl of aioli for Loy, and away we munched, half a kilo of squid vanishing in seconds. After a few bites I noticed that Seni wasn't eating any. "You don't like *cumi-cumi*?" I'd asked.

"I no eat your food."

Victor looked at me. I looked at Victor. In an instant I replayed in my head all the times I'd watched Seni preparing meals for us. I didn't think I'd ever seen her actually *taste* the food as she cooked. I remembered sharing my toast with her the morning of her interview back at Bali Putra and had just assumed she'd know that our food was her food. Apparently, I was wrong.

"What? Seni. This is your home," I said, stunned.

Victor, the sort of chef who is forever dipping his fingers into the pot or pan as he cooks, asked, "How do you know if the food is done or if it's seasoned right?"

Seni smiled her big Seni smile. "You funny, Victor. I know how the food taste. I cook all this food before many, many times in my house. I know in my head when is good."

Victor was having none of that sort of gustatory denial in his house, no. "Well, from now on you can taste whatever you want, whenever you want. Here, take a bite." He placed a fried squid into her mouth as if she were his girlfriend.

After that first squid tasting, we decided we had to have it again. Soon. Next time, we told Seni, she'd have to cook up a few more pounds. And next time we'd invite the neighborhood.

And so began the Friday night *cumi-cumi* ritual. The end of the week would roll around and the teachers would turn off their laptops, strip down to the bare minimum and wander over our way, some bearing a couple of six packs, some a fresh salad or bread, and some toting along a child or two. Sometimes three people showed up; sometimes we had ten or more. The invitation was always out there.

Cumi-cumi at Victor and Lisa's hut. Come one. Come all.

"You think you can shuffle over on your own," I asked Sinead, "or should I pay a couple strong Javanese boys to carry you?"

"Nah, they'd be too weak from fasting to carry this body. Don't worry, I'll be there. I may wait till after sunset, though, out of respect. It's the least I can do."

"*Tidak apa apa*, babe. See you tonight," I replied, before running back to my hut.

Of course, he wasn't on time: Aldo showed up when he wanted to. I was sure it was at Kumar's bidding that he would bother to keep his appointment today. He was John Hardy's heir apparent/lead designer/lapdog, and having to deal with the piddling needs of a teacher's wife seemed sub-par to him, I knew.

Now I was stuck at home, having to wait for Aldo. And darn, but I wanted to go for a walk before it got too hot.

Before it got too hot? I laughed at my own idiocy.

I heard Seni rustling around upstairs. I thought she was tying up Loy's mosquito net, but when a scattering of ant skeletons sprinkled down through the bamboo ceiling cracks and landed on the counter next to the kitchen sink, I knew she was sweeping.

I still hadn't acclimated to the sounds of daily life. When you move into a different house it generally takes time for the acoustically new to fade into the woodwork, so to speak. Floor creaks, door slams, kitchen-drawer rollers, all sound distinct and—if you're sound-sensitive like me—annoying as hell. The hot-water faucet squeals differently (even if nothing comes out of it). The tea kettle's sloshy echo reverberates more emphatically when you set it on another stovetop. The light in the master bath hums louder than you wish. But then time moves on and the din disappears; you pay no attention to the flush of the toilet or the draining of the washing machine or the clang of the bi-fold laundry-room door when your dog's tail wags against it. The vibrations—like a tattoo, weeks after inky needles repeatedly jab your skin—settle down and become part of your being.

I heard everything in Bali. And the sounds still didn't make sense. Barking dogs kept me awake. The constant drone of insects and birds etched away a piece of my soul a bit at a time. The drop of the toilet lid over the black plastic bucket startled me over and over again. As I sat on the couch day after day, trying to write, I tried hard not to listen as Seni tidied her way around the house, but I couldn't help it.

My mind played games, asking, "What's she doing now: folding clothes, dusting the shelves, or shaking out the blanket?" I listened for cues—the rustle of certain fabrics, the slight textural difference between netting and cotton.

"Lisa, you home? I no hear you!" Seni yelled down from the landing.

Apparently, *my* sounds had already faded into Seni's bamboowork.

"Hi, Seni," I said. "*Apa kabar?*"

"*Baik-baik, kamu?*"

"*Saya sangat panas.*"

It was always the same.

How are you?

I am fine, and you?

I am very hot.

Seni smiled, waved, and went back to making indefinable noises upstairs. I opened up my laptop and clicked on my novel-in-progress. I stared at the words, and after typing two measly sentences started to think about Victor. I thought about some of the reasons I loved him. I loved him for being an amazing parent. I loved him for being the friend everyone in the universe could lean on. I loved his intelligence and his honesty and ability to see the humor in every situation. I loved that his glass was always half full, no matter what the liquid. I loved how he used to look at me when I'd wake up beside him.

Back when we used to sleep together.

I loved him because he was the most grounded, most non-egotistical person I knew. Everyone who met him could tell that Victor had no baggage.

Perhaps because he was too busy carrying mine.

And now, I realized, he probably just wanted to let it all drop from his tired hands and fall to the floor in one loud crash.

Two Javanese men carrying a saw and a large bamboo pole suddenly appeared in the dirt outside my living room, five feet from where I sat. They both stared expectantly at me as if I were about to offer them tea. I shouted at them: "You're not supposed to walk through my yard!" but I knew they didn't understand me.

Seni appeared at the railing and yelled down at the men, too. They yelled back up. She said something else, fluttering her arms up and down then pointing at the road in front of our house, the road they were supposed to use instead of short-cutting between the huts. I felt a little like a ping pong ball, white and hollow, waiting to be struck by someone's paddle.

They shrugged their shoulders and sauntered off. "They no come through here no more, Lisa."

"*Terima kasih,*" (Thank you) I said to Seni, then blew her a kiss.

"Hellooooo?"

"Aldo! Come in," I said, pushing past both the dark sludge in my brain, along with the mosquito net, to greet him.

"Hello, Lisa. Good to see you." In his thirties, lithe and gorgeous, I had yet to determine Aldo's sexual orientation. I got the impression he functioned on a combination of beer, ego and adrenaline. Aldo was always on the go, vrooming from one building project to another on his scooter, scooting around the teachers' village and campus, making sure everything was aesthetically pristine. Whenever John Hardy made a public appearance you'd often spot Aldo hanging by his side—sort of like a machete.

Aldo had on a blue linen shirt with his sleeves rolled up just past the half-dozen spectacular silver bracelets with inlaid jewels—most,

I assumed, designed by him. The bottoms of his ankle-length grey slacks had been shredded, purposely, at the cuffs. You could tell he took longer than Heidi Klum to get ready to go to work in the morning.

"I'm busy as hell," Aldo allowed in a Euro-trash southern drawl that was both sexy hot masculine and alluringly feminine. "Let's get through this list pronto, okay?"

"Sure," I said, not bothering to offer him a drink of ice water.

We walked into the bathroom, and when I pointed out the lack of any sort of hang-worthy hooks, Aldo slammed his hand to his chest and his jaw dropped. "Lisa!" he shrieked as if I'd just shown him a dismembered squirrel. "Why is there so much horrible plastic in here?"

"Because all the shelves were moldy. We had them carted away and bought these bins instead," I replied, admiring the two huge, kid-colored Tupperware forgeries.

"Yes. It is bad in here, isn't it?" he said as he surveyed the long dark stain that ran the length of the India fabric behind the shower head. "It's bad from the outside, too." He put his index finger to his mouth and tapped. Tap. Tap. "I think I will have the gardeners plant some mature plants. Tomatoes. To cover it up."

Did he mean to plant them *in* the bathroom?

"What do you mean? How will that help the mold?"

He looked at me, almost surprised I was standing there. He'd been thinking out loud, hadn't he? "Oh, yes, ah … I am talking about how it will look from the outside, but in here, yeah, sure. We have to figure something out. Of course. What else? Kumar said there was an issue with ants."

"If you notice, we have no place to hang a wet towel or a sarong," I repeated. "Could you maybe install a few hooks in the beams here?"

"Great idea. But I have to design them first so it might be a while."

"You have to—what?"

"I can't just have *any* hooks drilled into the walls here." He ran his tanned hand along a smoothly sanded bamboo beam that held up the brunt of the bathroom. With the way Aldo worked, I figured we'd get bathroom hooks sometime around New Year's Eve.

There was always someone, I suspected, out there waiting for Aldo to design, or *redesign*, an object of importance. The teachers sparred with him right and left when it came to their classrooms. They had to wait for him to design paperweights, white boards, chalk boards, bookshelves, and pencils.

Yes, Aldo actually designed the pencils. Naturally, they were made from bamboo.

Rumor had it that the reason the teachers' houses weren't ready when we arrived was due to Aldo's constant change of mind. When we asked Richard, the engineer who built the school, for the inside scoop, he confessed that the construction crew had lost weeks while "Aldo dithered to make a decision on the layouts. When he'd finally make up his mind, we'd race ahead at break-neck speed to catch up, only to have him come along and fuck-all, wouldn't you just know it, change his mind again. More than once we buried a foundation that we'd already poured, because we had to move a building back by *one* meter, or he'd make us revolve the front of a hut another twenty degrees to the northwest. No one gave a shit about which way the houses faced. They all face the fucking bloody jungle anyway. We just wanted to finish the houses for you teachers who were coming in a few weeks' time."

"Let's move on to the ant situation. The gardener sprayed the Neem oil, right?"

"The organic pesticide that did nothing? Yes," I said. "He sprayed the oil. Many times. But they still come out every night."

I followed him up the stairs to Loy's room, after convincing him without much fanfare to add an outlet where Victor wanted one. Seni was swishing about in our bedroom and came out to see who was in her house. When she saw it was Aldo, she quietly about-faced and went back to tying up our mosquito net.

I watched as he stared up at the coconut tree growing through the middle of the hut. Tap tap tap, went his finger on his lip.

"Nope. Can't cut it down."

"Why not?" I stayed calm and didn't hurl stories of my child's nightly terrors at him.

"I'm going to send a climber up first. To see what's at the top. Maybe there's a nest and all we need to do is find it."

I found that to be a reasonable assumption. "Okay. But do it soon. Wait, before you go downstairs. Look over there. That's one of the places where the roof leaks; it's where most of the water gets in."

He stared up again.

Tap. Tap. Tap.

"You going away during the *Eid-ul-Fitr* holiday?"

"Oh yes, oh yes we are. I have no idea where yet, but for sure we're going somewhere."

"That's great," Aldo replied, skipping easily down the looped staircase he designed. "While you're gone, we'll get a crew in here and fix the leaks."

"Why not do it now?" I hadn't gotten the hang of living on "Bali time," which pretty much means getting done what needs to be done *whenever*. "I mean, it rains every day, Aldo. And every time it does, we have to move all this furniture into the middle of the room."

When the rain stopped, we moved it all back into the sun to hold off that mold, that devilishly moisture-lusting beast, from spreading even further into—

"I'm sure you can live with it a little while longer," Aldo contended with the assurance of someone who so obviously did not live in a leaky, moldy house.

Seni came downstairs and took the ham for Loy's lunch out of the refrigerator. I suddenly had this wild urge to check on my daughter's benign rash and to see my husband. I looked at Aldo who stood in the middle of the room in a model's pose, relaxed hips back, right hand in his pocket. He was thinking about something else altogether; maybe a new ring design based on the delicately swirled pattern the mold left on the fabric. All the world was Aldo's easel and he was anxious to get back to painting its perfect colors.

"Okay, then," I said. "I have your word that by the time we get back from holiday the leaks will be fixed and the ants will be gone?"

"Promise."

"And you'll install some bathroom hooks and put in an outlet there?"

"I swear." He held his hand to his chest the same way he did when he saw the dreaded plastic.

I stopped by Philippa's hut to say hi on my way to Loy's classroom. She and Johnny were two of the most genial people we knew in Bali, and I regretted not spending more time with them. But Johnny, the 3rd/4th grade teacher, was just as busy and aggravated as Victor was, and Phillipa, when not contending with her own two children, had been asked to step in for the missing school nurse whenever emergencies beckoned.

"Hello, Pip," I yoo-hooed from her steps. "Just wanted to check in. I'm on my way to campus. Need me to bring anything up to Johnny or Elliott or Emily?"

Phillipa came out of the bathroom with a tube in her hand. "Lovely of you to ask, Lisa," she said in her sweet New Zealand twang. "Actually, yes. Ells has some new, rather nasty bug bite infections on his legs, and he forgot his salve. Do you mind standing over the boy to make sure he spreads it on?"

As she handed me the homeopathic medicine, I thought I could smell warm milk coming from her skin. What was it about school nurses that made you want to fall into their arms and cry out all your boo-boos?

"Of course, I don't mind," I said, backing away before I fell over the gate and shared my grief.

"*Cumi-cumi* at your place tonight?" she called after me.

"Absolutely," I yelled over my shoulder. I headed down the slippery rock stairs that would bring me to the path toward the west side of the campus. I nodded to Edie, the Balinese boy who swept rocks and leaves and garbage from the trails. Waved to Wayan who had apparently been promoted from Front Gate security guard to School Footpath security guard. "*Ibu* Lisa. *Selamat pagi!*" he shouted while waving his walkie-talkie at me. I crossed over the magnificently structured, bamboo bridge that was on every brochure, every page of every online site that mentioned John Hardy or Green School, due, in all fairness, to its supreme beauty. I paused halfway across and stared down at the Ayung River. Upriver, I saw an old man squatting down in the water with his eyes closed. Downriver, I saw two men fishing from a rock.

On the far side of the bridge I passed the "vortex," another absurdly unworkable but highly PR-sexy invention from the incessant mind of John Hardy. According to the literature handed out at the Admissions Office, the school derived most of its power from the river-powered vortex, but at the moment no generator had been hooked up to the swirling waters. Nor was there a turbine to turn the missing generator.

I remembered Richard pointing out that even if all the parts were there, the vortex wouldn't be able to power anything more than a dollhouse. Plus, some of the villagers had started complaining that the vortex was changing the flow of water downstream. A meeting was held and, supposedly, knives were drawn, but ultimately the locals backed down. It might have been because Hardy paid off the village head, or because he offered many of the men jobs at PT Bambu; but I'm only speculating.

I passed five men carrying a bamboo pole at least five car lengths long. I smiled at them. They looked away from me, said something in Bahasa, then laughed. I knew they were laughing at me, but I had no idea why. Because I was white? Rich? Because my sarong was crooked again?

I quickly looked down at the ground, sharply aware of how distinctly I stood out amidst the hundreds of Javanese and Balinese people who swarmed the campus each day: the gardeners and animal wranglers, compost cleaners, walkway sweepers, pole carriers, construction workers, teachers' aides and guards, cooks, food servers, drivers, as well as the many *pembantu*.

I discarded my self-conscious white-ness and turned right up the steep steps that took me up to the classrooms. I was thoroughly soaked and drained by the time I got to Loy and Elliott's 1st/2nd grade room. I waved hi to Miss Andrea, their teacher, and sat down in the back of the room to wait for lunch time to begin. After wading through the noise of small children infused with the musical sounds coming from Johnny's classroom just a few feet away, and the hammering from the bamboo construction zone behind us, I finally gathered that Andrea was in the middle of teaching them the parts of a plant in English and Bahasa.

"Can anyone tell me what the *batang* is?"

Loy raised her hand first. "Stem!" she said proudly.

My kid. Yes. Mine.

"Correct. And what do we call the flower in Bahasa? Anyone?"

A bout of ADD swept over me and I became increasingly disinterested. I closed my eyes.

"*Bunga.* That's right, Ava."

I was afraid I'd fall asleep instantly, so I opened them and contemplated the thick stream of ants crawling up and down the two ropes from which the chalkboard was suspended. I followed the mass of them up into the *alang-alang* and noticed that there were two bats fast asleep in the corner of the roof, their small bodies snuggled tightly into their own wings. How neat is that, being equipped with your own blanket. Hugging yourself to sleep.

"And the *akar*? What's that?"

Sleep. I was getting oh so sleepy. My eyes heavy ... the words melting ... I suddenly fell forward, and then jumped awake.

Loy was standing in front of me. "Hi, Mommy. You have my lunch?"

"I do, baby. Ham and mayo. Sound good?"

"Yeah, thanks." She snatched the container from me and ran to the Mepantigan, the grand open-aired building that served as Green School's auditorium, gym, and cafeteria. It was also where the occasional performance of Mepantigan, the Balinese mud-wrestling-cum-martial arts practice, happened.

I grabbed Elliott's medicine and followed behind her.

The large space was awash in noise and smells and thick humid heat. In the back of the room, two women served a Balinese lunch from a buffet table. Today's choice was either pork or fish steamed in banana leaves, brown rice, and slices of watermelon.

John Hardy, the man who professed to know what was best for the Balinese people, insisted everyone be served organically grown, brown rice. A treat for us, most definitely, but given all the centuries of white rice consumption here, it was no wonder most of the locals often pushed their rice to the side of their banana leaf plates. Watching them eat around it was like watching Loy try to hide her peas under her mashed potatoes.

At the edge of the space, I noticed John Hardy himself looming over a group of well-dressed white people. Parents? VIPs from another venture he was dabbling in? He had on his usual outfit: a wrinkled, sweat-stained, men's dress shirt, sleeves rolled up and, instead of trousers, he wore a sarong, just like all Balinese men did. I got that he'd been living in Bali for decades, but the whole white-person-going-native thing seemed a little silly on such a large man with a huge belly hanging over it. He reminded me of someone—of course—I flashed on the staff's nickname for him: yes, he *was* Marlon Brando playing Colonel Kurtz in *Apocalypse Now*.

Next to the Colonel was Daniel, the school's resident videographer who photographed or videotaped every John Hardy and every Green School moment. Hardy made a sweeping gesture up toward the roof, showing his guests the four broad bamboo arches and the forty-meter-long end-to-end skylight. Daniel, as if it were attached to his hand, simultaneously panned his camera up and across the long span of the ceiling. Hardy was undoubtedly gloating over the bamboo vision he'd created.

Not that anyone could fault him for wanting to boast. Aesthetically speaking, the Mepantigan, the classrooms, the huts, were nothing short of inspired; true engineering miracles. And he assumed correctly that "if you build it they will come," because come they/we did. But what needed to count now weren't the sexy structures but the *contents* inside them—those little beings running around the dung/mud/concrete-floor, as well as the teachers who taught them.

Had John Hardy truly built Green School as a shrine to some noble purpose, like education or environmental responsibility, I wondered. Or as a shrine to himself?

I let go of my cynical presumption and went to find Elliott.

"Elliott," I said to the dirty blond-haired child splayed out across a row of dusty stone steps, "your mom wants you to put some of this stuff on your bites."

"Yeah, sure." He looked up at me with large sad eyes. "Can you do it for me?"

"Can I—what?" Phillipa had said the bites were infected. Infected with what? Impetigo? I looked around. Maybe I could offer to pay one of the *pembantu* to do it? Or—I undid the top and started to smear the thick ointment all around his legs, using only my right forefinger. Holy cow, but insects liked this kid. Was Pip not as paranoid about dengue as I was? Was anyone?

Speaking of dengue, I looked up to see where Loy was eating lunch and saw Victor and Sara sitting side by side on floor mats, talking and eating. She said something and he laughed. She put her hand out and pulled a loose string off her skirt. Then she brushed some crumbs from Victor's sleeve.

Did they not see me over here next to the kid with the angry bug bites?

I closed the tube, wiped my healing finger on my sarong twenty times, then went over to Loy who was jumping rope with another girl.

"Hi, Loy. Let me see your rash."

"Mommy, it's gone. Look."

"You're right. I'm so glad."

"Can I go back to jumping now?"

"Absolutely. I love you. See you at home."

"I love you more."

My heart went soft. We used to say that to one another every night after I kissed her. "I love you more." "No, I love you more." "No, I love *you* more." Over and over until her eyes got heavy and I backed out of the room.

"No, Loy," I said to my jumping child who couldn't hear me over the cafeteria's din, "I love you more than you will ever know."

I looked back at Victor and caught his eye. I expected he'd get up, but he just waved then turned back to Sara.

What the heck? Were they talking about some important school issue ? Should I go over there, or should I stand in the middle of this room, making a scene because my husband would rather be talking to his co-teacher on a dusty dirty floor than getting up and coming over to me?

I almost squeezed the cap off the tube of ointment in my hand, I felt so frustrated and hot and out of place. I went over to the food and asked for a slice of watermelon, and, as I munched it down I watched my child, the one who loved me from the earth to the moon to the stars that existed beyond infinity. She was my forever. I swallowed a seed as she ran in circles on the floor in her bare feet, her DEET-stained denim capris and a T-shirt with the rows of exotic fish across the front. She seemed positively joyful.

Even though her parents weren't certain they were meant to be together for eternity. Even though she had to sleep with the ants. Even though she left all her friends back home in California. Even though her mother gave her too little yet expected so much back.

I drank in her unconditional bliss and headed for home.

I returned to my mosquito-netted refuge and decided that I'd had enough of thinking about Victor and our marriage and my future for a day. What I needed was to get back to my writing. Back to being a writer. I didn't have to win a Booker: I just had to tell a good story. I could do that. I'd done it before.

I'd wanted to be a writer since I was in the sixth grade. That was when I was supposed to write a book report, but was too distracted by my crush on Tommy Boehm to read the book. When it came time to write the report, I just made up a story.

My teacher, Ms. Robinson, kept me after class.

"Lisa," she said, holding my book report in her hand, "you didn't read the book, did you?"

"Uh, maybe?"

"Well, I have read it, and your book report has nothing to do with the actual book."

I was busted. Now I was going to get detention and my parents—

"But what you wrote is incredibly mature," she continued. "I think you've got real talent."

"You do?"

"I do. In fact, I'm nominating you for the school district's creative writing program this summer."

While my friends practiced archery, macraméd potholders, and experienced their first kisses at summer camp, I spent six weeks hunched over a spiral notebook, learning how to corral my adolescently feral imagination into the written word.

From then on when people asked me what I wanted to be when I grew up I said, "writer."

A teller of stories.

After Victor and I moved from Seattle to the tiny town of Nevada City, I told him I wanted to try writing a novel. Living off his teacher's salary would be tough, but he was his usual supportive self. "Let's give it two years to see if you can make a go of it. If you can't," he said, "you've gotta get a real job."

So I wrote. Or started to, but then one day while on a walk with our dog, Rivers, I passed by a beat-up, old, white house with a FOR SALE sign in the front yard, one littered with rusty pipes and trash. A dirty toilet lay sadly on its side in the shade of an ancient Cedar tree.

I hopped the low ruined fence and squished over the brown mounds of rotting pears that had fallen from a gnarled pear tree, the sharp alcohol-y smell of decay heavy in the summer air. I peeked through the windows and saw the abandoned kitchen with its antiquated O'Keefe and Merritt stove, crusted over with a hundred years of grease and spills. I saw the stained carpet in the living room, the cracked shower door in the bathroom, the gaping hole where the toilet in the yard obviously belonged.

I ran home and got Victor who stood next to me on the crooked porch, his hands shading his eyes as he peered into the same windows and saw the same magical potential that I did.

We bought the 1871 miner's cabin and transformed it back to its youth. When I wasn't tapping out stories on my keyboard, and Victor wasn't teaching, we scraped and sanded and cleaned and caulked and nailed and plastered and painted and taped and swept.

Oh dear lord how we swept.

In a little less than a year we moved in and—like any bird who has just finished building her nest of twigs and spit and leaves—I got pregnant.

"Rivers! You're going to have a baby brother or sister," we said to him, after looking at the double pink lines on the plastic stick. A few weeks later, we rented a drafty cottage on the Sonoma coast. I trolled the beach for shells to use for a mobile over our baby's crib.

We threw the same stick into the sea a thousand times, grateful when Rivers finally collapsed exhausted onto the sand in front of us. After we watched the sunset, Victor stood and put his hand out to help me up. It wasn't until I was in his arms, the cold breezes whipping my hair across my face, that I felt the wetness in my crotch.

I was having a miscarriage.

I went back to writing, every so often touching the small box of unused shells I kept on my desk. I focused on the stories, the pictures in my head, the dialogue. I let writing soothe the ache in my heart and the emptiness in my belly.

Right after I completed *Other Fish in the Sea*, a collection of interrelated stories about a young woman named Elly, I discovered I was pregnant again. And while that healthy new fetus swam contentedly in my womb, a passel of New York editors read my book and fought over it, Hyperion offering me a two-book deal.

After I turned in *Hat Trick*, the second book, we moved out of town. I craved quiet. Loy needed a backyard bigger than a postage stamp, and Victor still hadn't found a porch he could pee off. We bought a blue house on five acres of rolling fields and meadows, next to hundreds of acres of creek-fed wilderness. We converted the small cabin on the property into a writing studio.

It was there that I spent two years writing *Mary's Crossing*, a WWII love story.

It got rejected by ten publishers.

Undeterred, I did as my agent suggested. I put the book out of my mind and started kicking around ideas for another book. When Bali blew me a come-hither kiss, the writer in me zealously acceded. Bali would inspire me. In Bali I would write my best work yet.

Now, as I opened Word, I tried to ignore my skin's increasing incandescence, as well as the noises surrounding the hut. I thought through what I'd sketched so far: Miles Caswell, the protagonist, will have anosmia—he will have no sense of smell. Debilitating as this is, he will use this sensory lack to his advantage. The story will begin in

Alaska, where he guts fish on the slime line, and is the only worker who doesn't complain about the smell. He is renting a room in a former monastery with an ex-monk who lost his religion because of a woman he'd—

From the cemetery across the road came the gasping, raspy roar of a high-powered propane torch. Somebody's useless body was about to get incinerated. A few seconds later a gamelan orchestra started up. Dammit. I bowed my head and prayed that I'd go deaf, at least until the funeral was over. All funeral pyre smoke aside, I'd recently developed a severe aversion to gamelan, that repetitive drumming xylophone-y ensemble played all over Indonesia. No cremation or celebration in Bali is complete without it.

The first dozen times you hear gamelan, you sort of dig its persistent reverberations filling your entire being with an almost trance-like power. Then one day you're sitting on your bamboo couch answering emails; and you realize that for the last hour a gamelan orchestra has just been playing at someone's cremation next door, and you hardly noticed. Then, around the twenty-third time you hear that same pulsating clangorous cacophony, you get this unreachable metallic itch inside your chest. And you have to immediately put on headphones and scroll down your iPod to Coldplay.

Smoke. Gamelan. Either I could freak out and hold my fist up at the smoky grey sky or I could try to settle down and embrace the moment. I shut my computer, pushed aside the mosquito net, went into the downstairs bedroom, and unrolled my yoga mat.

I sat cross-legged and chanted "ohm" to get my myself grounded. "Ahhhhhhoooooooooooooooooohhhhhhhhhhhhhhhhhmmmmm."

"Lisa! You saying something to me?" Seni yelled through the floor of our bedroom directly above my head.

"*Tidak*. I'm doing yoga."

"Okay. I stay quiet."

I unfolded my legs, turned over and stretched into child's pose. What was Seni doing in our bedroom this late in the day? Had we gotten a laundry delivery? No; there's never a laundry delivery on Friday. What was she doing? What was that sound?

I uncurled and yelled up through the ceiling. "Seni? Whatcha doing?"

"I cleaning many spiders from your room, Lisa. This is okay?"

"Yes. Of course." I moved into downward-dog pose, held it, stretched my calves—right then left then right then left—then walked my legs forward and hung down, letting my head fall freely, before rolling up one vertebrate at a time.

"Lisa. You want I am making the *cumi-cumi* tonight, *ya*?"

I stopped mid-sun-salutation. "Yes, Seni!"

"Okay."

Two more sun salutations. Then I shifted my weight to my left foot, tucked my right foot up into the inside of my left thigh, and raised my arms straight up.

Tree pose.

I breathed in the warm air, held myself still. Listened to the whoosh of the ceiling fan. Let the gamelan bells wash over me. Felt something large start to crawl across my foot—

What the? I dropped my right foot and kicked my left leg out, flicking the cockroach-like creature against the wall. I walked over to where it lay, stunned, on the floor, tiny stars, I assumed, floating like a solar system around its bristly bug head.

I rolled up my mat and went out to the kitchen to eat papaya.

"Lisa, you finish yoga?" Seni said as she came downstairs. Seni loved to state the obvious.

"I wasn't that into it today."

"You go see Loy and Victor?"

"I gave Loy her lunch, but Victor and Sara were talking, and I didn't want to interrupt them."

"Oooh, I like Sara. She very nice. And so pretty *ya*. Do you think?"

"Do I think Sara is pretty?" While fairly new to teaching, Sara was a lot like Victor. She always smiled, always had a nice word for anyone she met, and she saw the positive in every situation. She was dedicated to the kids and even more so to Victor. When I first met her back in July she told me how fired up she was to have such an experienced teacher as a mentor.

"I am going to learn so much from your husband," she'd gushed to me as I handed her a cup of tea.

And, yes, she was quite pretty. Now that I thought about it, she looked a lot like Taylor Swift.

"Yeah, she's pretty, sure," I said to Seni. "What's your point?"

"What you mean, *point*?"

"Nothing. I mean nothing by it."

Seni opened the fridge and took out the packages of squid. "Sara will come for *cumi-cumi* tonight?"

"I assume so. We bought enough for an army."

While Seni cleaned the large mound of slimy white invertebrates, I boiled some jackfruit seeds and salted them. They went perfectly with beer.

By the time we both finished, Loy and Victor were home from their day in jungle school, looking hot, exhausted, and in dire need of refreshments.

"Oooh, nuts," Loy exclaimed, scooping up a handful.

Victor headed straight for the cold shower. When he emerged minutes later in a towel, I handed him a cold Bintang. "How was your day?" I asked.

Do you still love me? I did not ask.

"Hot. Long. Frustrating."

I watched Loy try to open a container of cherry yogurt that she grabbed out of the freezer then hand it to Seni to pry off. "Why frustrating?"

"For one thing, they shouldn't have put ninth graders in our class."

"Why not?"

"I know the school needs as many kids as they can get, but remember I was only supposed to have eighteen kids?"

"How many do you have?"

"They enrolled another kid today, so now we have twenty-four, and you know, we just can't give them—their parents are starting to get more pissed off that we're not giving them what they were promised. And oh, get this: Brad informed the staff that the Hardys just lost a ton of money in the stock market and so from now on we're going to have to make do with less."

I swallowed a nut and gasped. "What? Less what?"

"Less everything. We're going to have to dial down the curriculum. No foreign language teachers. No PE teacher. No drama teacher."

"But I thought they were so rich? I don't get it." I thought of John Hardy with his tour group today. What had he told them about the school? Had he described it as a place where resources are plenty and no expense is spared for the sake of the children? And in the same breath did he ask them to help cover the cost of tuition for a local Balinese child, like he always did?

I imagined that after showing them the Mepantigan he strolled them over to The Heart of School—the massive three-story construction project going on in the center of campus—a great expanse of sticks and scaffolding and sound. It was going to be, when finally finished, the world's largest bamboo structure. It would house the school's library, computer lab, administrative offices, upper grade classrooms, art rooms, and more.

It would be the apotheosis of Hardy's vision.

And, if you forked over a couple thousand dollars, you'd get to have your name carved into one of the bamboo poles used to build it.

"Yeah, well, according to Brad they're pretty much done giving money. He made it sound like the gravy train is gone, and we shouldn't ask for any more things for our classrooms, which means we'll probably not see any computers for the kids any time soon."

"But does that also mean you'll—"

"Hey, you know what? I'm done talking about this right now. I'm gonna go get dressed."

I wanted to keep talking about it. I wanted to know the implications for us, the school, Victor's job. I was about to follow him up the stairs when Katy appeared at our gate.

"Hey there! Can I come in?" Katy, who lived next door, had been working in Jakarta, but had gotten sick of the city's noise and pollution so she took the job at Green School. Why should she have suspected that she'd find a lot of the same noise and pollution in Bali? Katy regretted coming to Bali almost as much as I did. We often commiserated over our imaginary fence.

"At least you have your family to whine to," she pointed out the other day, a little too accusingly, I might add.

"Katy! Come in. We've got fixings for gin and tonics if you want to make some."

"Excellent. I'm on it."

"Hi guys."

"Sinead!"

"Sinead, you walking," Seni yelled, running toward the gate. "Here, I help you. You sit here and I bring you food, okay?"

"*Suksma*, Seni. Are those jackfruit nuts I see over there?"

"Who needs a beer?"

"Did someone say 'beer'?" That was Sam, the 5th/6th grade teacher who took over for Carol.

"Thanks for dropping off the beer, Sam," Sinead joked from her chair. "We'll call you if we need more."

"Don't get up, Sinead. I'd hate for you to have to move anything more than your mouth."

"May I come in?" Sara asked from the stoop.

"Sara. You came." Victor walked past Sam and opened the gate for her. "Can I get you a beer?"

Why was he so pleased to see her? Didn't they work together ten hours a day?

"Sara!" Seni yelled. "You look so beautiful in your skirt. Come eat *cumi-cumi*. You so skinny, you need to eat, okay!"

"Okay," Sara said with a laugh. "I will. Thanks."

Johnny and Phillipa and their children Elliott and Emily came next. Loy and Emily disappeared upstairs to her room while Johnny told the rest of us about a Balinese helper getting hurt today. "The wind came up just as she was passing by Heart of School. A massive bamboo pole fell over and knocked her down. Pretty much flattened her."

"Oh, no!" Sinead said before sticking a fried ring into her mouth. "Is she okay?"

"She was taken to the hospital." Andrea, Loy's teacher, appeared at the door just in time to respond. "John Hardy was about to bring a tour group through, and he made sure she was whisked away before they saw what happened. I heard that she got bruised pretty badly, but there's no internal damage. Anyway ... is there any squid left?"

Andrea complained about her hut more than I did, and not just because of the mold. She hated the lack of privacy as well as the lack of shelving for her clothing. No one on the staff looked as put together as Andrea did. She never left her house until she blew her hair straight and ironed her skirts. By the end of the day, though, when everyone else looked like a squashed up piece of litter you might kick aside, I was relieved to see that she did, too.

"There's plenty. Come in. Come in," I yelled from the couch.

Sinead turned and asked me, "Hey, you think maybe they'll fire the helper for getting hurt?"

"Ha-ha. You want something else to drink?"

"Another beer would be marvelous, darling. Thanks."

When I walked into the kitchen to get a cold beer from the freezer, I had to squeeze past Victor and Sara, who were huddled up near one another, talking in hushed intimate whispers.

"Hi, guys," I said as casually as I could pretend to be.

"Hi, Lisa. Do you need something?"

"Me? No. What are you two talking about?"

"Sara was just telling me about the school in Korea where she taught and how they spoiled the new teachers."

"Spoiled? I would have been happy with a hello and a wilted bouquet of flowers," Pip said as she came up next to me. "When we landed, there wasn't anyone to greet us. No one told us where to buy food or anything. We were left to fend for ourselves. It's a good thing Johnny knew some Bahasa or we'd still be waiting at the airport."

"You guys have no idea what most international schools do for teachers," Katy slurred more than spoke. "In Jakarta? Oh man. I'm talking welcome wagon galore. New teachers get put up in a five-star hotel for their orientation weekend. They're wined and dined. They take care of everything for you—your work permit and visa crap—all the legal stuff they take care of it, and they teach you about living in Indonesia. They—where's my drink? Oh, here it is in my hand! Ha-ha!"

We waited for the ice to stop clinking. "What's housing like?" Andrea asked.

"It sure isn't moldy, kiddo, I'll tell you that. I lived in a huge apartment complex with the other internationals. Fully furnished. Air-conditioned. They hired everyone a cook and a housekeeper. After the first week, there's a big-ass welcome party for all the teachers. Unlimited food and alcohol."

It only then dawned on me that neither John Hardy nor his wife Cynthia had ever acknowledged our arrival. Neither of them once said, "Hey, by the way, thanks for coming halfway around the world to teach at our school."

And when we finally did move into our finished hut, we found no note, no hut-warming present other than some laundry detergent and an enormous jug of mosquito-spray. Everything else, from the forks to the toaster to the dishes and glasses to the salad spinner, we had to find on our own.

"Come on, people!" Sam interjected from the dining room table where he sat with his feet up on another chair. "Let's not forget that we're pioneers here!"

Now the whole hut erupted in laughter because every teacher and every spouse and every child in the room had had to sit through (some more than once) John Hardy's famous speech comparing the lot of us to the pioneers who forged the Oregon Trail. Like the brave souls who pushed on into uncharted territory in the 1800s, we, too, would have to endure hardships if we wanted to make the school a success. Being the first at something required a real "pioneering spirit."

Come to think of it, he wasn't far off comparing us to those early emigrants: they also slept out in the open and had to contend with miserable weather and deadly diseases.

"Speaking of visas," Sam added. "Does anyone know if we'll ever get work visas?"

Victor had been dealing with that very issue, and it was like a fresh cut to him. Green School had not yet gotten a legitimate license to operate a business in Indonesia. Technically, it wasn't allowed to employ any non-Indonesian workers. Putu in human resources had recently informed him that we had to hand over our passports so she could get our social visas extended for a third time.

"We're totally working illegally," Victor announced.

"Well, that's comforting," Sinead said.

"As long as you don't try to leave the country, it's probably no biggie," Sara stated as randomly as if she were remarking on the deliciousness of the salad greens.

Not try to leave the country?

"You guys hear about the possible change of schedule for the conferences?" Johnny asked from the living room chair. He had his feet propped up on the railing and his son Elliott raced around in circles, ducking beneath his father's legs every 360 degrees.

"What?" Victor said, moving away from Sara. "What are you talking about?"

"Now don't get all excited, Victor, not till it's a sure thing, but I heard that CNN is coming to do a story on the school. Cynthia said if it's during parent-teacher conferences, we'd have to cancel them."

"Why?" Sam asked.

"Because she wants them to film the campus when it's filled with kids."

"That seems fair," Andrea said.

"No, it doesn't. It's idiotic," Victor replied. "We need to have those conferences."

Sara added her support. "Do you guys know how many parents are already freaking at this point?"

"I'm freaking at this point," Sam offered through a mouth full of salad. "I think we're down to three beers."

Sara put down her beer. "Seriously. Oki's mom sent Victor and me an email yesterday. She and lots of her friends are really *concerned*," she said, forming quote signs in front of her low-cut blouse with a green-flowered print that perfectly matched her hair band.

During the dramatic pause, I heard Loy and Emily playing dress-up in our room. Obviously the killer ants had already taken over hers.

"She's pissed that there's no music program. She's pissed that the kids still have no computers."

"Yeah, that sucks."

"And no library."

"Let's not forget the safety issues, folks," Phillipa, the substitute nurse, added. "The fact that kids are getting injured every day—falls, cuts, and we still have no one but me to mend them. And we've yet to talk about fire drills or evacuation plans."

Andrea scraped together some of the burnt squid crumbs and dropped them into her mouth. "What are we supposed to do if a kid wanders off into the jungle?"

"Or falls into the river?" Sinead said. I could tell she wanted to add a *What if someone falls through a bamboo shower floor?* but she managed to keep the conversation child-centric. I went over and took her empty plate and patted her shoulder.

"I get all that," Victor said. "But what you're missing is the fact that more than half the kids in our class are below grade level, and the parents still have no idea. Their little darlings are academically so far behind their peers in the States and Europe. And Sara and I are going to have to break the news to them sooner rather than later."

"You mean *if* the conferences take place," Katy said.

"Oh, they'll take place. If Hardy cancels them, I'll quit."

I did a double-take and my beer sloshed onto my foot. I saw a look of surprise wash over Sara's face. Everyone's eyes seemed to get larger.

"You won't quit over that," Katy protested from the floor where she languished, her wiry tanned arms and legs tangled around three purple cushions.

"Watch me," Victor replied.

During a call to my mother in San Diego, she asked me why Seni is called Seni if Balinese children are named according to their birth order.

"I don't know. It's complicated."

"What's so complicated that you with the almost Ph.D. can't figure it out?" came her insistent voice through my computer headphones. "Are you too busy to find out?"

After closing Skype, I did some investigating and concluded that the Balinese naming system is mystifying. Nonetheless, I ascertained that there are four castes in Hindu Bali. In descending order these are *Brahmana* (priests); *Satriya* (nobles, ruling officials, and warriors); *Wesya* (lower nobility, merchants, and bureaucrats); and the *Sudra* caste (everyone else, i.e., ninety percent of the population).

Both *Wesya* and *Sudra* male and female names begin with *I* and *Ni* (pronounced "ee" and "knee"), respectively. Only those born into the *Sudra* caste are named for their birth order:

First-born = Wayan or Putu
Second-born = Made (pronounced "Mah-day") or Kadek
Third-born = Komang or Nyoman
Fourth-born = Ketut

These are followed by a name which is supposed to have some spiritual meaning, but from what I've discerned, it's more of a description or a pet name (*Seni* means "art"). Lastly, comes the family name (which does not change when you get married). The legal name of our beloved *pembantu* is Ni Ketut Seni Nurnaningsih, but she prefers to be known as Seni, not Ketut.

For some strange reason, second-born males in Bali seem particularly drawn to the transportation industry. Of the six drivers' names we had in our cell phone, five were I Made's. And which one was going to drive me to Ubud today to get waxed, so that when I put on a bathing suit in two days, people won't mistake me for a dog? I called I Made Subayasa, the one we referred to as "the nice I Made," the one who smiled all the time and had infinite patience. The one who adored Loy and drove at a safe speed.

After he dropped me off at the spa where I'd made my appointment, the young man behind the desk informed me that Kadek, the waxing chick, "no come yet. She come later. You come back."

"*Kapan*?" I asked. Are we talking a couple of minutes here, or more like later this week?

I heard "*dua jam*" in the midst of a long polysyllabic reply, so I thanked him and went outside to figure out how best to kill the next two hours. I looked up the street in the direction of Ubud's huge traditional market, as well as Bali Buddha, the quintessentially hippie oasis that sold overpriced ginseng smoothies, spelt pancakes, hummus plates, and the cinnamon raisin muffins that Sinead had begged me to buy for her if I should pass by during my day in town.

Then I looked south toward our old haunts: Bali Putra and Pizza Bagus, and the Sacred Monkey Forest Sanctuary.

If I turned right, I could squeeze through the multitudinous aisles in search of a hand-hewn machete that'd go dull after slitting a throat or two; or a rainbow's worth of flip-flops; or any one of the thousands of hand-made, hand-woven, hand-sewn, hand-carved, thoroughly useless, plastic, bamboo, or wooden trinkets that tourists buy for their friends back home.

Or I could go grab a couple of muffins for Sinead and drink down a mango/watermelon/ginger smoothie, while eavesdropping on the

American hipsters who lazed about all day in their expertly cinched sarongs, dusty leather sandals, and tie-dyed headbands, smoking clove cigarettes.

If I turned left, I had the option of grabbing a slice of *jamur* (mushroom) pizza at Pizza Good, or shooting the breeze with our old pal, Putu. Or I could walk a couple blocks beyond Bali Putra and go hang with a couple hundred, long-tailed macaques at the Sacred Monkey Forest Sanctuary.

Monkeys.

For a long time now, I hadn't wanted to be within spitting distance of a monkey. Before my phantom death by head monkey man, I'd loved them, reveled in our genetic cousinship. I took great delight in watching them use their opposable thumbs.

Until one of them almost bit me.

I pictured monkeys playing running jumping through Balinese temples in the midst of a thick shaded jungle. I saw a quiet, ruminative scene. I saw myself not letting the past crack a whip at my present.

I picked the monkeys. The monkeys who live down on Monkey Forest Road, which is just over from *Jalan Raya Hanuman* (Monkey God Street).

I wiped off some underarm sweat with the back of my wrist and crossed the football field, passing by a long line of men holding—what the? All of them were holding roosters while stroking and talking to them. I walked past, trying not to stare, but there was A LINE OF MEN HUGGING CHICKENS. How could I not stare? And there at the front of the queue was a Priest who was, as far as I could tell, anointing those birds with some heavenly powers.

A Blessing of the Cocks.

I knew Loy would be bummed that she missed the show of birds on display. She'd recently brought to our attention that she wanted to see a cockfight up close—that peaceful gathering where small steel daggers (*taji*) get attached to roosters' legs and two of them are thrown into a ring together to fight to the death. As it's a betting game, the (human) winner earns cash. He also gets to take the loser home and doubtlessly turn it into a nice *soto ayam*.

There was no way Loy would be watching a cockfight any time soon.

At the bottom of the street, I saw our formerly favorite *makan padang* spot, which I believe translates into "Muslim-friendly-no-pig-eat-in/take-out buffet-style-restaurant." There are more than a handful of such *warungs* (small food stall) around Bali, catering to the small minority population who, besides fasting during Ramadan, do not worship monkey Gods.

Back when we lived in Ubud, Loy and I stopped in one day and watched other people order before figuring out the proper technique: you go up to the lady standing next to some twenty or so different dishes displayed in the window and say, "*Satu, silakan.*" One please. She scoops out an enormous glob of white rice from a pot and drops it into the middle of a large bowl. Then she waits for you to tell her (or, in our case, point to) which of the dishes you want her to put on the rice. The fare included fried potato cakes, fried chicken, some kind of curry fish, meat of some sort in a tomato sauce, water spinach in a bland sauce, chicken in a spicy sauce, and hard-boiled eggs in yet another sauce. We both picked five or six different foods to try, then sat in folding chairs at one of four family sized tables. A broken fan teased us from above.

Including two bottles of iced tea and two bottles of water, the bill totaled $.90.

Yes. Ninety cents.

When I got to the Monkey Sanctuary I paid my 15,000 rupiah ($1.50) entrance fee, and started down one of the winding paths that crisscrossed the twenty-seven acres of jungle. I was stopped by a little boy offering to sell me a bunch of bananas to feed to the monkeys. I declined. I had no desire to get within feeding distance.

I wandered over to one of the three temples inside the sanctuary and sat down midway up the steps, under the shade of a large banyan tree. If I'd had on a sarong I would have gone onto the temple's grounds to set a spell, but I'd worn my blue cotton pants with a pull tie. It's disrespectful—for both males and females—to enter temple grounds without wearing a (properly tied) sarong. I couldn't go in if I had my period either. Or if I was carrying a baby who was less than four days old. And, according to the sign, if I'd "resontly" lost a relative, I'd have to wait until three days after that relative had been cremated or buried before being allowed entry.

The steps were fine. It would be only a matter of minutes before some curious food-seekers would come by to check me out. While I waited, I closed up my purse and tucked it behind me between my lower back and the next step. The monkeys were famous for stealing stuff out of tourists' hands and disappearing into the jungle. There were signs all over the place warning visitors that the monkeys WILL pick your pockets, grab any jewelry or watches you wear, or rip your expensive camera off your leather strap and go far away with it.

An American, or possibly Canadian, family was descending the stairs behind me (wearing none of the aforementioned compulsory sarongs), while in front of me a family of macaques had just dropped down off a tree to see what was happening.

The older monkey male busied himself with crotch-scratching while the female picked fleas and other assorted detritus from her baby's fur, eating what she found. The two juveniles hissed at one another with their teeth bared, playacting aggression. While one rolled over onto his back and appeared to fall deeply asleep, the other one climbed a tree, hollered down at the humans, jumped down off the tree, yawned, played with his feet, fiddled with some rocks on the ground next to him, scratched his legs, bit his own foot; then pounced on his sleeping buddy, pulled his/her tail, and ran up the stairs a few inches from where I sat, his rudely awakened friend in hot pursuit. They chased one another up and over and around the temple walls for a few seconds, then barreled back to their friends/ family, smacked each other around Three Stooges–style, and collapsed onto the dirt.

I slouched low and pretended to be lost in thought as the dominant male human ordered his two small offspring to go stand by the monkeys and pose for the camera.

"Go a little closer, Mattie," he demanded. "That's it; now hold out one of those bananas—who has an extra one—here give me one of yours, Sue. Reid—here; feed this to that little guy."

And just as the small male hominid reached out to offer the *other* small male hominid a banana, the mama monkey suddenly screeched at what, I guess, she considered a pathetically tiresome scene. She grabbed her baby, tucked it up under her belly and fled, causing the large male to leap onto the humanoid father's back, pull his hair, reach across his chest and attempt to yank the camera out of his hand, whereby the father yelped, "What the hell? Ow!" which startled his son into forgetting to let go of the banana gift he was in the midst of offering, precipitating the slighted juvenile monkey to snatch it directly from the kid's hand, inadvertently scratching his skin as he did so.

When the boy yelled in response to the unwelcome snatching/scratching, Mattie wailed into the air for no good reason other than that she was a five-year-old child and the world around her had devolved into monkey chaos.

At the sound of the human howl, the monkeys bounded off, one banana richer. The family waited for Mattie to calm down before walking off and leaving me alone in the humid shade of a Balinese jungle.

Relieved beyond words not to have had to witness fangs or gushing blood, I strolled down to the temple pools to watch the monkeys splash about in the water, ducking their heads under and out like small children.

A couple minutes later I was standing up to leave, when two American women in their thirties—both reeking of far too much perfume and wearing inappropriately short shorts—alighted not three feet from where I sat. One of them said something that made me lower my butt to the wall once more.

"He blames all his sadness on me and the rest of the world. He thinks that if he was with someone else, or doing something else, he'd be happy."

Why did that ring such a loud bell?

"What do you mean? Does he want to have an affair?"

"I don't think he does," the fretful one said, not bothering to notice the monkey antics taking place in front of her. "But he's so manic. One day he's happy-*ish*, then he's depressed."

"Do you think he needs drugs?"

"No. Counseling would be good, but no way he'd go."

"Why not?"

"He can't have anyone else tell him he's wrong or sad or anything but what he is. He needs to be right all the time. He needs to, I don't know, *win*."

"Win what?" the friend inquired.

She laughed and a gold bracelet jingled. A monkey looked up. Oh no, little monkey, I said to myself, stay right there and keep playing. Don't bother the smart lady who is telling her friend all about me.

"Exactly," she replied. "Win what? That's what I ask him all the time. I say, 'I didn't realize we were in a competition and someone has to win,' but he doesn't get it. I mean, for him to win, does that mean the rest of us have to lose?"

I don't know. Does it? I also felt that way sometimes; like when Victor and I fight, I get so hooked onto the winning part I can't even remember what we were tussling over in the first place.

"Why can't we all win?" she said, adding much to my rapidly expanding non-Biblical book of revelations.

The unfretful friend took out a compact from her huge, trendy, leather bag and dabbed some powder on her rapidly melting makeup. I worried that one of the wet monkeys would try to snatch it. "So what are you going to do?"

Yes, what are you going to do?

"Heck if I know." She smiled at a small monkey that padded over to her. I wanted the monkey to go away and stop distracting her. I wanted her to keep talking. "I just wish he'd take *some* responsibility for his own happiness. And not keep thinking that it's everyone else's job."

Both women cooed at the little hairy intruder. The friend stood up and tugged her shorts down. "I don't get it, Lindsey. I don't get people who aren't just happy because." She knelt down and put her hand out toward the monkey. I prayed he wouldn't bite it or jump on her head. "Mike should just look around him and see what a great life he has. Shoot, his work flies you guys to Bali for free and all he's doing is complaining about the food."

"No. He's having some fun here, for sure, but, I don't know…"

I looked at my cell phone. I had to leave. Hurry. What? What?

"…I think Michael is waiting for everything in his life to change so that he can be happy."

When had I stopped being *just happy*? I wanted to believe I'd been an undeniably happy person back in California, but the more I thought about it the more I realized I wasn't all that different than I was now. Ever since my third novel got rejected, I'd been moody. Too quick to anger and accusation. I was often a dark presence, hovering over Victor's life like a bitch balloon: a Pigpen cloud of ugliness following me around. Sometimes, I remembered, no one, not even me, wanted to be with me.

Now and then Victor had referred to "us" as if it were a thing that could be gotten rid of. Occasionally Loy threw tea parties without inviting me. If I'd bothered to look, I would have seen the questioning looks on their faces when I walked into the house at the end of each day—the days I'd spent locked in my studio, pretending to write, trying to find my way back to the person I used to be. I no longer knew how to appreciate all that was good and beautiful in my life. I was stuck.

Could that be why I was so desperate to move to Bali? And why Victor had been more than agreeable? Did he, like me, mistakenly think that moving to Bali would change me back to the woman I was before? The smart, sassy, smiling woman he'd fallen in love with?

It didn't matter where I was living because it wasn't the *place* that was going to change me. What was the saying?

Wherever you go, there you are.

I'd been using Bali as an excuse.

"He doesn't get that happiness doesn't just *happen*. It's a choice you make every moment," Lindsey's friend stated.

She was right: happiness is a choice. It's not what *happens* to you. It's not where you live. Or who you live with. It's what you make happen on your own. It didn't matter if I stayed in Bali or went back to California. Neither place was going to make me truly, unconditionally happy.

"That's perfect. I should say that to him. I will tell him that it's *his* choice. He can *choose* to be happy or he can stay sad. Period. It's never going to work between us if he doesn't figure that out."

"Will you quote me?" the friend said with a laugh.

"Naturally. So, you wanna go or walk around some more?"

"Nah. I'm over the monkeys. Let's go back to the hotel and go for a swim."

They walked away, barely acknowledging the darling monkey, who was, like I, staring up at the sky, contemplating the universe's seemingly infinite wonders.

As I wiped the layer of green mold from our big, black Eagle Creek suitcase, I clung tight to the wisdom I'd received from the Monkey Forest School of Consciousness. I threw the damp bag on the bed and, while Loy and Victor ate their toast, cereal and sliced mango, I packed for our very first Balinese holiday.

I'd gotten us a KITAS rate at the Bali Hyatt. KITAS: an indecipherable acronym for the working visa Victor and the other western teachers were supposed to have been given upon their arrival. Besides the issue of how much exactly to pay off the officials at the immigration office, there was the fact that Green School hadn't yet been fully approved by either a structural engineer or the head priest, both essential prerequisites. Until then, we lived in Bali on repeatedly renewed social visas.

Once we got our KITAS, though, we'd be able to get "local," far cheaper rates at western hotels, restaurants, spas, etc. When I made our reservations, I'd lied to the Hyatt reservations agent, saying we had a KITAS. I was hoping they wouldn't ask to see it—whatever *it* looks like.

Regardless, it'd been ages since we'd gone anywhere and I felt aflame with anticipation.

I felt aflame with sweat, too. At this point I'd have walked on glass to get to an air-conditioned hotel room with walls. We'd moved sixteen time zones away to an island in the Indian Ocean, and had yet to see the sea. Finally, we were breaking out of our bamboo prison and going on vacation, a wacky thing to say considering we were living in Bali.

I phoned I Made, our favorite driver, to confirm that he'd be by to pick us up at ten. "*Ya, Ya.* Two-hundred and fifty thousand rupiah," I said, agreeing to the price of $25. "*Tidak apa apa.*" No problem.

I took another cold shower, put my hair up in a fancy bun, looked at Victor's watch, and sat down to wait.

"Loy, we're going to a nice hotel. Take off those stained shorts and put on a dress—where the hell is I Made?"

"It's still early, Lisa," Victor said from his breakfast bar perch where he sat typing on his laptop. "I thought we can't check in till three."

"So what? We can show up early and drink umbrella drinks on the beach while they get our room ready. Why are you still working? You should go upstairs and finish packing."

"It'll take me all of forty-five seconds to throw a few shirts into the suitcase," he replied without bothering to turn around and face his impatient spouse. Loy, meanwhile, stood behind me with her elbows on the back of the couch, making short breathy sounds through her nose, taking in the exchange as if she were a scientist contemplating the paradox that is marriage. "What are you doing, baby? Why haven't you changed your clothes yet?"

"What's an umbrella drink?" she asked skipping across the room.

"It's something you only drink on holiday," I said, wondering if I needed another shower. I really wanted to step into the hotel lobby looking cool and collected, not desperate and soggy.

"Will I get to drink one?"

"Yes, but yours will be virgin ones. Like a virgin piña colada or a virgin daiquiri."

"What's a virgin?"

As if I didn't see that coming a mile away! "Something that's been untouched," I replied.

"But if no one's touched the drink then there's no drink to drink!"

"The juice is touched—I mean, there's juice in everyone's drink, but Mommy's will have rum in it, meaning it's been, ah, touched a little more," I tried, then gave up and went over to Victor, where I took my turn hovering behind him, breathing breathy sounds through my nose.

"Lisa, please. Let me finish. Brad's waiting for this."

"What is it?"

"Yeah, Daddy, what is it?" Loy asked. She pulled one of her hungry dolls out of the bamboo toy basket and began to nurse it.

"No one has created any scheduling or protocol forms for the parent-teacher conferences, so I guess I'm the one doing it."

"But you're on holiday."

"Yeah, well. I'm also coming up with a fire drill plan."

"Shouldn't they have done that before school started?"

He ignored that question because we both knew it was rhetorical.

"Well, just … finish," was all I could say because if he didn't get the documents written now, he'd work poolside. And that would be *tidak bagus*. No good.

I thought of calling Sinead, who I knew was on her way to the airport. Flying to Singapore to get an MRI so that everyone would know how bad her injury was, had been my idea. Getting the school to pay for the flight had been hers.

"Plus, you'll get to see your fiance," I'd said, wishing her *bon voyage* and hoping like hell she'd come back to Bali. Besides *Ibu* Sinead, I had no real friends in Bali. Victor, my former best friend in the whole world, had become more of a roommate and parenting partner. We no longer laid side by side in bed at the end of his interminable days, me listening with interest while the finger holding my place in my book slowly lost feeling. Now he barely finished his sentences with me during dinner. And he slept with Loy every night, using the scary ants as more of an excuse than both of us dared to admit.

Instead, I listened to Sinead's stories. I nodded and empathized and caressed her wounded back and told her she was too good for this place. All the stuff I should have been doing for Victor.

I drank a glass of water, wiped up a line of ants from the counter where Loy had left a milky trail, looked out the window hole, waved to the gardener lady, went upstairs to again check that the door to the wall safe was locked, packed another sarong for me and another sundress for Loy, sat on the bed next to the suitcase, picked my thumb nail, and sighed.

"Hello? Can we come in?" came a voice from below.

I looked over the railing and saw Aldo, prince of impeccably bad-timing, standing next to a short, wiry, bald Balinese man who held a machete as long as his arm.

"Aldo? What's going on?" I asked, guessing by the presence of the machete that the umbrella drinks might have to wait.

"I promised you I'd get rid of those ants, right? I've got your man right here."

"I know. But why today? Why right now?"

"Lisa." He smiled and raised a knowing eyebrow at the small brown dude by his side. "This is Bali, remember? These guys are on Bali time. We take them when we can get them."

I felt icky talking about machete man in third person so I came downstairs and we made introductions all around.

"*Selamat pagi. Nama saya* Lisa. *Suami saya* Victor. *Saya anak perempuan* Loy. *Apa nama Anda*?"

"My name *Pak* Tri."

"Your name is Mister Tree?"

"Mommy. His name is Tree?"

"*Ya.* Tri. Is okay?"

"Sure. Very okay. Let's go upstairs, alright? Aldo, aren't you coming?"

"You don't need me. I've got to get a crew of men ready to bleach Katy's house."

"Fine. Sure. See you later."

"Text me if there's an issue."

Pak Tri followed me up the stairs to the landing. "*Di sana*," I said, pointing up the offending tree. "*Banyak semut.*" Many ants.

But how was he going to get up there? Did he carry a ladder in his back pocket? Did Aldo expect—oh, man, look at him go! "Loy, Victor, you gotta come see this."

Loy ran upstairs but Victor continued to type as if it were an ordinary occurrence to have a man climbing up a tree through the middle of your house. Loy and I stood mesmerized as our resident tree-meister, with his machete hanging by a string at the back of his shorts, crawled up the tree like a monkey. With his feet flat on the sides of the rough bark and his arms hugging the trunk, he pushed his feet to straight, grasped the tree, pulled his feet up a few feet, then started over. Halfway up we lost sight of him so we ran outside to watch him ascend the final twenty feet.

When he got to the top he yelled down, "*Ya! Semut! Semut!*"

He'd found the ant hive. Farm. Nest. Lair. Whatever it is they call it, he'd found it. He grabbed his machete and began hacking away. I pulled Loy out the way as three giant leaves came hurtling down.

Those leaves were teeming, I mean TEEMING with ants.

No, actually, they were writhing with ants.

Pak Tri slid down the tree and came outside to observe the mess he'd made on the ground in front of us, Victor close behind.

"Now what?" I asked no one in particular. It'd take us about a week to stamp them dead. "Should we drag the leaves over to the forest and set them free?" Sure, this wretched ant gang had been tormenting our family for ages now, but I had no wish to see them murdered in cold blood on the ground. It'd been *their* tree, their home. Their peaceful pheromone-rich ant pad. Then a bunch of design-silly humans came along and constructed a house around their house. They had no choice but to crawl and bite their way through Loy's princess dresses.

"In the spirit of fairness I say we—"

"I make fire now," *Pak* Tri said, grabbing a can of gasoline out of what seemed like thin air. And before any of us could protest, he shook the can empty, dousing, splashing, sloshing those ants with so much fuel, I suspect most of them drowned before he tossed on the lit match.

In a flash the leaves crinkled and the ants smoked. We four stood wordlessly watching the flames lick the ground clean, leaving scarcely a trace of ant or leaf. Someone touched my shoulder and I jumped.

"Oh, I Made. Hi."

"*Ibu* Lisa. I am here now. We go to Sanur today, *ya*?" he asked, probably wondering why a family about to go on a beach holiday was standing around a smoking pile of dead ants. Did he think maybe it was an American custom to sacrifice insects before embarking on a road trip, just to be sure we had a safe journey?

"Yes," I said, moving off toward the house. "We go to Sanur today."

One of the reasons I chose the Bali Hyatt resort was because it's in the village of Sanur, which a lot of the expats nicknamed SNORE due to its relatively low-key, non-disco-y vibe. In Sanur you'll find few, if any, rabble-rousing, Bintang-swilling, twenty-somethings trolling the streets and beaches for an all-night party. In Sanur you are more likely to bump up against rich British retirees or sunburnt German honeymooners, than half an Australian rugby team looking for a good fight or a cheap tattoo.

Not to discount or insult or downplay any of that other stuff. I'd spent many a week—pre-Victor—rousing rabble with friends. But I was a grown-up now with a husband and delicate child and a hatred of all things noisy and crowded. If we'd desired that sort of rollicking frat-boy vay-kay, we would have gone to Kuta, the site of the infamous Bali Bombings back in 2002, where lots of young, dancing, drinking rabble-rousers got blown up.

The bombings were the reason we were immediately halted by three machine-gun-fondling policemen when we turned into the long drive to reach the hotel. They looked through the windows at the four of us. They opened the back of the car and pushed our suitcases around as if jiggling them would give away our concealed plastique. One of the guards ran a long mirror—like the kind the dentist uses to check your back teeth, only one thousand times the size—underneath the car.

Did I look like someone who wanted to blow this place up or did I look like a lady in desperate need of some R&R? "Why is this taking so long?" I asked the windshield.

"Relax, Lisa."

"Yeah, Mommy. Just relax."

Twenty minutes later, I was sitting on a saffron-colored couch in the marble-floored, open-air lobby of the hotel, sipping a complementary tropical fruit drink through a red straw. Around my neck hung a frangipani necklace.

The nice man at the front desk had been tickled when we greeted him, complimented the hotel and then thanked him, all in a pidgin-y mix of Bahasa Indonesian and Balinese. Which may have accounted for the reason he said—after we apologized for arriving so early—*"Tidak apa apa*. Your room will be ready very soon. Please, *Ibu*, *Pak*, please have seats there. We bring you cold drinks, *ya*?"

"*Ya. Suksma.*"

We glanced around at the other arriving guests and realized we were the only "locals." Everyone else had that just-off-the-plane-after-more-than-thirty-hours-of-flying, chalky-skinned, desiccated look about them. A middle-aged American couple hardly bothered to notice the view of the Indian Ocean beyond the two huge sparkling swimming pools. The pools that Loy had eyed within seconds after slamming the car door shut.

"Why can't I go swimming? I want to go first to the blue pool. Hey, you can sit on a chair in the middle of the pool and order food. Oooh, can I drink one of those big drinks with the pineapple on the glass like that lady is drinking? Is that a virgin drink, Mommy? And then I want to get out and jump in the green pool. It has a waterfall; I can see it from here. Why do you think it's green? I think it's green because they don't clean it enough. Or maybe they use green water. Guys, I really want to go swimming. Why can't I go in right now?"

"Because."

"Why?"

"You're not wearing your bathing suit. This isn't California. They throw you in jail here if you swim naked."

"But we can just open the suitcase, Daddy. It's right over there."

"Loy. Just wait."

We were finally shown to our ground-floor room, a room with air-conditioning and a beautifully tiled bathroom with two thick white robes and a king-sized bed with clean white ironed sheets and a perfectly functioning cot for Loy and a television that had hundreds of channels and three bottles of drinking water and a bowl of fruit and a sliding door that opened onto a little patio which overlooked an expansive green lawn leading to the ocean about a hundred yards away. I touched and sighed and made Victor tip the guy something like a day's worth of wages.

Loy and Victor got into their bathing suits and left for a swim while I lounged on top of the bed, clicking through the television, letting the drone of CNN International and the freezing air from the AC coddle my brain into much-desired flaccidity.

My family came back refreshed and full of pool stories, Loy grabbing for the remote and clicking over to any cartoons she could find. She didn't care that they were in Bahasa, and neither did I—it was all fascinating. After a few minutes of watching, we noticed a discouraging trend in Indonesian advertising: up until then we'd had no idea how important it was to have WHITE skin. How had I missed that aisle in the supermarket, the one that sells the many hundreds of products for skin-whitening? I hadn't realized that having dark skin—according to the commercials—is *jelek* (ugly), whereas those women with light, bright, European-white skin are oh so *cantik* (o so beautiful).

It was all very Michael Jackson-y and I loathed watching it, but Loy refused to relinquish the remote.

Victor supined himself next to me with a magazine. He smelled like sun and chlorine and damn if that wasn't the sexiest smell I'd smelled in months. I wondered what our tourist neighbors would think if we locked Loy out on the patio with a good book to read and a doll to suckle, while we made love in the crisp dry air.

Make love? Who was I kidding? We hadn't made love since, since before we'd left California. Having sex in outside-only Bali felt like coupling with fly strips attached to your bellies.

I turned my body on its side, rested my head on my right hand and put my left hand on his chest. I felt the rhythm of his heart, his big beautiful heart; the heart I'd been breaking for God knows how long. "I'm sorry I'm not a better person," I said.

"Thanks," he replied without taking his eyes off the magazine.

Monkey enlightenment nothing, I came *this* close to ripping it out of his hands and throwing it across the air-conditioned room. But I did not. I rolled over and shook it off. I had two more days to pull some Monkey Forest magic out of my hat; beginning our holiday with a screaming fight about whether or not he still loved me would not be very favorable.

Even I, the dejected, sweat-free woman in the bed next to him, realized that.

Just as the cartoon kids Max and Emmy and their dragon friends became as grating in Bahasa than they are in English, Victor jumped up and said, "I'm starving. Let's go eat some food that's not Balinese."

At Massimo's, supposedly the finest Italian restaurant in SE Asia, we were seated at a table-cloth-covered table.

"I'm not even going to complain that there's no air-conditioning," I said as I placed a white linen napkin on my lap.

"Good thing," Victor said. "The fans are fine. It's a cool night. Please use your napkin, Loy. This is a nice restaurant."

I was going to sit back, order up some lemongrass-free food, and relish the moment.

Victor hugged his menu against his chest and declared, "You guys, don't even look at the prices. Let's get whatever we want, okay?"

"Really, Daddy?"

"Victor, really? It's super expensive."

He laughed loudly enough for the old white couple next to us to glance over. "Do me a favor. Close your eyes. Just do it. Now pretend we're in New York. Now open them."

I looked again and saw prices that probably hadn't been seen on a New York City menu since 1962.

So with caution thrown to the warm wind, we ordered mushroom and cream soup with garlic croutons; fettuccine with four cheeses and prosciutto; homemade agnolotti with sausage, mushrooms and cream; as well as a pizza topped with tomato, mozzarella, fried eggplant, garlic and hot pepper.

All of it ... every last bite ... *enak*. Delicious.

Signor Massimo had a gelato cart stationed out in front of his restaurant, and attempting to walk by without buying some proved impossible. "Loy, how can you want an ice cream? We just ate so much!" I said trying to steer her away.

As if.

I got fig. Loy picked peach. Victor requested a small scoop of hazelnut.

"Do you think the food was really that good or is it just because we've been eating fried rice and fern tips for so long?" I asked as we strolled slowly through the village, licking our cones, browsing the craft stalls along the sidewalks.

"I don't know," Victor said, stopping to try on a sun hat. "But I'm really glad nothing came stuffed in a banana leaf."

We all three had a good chuckle the next morning when we arrived at the hotel's breakfast buffet and watched the other vacationers heaping spoonfuls of Balinese-style fried rice and Balinese-style fried noodles onto their plates. As for us? Loy loaded her plate high with pastries. Victor ate a bowl of multi-textured granola mixed with fresh yogurt. I joyfully worked my way through about a kilo of *manggis* (mangosteens), one of God's loveliest and sweetest creations.

To eat a mangosteen you take a sharp knife and slice a circle around the hard, dark purple skin. Firmly twist off the top of the fruit to reveal the white fleshy sections. And though they might look like snow-colored mandarin-orange segments, they taste like Concord grapes, Granny Smith apples, and cherry Starbursts all rolled into one heavenly bite .

Overly full again, we retired to the green pool where we pushed together three lounge chairs and christened our little piece of poolside HOME. For the next six hours, we hung out there, dozing, reading, swimming in the blue pool then the green pool then the Indian Ocean pool, and eating yet more pizza and drinking many piña coladas—both virgin and deflowered—delivered with a white, even-toothed smile by Wayan, the waiter.

"You speak the Bahasa?" he asked me after I said, "*Terima kasih.*"

"*Tidak. Saya bisa sedikit.*" No, just a tiny bit really, but thanks for chatting, and now, if you don't mind, I'd love to get back to my novel. Bye!

"You have only this one children?"

Great, I was trying to be nice and now he's going to rag on my family tree.

"*Ya, satu perempuan.*" One daughter.

Of course, he frowned.

The ugliest word in the Indonesian language has to be the word for female: *perempuan*; while one of the most whimsical words is the male equivalent: *laki-laki*. Whenever a Balinese person asked me, "*Berapa anak?*" (How many children do you have?), and I answered, "*satu perempuan*," there'd be a universal sigh of despair, disappointment, even grief. Apparently I had not been smiled upon by the gods and been blessed with many *laki-laki*. Having only one child was bad enough. But having only ONE GIRL ... well, poor pitiful you, the look always said.

"No *laki-laki*?" Wayan asked, disbelieving me, as did every other person in Bali whenever I stated my present state of progenitorship.

"*Ya. Satu.*" But you know what, buddy? It's all good. She's great, this kid. See how she's lying there all wrapped up cozy in her towel, reading her *Magic Tree House* #18 through #23 books, and not bothering either her mother or father? Look over there at that family, the one with the two boys, and tell me what *they're* doing. Not a lot of reading going on, is there? No—wow, did that kid just throw a fork at his father's face?

"So, is this what you'd hoped for?" I asked Victor after Wayan left us the bill and moved on.

"Sure," he said, not looking up from the two-month-old *The New Yorker* he had borrowed from Sam.

Again with the not talking about us or him or anything intimate. He didn't want to hear about my change of heart, but I needed to hear about his heart before I died of self-doubt.

"What? You hate it here."

"No, I don't. But you know I'd never go to a place like this if I didn't have to." As if on cue, a gang of Balinese men and women carrying carts and baskets full of tourist crap began setting up a small market next to the pool area.

"You didn't have to," I remarked, painfully aware of a guard in a Bali Hyatt uniform standing by, watching their every move.

"You're wrong. I did have to." He finally looked at me, glanced over at Loy, then at the makeshift bazaar. "I had to get away," he said wiping the sweat from the place between his sunglasses and his nose.

"From school?"

"From all of it. From the house and the school. From the kids. The administration. The mold. All of it."

I could have added more to his list, like the bugs and the smell of burning plastic and burning bodies, but there was enough on the table already. "So then it's good," I said more than asked.

"It's fine, Lisa." He went back to reading.

I put down *The Birth of Venus* and rearranged the towel to cover my feet. "But being here does make you feel like you're away from it all."

"This is so not us."

He'd used the word "us," and as tempting as it was to ask if there still was an "us," I knew it wasn't the time. Not yet.

"Why not? What's wrong with it? I think it's perfectly nice." It was perfectly nice, but the scene sort of depressed me. All these honeymooning couples who flew halfway around the planet to lay by a pretty pool and pay large sums of money to eat white coconut flesh and get massaged by straight-teethed Balinese women. I'd made us come here instead of hiking up Mt. Batur, or snorkeling in Candidasa. I'd wanted a calm civilized holiday.

"Sure, it's nice."

"Where would you rather be?" I asked, figuring he'd say hiking up Mt. Batur, or snorkeling in Candidasa.

"California. New York. Kansas. I wouldn't fucking care. Oops. Sorry, kid. You didn't hear that."

"Didn't hear what, Daddy?" Thank goodness that child of ours got her father's power of concentration.

"I didn't realize you thought it was so bad," I said. "I mean, you don't really complain. Other than about the heat and stuff."

"You complain enough for the both of us."

"That was mean," I said.

"I don't mean it in a mean way," he said, finally putting the magazine down and facing me. "I'm just being honest. I can't remember the last time something positive came out of your mouth."

"But, I, ah..." Before I could conjure up something that was the opposite of negative to say, a large group of Spaniards decided they had to get to the pretend market immediately, and the quickest route there was the narrow slice of concrete between our row of chairs and the pool. As they made their way past, every one of them bumped every chair along the way. The French man next to us raised his head about two inches off the mat, squinted an eye at the Spanish procession, then dropped back to sleep. His pretty wife, as if disgusted by the ogling eyes, threw her *Voici* magazine to the ground, untied the string of her fancy French bathing suit and turned over to tan her back.

"Don't they know they can just walk down the street and buy all the same crap for a fraction of the price?" I said.

"Yeah, but that'd be too scary for them."

"You think so?" I watched a woman actually trying to haggle over a bamboo wind chime. She was probably paying $300 a night to stay here (our KITAS rate was a lean $88/night) and she didn't want to pay $4 for some hanging mold sticks.

"Half the people who come here get off the plane, take a taxi straight to the hotel, and stay put until it's time to fly home again."

"And they tell their friends all about Bali being this amazingly clean, exotic paradise."

"Exactly." He gulped down the rest of his drink and stood up. "That's why this is a stupid place," he uttered before diving into the pool.

Loy and I followed him in and we swam as far from the sounds of gamelan as we could get. We doggie-paddled through the fake rock cave, under the waterfall and over toward the steps where a boiled-lobster-colored German couple sat drinking beer.

I sidled up to my husband. Loy was practicing standing on her hands underwater. I waited for her to dive under. "How bad is school going?" I asked.

"It's pretty bad. I'm already dreading going back. You know I'm always up for a challenge, but this isn't a fun challenge. There's nothing fun about it. Pioneer spirit or not, I'm worn out. That was really good, sweetie. Do another one, but see if you can straighten both legs up this time," he said to Loy, I'm sure to keep her from hearing him complain. He never liked to let her see him sad.

I, on the other hand, let her see me sad and mad and while I'm at it, hateful and ugly and—God, I'm already picturing her memoir—*Mommy, You Sucked.*

"I'm worn out," Victor said, running his hand through what was left of his hair. "It's fucking tiring to teach a first-world high-achievement curriculum to twenty-four kids in a third-world setting. It's not working."

Loy popped her head up, a huge smile on her face. "Guys, did you see that handstand? I held it for like ten minutes."

"We did," Victor replied. "It was amazing."

"Amazing," I repeated. "You are like the best hand stander in all of Bali."

"Do the other teachers feel that way?" I asked after she went under again.

"Honestly, I have no idea if they think they're being successful teachers or not."

"But you guys all seem so close. What about our last *cumi-cumi* party where everyone bonded over the bad housing and the—"

"Sure, we're socially close. I mean, we all basically came here because we believed in what John Hardy was selling. But from an educational perspective," he dunked under then came up, "there's no cohesiveness. We have no vertical alignment whatsoever."

An Australian couple and their three children splashed past us, racing for the other side of the pool. For the fiftieth time since having Loy, I wished I'd started having babies at a younger age so that we, too, could have been a raucous self-contained party instead of the quiet threesome we were. Loy and Victor swam back to the rock cave and splashed under the waterfall. I caught up to them and asked Teacher Victor if he could please translate what he'd just said.

"What I mean is that as the kids go up from grade to grade there's no continuity. I teach what I want. Sam teaches what he wants. There's no connection between what they learn in fifth and sixth grade and what Sara and I are teaching them in seventh/eighth. Sam should be preparing kids for our physics curriculum using the river, but for all I know he's teaching them Marxist theory."

"Come on: why can't you just teach the dialectics of flow dynamics?"

He ignored my lame humor and added, "What's particularly worrisome is that a lot of the kids in my class are going on to other international schools—or worse, they'll go back to schools in their home countries—and there's no way they'll be ready."

"That's crazy."

"No shit."

I watched Loy climb out of the pool and grab a white plastic ball that appeared to belong to no one. "Let's play Monkey in the Middle. Mommy, you be the monkey."

"Is Director Brad doing anything to fix any of this?" I asked, jumping up and narrowly missing Loy's throw over my head.

"You mean Buddha Brad?"

"That is so funny. Is that what you guys call him?" I caught Victor's toss and made him the Monkey of the Moment.

"A few teachers do, yeah. You know what's really funny is that just this week I remembered something he said to me back in July. I let it slide then, but I totally get it now."

"What'd he say?"

"Something like, 'Yeah, I'm a Buddhist but you never want to cross me. You never want to see that other side of me.'"

After retrieving Loy's errant throw, I came back and asked, "He really said that?"

"He did, and now I realize it's the only side he knows how to show the teachers. A lot of them are totally intimidated by him."

"Still?"

"Sure. I mean, the minute someone complains about supply issues or the constant meetings, anything, he *still* threatens to replace them. I've heard him say more than once that for every position at the school, there's a hundred people waiting in the wings to take over. I don't think he realizes that not a lot of people at the school have any respect for him."

"Mommy! The ball is behind you!"

"Sorry. Where—oh there it is." I threw the ball over Victor's head while remembering what happened at the teachers' meeting the day before school started: the day everyone felt too unsafe around Brad to share the truth. "But Sinead said Brad is just Hardy's puppet."

Victor caught my throw and handed the ball to Loy. "I'm done playing, pickle. I've got to go take a nap before I fall over."

"Okay. Mommy, can we go look for shells?"

"Sure, but let's put our shoes on so we don't burn our feet."

We swam back to the wall by our chairs and climbed out. Loy dutifully tied her sunhat straps under her chin as Victor lowered the back of his chair down to flat. "You never answered me about Brad," I said, slipping on a sundress and flip-flops.

"I don't know. I don't think I would go as far as saying he's Hardy's puppet. He's just in way over his head. Plus," he said while smearing a big glop of SPF-60 all over his shoulders, "he has to battle it out every day with a crazed school founder who holds the purse strings. Hardy has the final say on everything." He tied his bandana around his head and turned over onto his belly.

"So, is there *anyone* you can—?"

He looked up at me, shook his head. "Kumar is about the only person I trust to be honest anymore, but he knows nothing about education, so he's no real help," he replied before dropping down once more.

"Kumar? But he told Sinead—"

"Lisa. Can you please go so I can take a nap?"

"Going." I took Loy's hand and we headed off to see what manner of treasures lay buried beneath the hot sand of a Balinese beach.

We ate yet another indulgently creamy meal at Massimo's that night. After a quiet swim in the green pool, Victor and Loy instantly fell into a deep, bug-free sleep. I stayed awake with the TV on mute, trying to let the empty images smooth out my tangled thoughts. Thrilled though I was to have Victor in bed with me again, I still had no idea how to close the gap between us. Sure, we were friendly enough, but his benign civility was starting to eat away at me.

Where had our passion gone?

Loy turned over and sighed a pink-tinged, innocent sigh. I got up and padded into the dark bathroom and sat on the toilet, relishing the feel of the cold white porcelain under my butt, the cool flat white tiles beneath my feet. I rested my head in my hands long after I'd finished, it felt so good sitting there.

I thought about what should come next. Whether I could stay on in Bali as a happy person, or if the best laid plans weren't so best anymore.

Because, honestly, all that heart-bursting *we-ness* that Victor and I had known so long ago was gone.

We'd killed it.

Or, really, I'd killed it: let it devolve into *me-ness.*

Meanness was more like it.

Fucking hell. I was clueless. Useless. Hopeless. Worthless. Careless. I crowded my brain with lots of LESS words and soon a picture of me formed out of the jumble: a picture of a forty-seven-year-old woman sitting on a toilet in the dark in a hotel room in Bali. Her chin in her hands. Her elbows on her knees. Naked. Alone. And unbelievably unhappy and uncertain about most everything.

I got back into bed, clicked the television off and rolled over to spoon Victor's back. He grumbled once, and I stiffened, but thankfully, he let me stay there. I fixed my mind on the ceiling and looked down at us, the two larger bodies, still under the thick blanket; the smaller figure next to them, it's short left leg dangling out from the knot of sheets.

"Either you change or go back to California," Victor had said.

I pictured our hut back at the school and instantly I got hot and had to move to the other side of the bed. I hated Bali. I hated myself for hating Bali. I mean, who hates Bali?

I could hear my friends' reactions: "You didn't want to stay because it was too hot and there were too many bugs and too much smoke?"

"Really? You *left* Bali?"

"Victor is still there? You left him alone with that pretty teacher you're so jealous of, whatshername—Sara?"

"Are you like the stupidest person on the planet?"

Change or go.

Enough of the blaming and the rage. I had to change.

In the morning, we went to the front desk and used our semi-fluent Bahasa to beg for a late checkout so we could have another almost-full day at the resort. Another day for taking hot showers. For eating food not flavored with turmeric or galangal. For Victor and I talking without having Loy around. First, though, we had to convince her that a morning of flying kites, making cookies, and learning Balinese dance in the hotel's Camp Sanur for Kids would be far more entertaining than she could possibly imagine.

"I wanna be with you guys," she protested through a mouthful of croissant stuffed with raspberry jam.

"You will be, honey. Mom and I are going to take a walk together for a little while."

"Then we'll come get you and we'll go swimming," I added.

Victor and I kissed her goodbye in front of the child-filled activity room and promised we'd be back well before they served her a Balinese-style lunch. Then we walked over to the sidewalk that ran along the beach, and started south.

It was early enough that the crew of garbage sweepers was still at it, raking up pounds of tide-returned plastic bags and food wrappers, bottles and cans. We could smell the trash fires burning behind us, north of the hotel.

I watched a pack of skinny strays fight over a bag of something green.

We passed by another resort and saw, tucked back a little from the beach-front behind large cement walls, a huge private residence. "Who lives there, I wonder?"

"My guess would be expats."

"Maybe their kids go to Green School," I said.

"Could be. Half of our kids commute over an hour every day from their beach houses."

"You mean they get driven by their drivers."

"Right."

"That's sick, making a five-year-old sit in a car for two hours every day." I pictured those tiny people on the winding, crowded roads sitting in the backseats all alone, without seatbelts.

"Tell me about it," Victor said, agreeing with me in the most vehement way.

What kind of parent does that? I thought about the many expat parents I'd met since moving to Bali. There are those who want to escape the rat race. Those who want to re-create the rat race in another part of the world. And those who are just, well, rats.

They move from China, Japan, England, the US, the E.U., Australia—all those nations that at one time or another ruled other nations. And they come to Bali where they can live large. For not a lot of money they build/buy/lease themselves enormous villas by the beach, or in the middle of many acres of rice paddies, complete with swimming pools and at least six *pembantu* who do for their children that which they themselves no longer have to or want to do; like sleep with them, feed them, dress them, bathe them, play with them, drive them around, cook for them, wipe their butts.

"You were talking the other night about how you have to tell a bunch of parents that their kids aren't even at grade level," I said as we passed a group of dirty Balinese children poking sticks through a pile of garbage.

We stopped walking and sat up on some resort's low cement wall. Behind us their pool area was just beginning to get crowded; people were already throwing their towels and paperbacks down on chairs to save their spots. I hated when people did that. Travel the whole world over and you can't escape it.

"Remember before we moved to Bali, I'd said that part of the reason I was so excited was that Loy would be going to an international school and she'd be getting an amazing education?" Victor was staring out at the sea. "I assumed these kids would be really smart and sophisticated. I mean they're well-traveled. They're exposed to other cultures."

"Yeah. But?"

"But the fact is they have relatively low academic skills, and even worse, they have absolutely no critical thinking skills."

"What's that mean?"

A speaker over the pool bar began blasting gamelan music. "You can't get away from that, can you?" he said, jumping down. I leapt off the wall, and we started down the beach again. I walked closer to Victor, thinking maybe he'd take my hand, but he kept his hands to himself. "They can't solve problems that do not have clear right or wrong answers," he said.

"Oh," replied the person who for sure lacked her own critical thinking skills.

"I mean, come on: these kids are basically raised by servants who do everything for them. They make their beds. They cook their meals and do their dishes. They put away their bikes. They make sure—"

"I get your point," I said. "But lots of kids in the States are raised like that, too."

"Yeah, but in the States, they're part of a larger culture. Here, they're not a part of it. They're to a large degree a different class. They're outsiders. There's not a whole lot they need to figure out on their own."

"And they're totally spoiled."

We stopped at the next resort down where the gamelan had yet to be turned on. We sat on a long bench obviously put there for hotel guests. Victor splayed his arms out to both sides so it almost felt like he had his arm around me. "They are not so much spoiled, no. But they ... they're—how do I put it? They seem melancholy to me, like they're living a life of relative emptiness."

Who could blame those poor kids? Like any child whose parents move their yachts from sunny sea coast to sunny sea coast, pulling up anchor whenever the wind blows the wrong way, they've had to learn how to survive, adapt, cope with being dragged all over the world, school to school, giving up friends right and left.

What about Loy?

Would a year here bruise her brain?

Should we not have dragged her all over the world?

Would she forget how to tie her own shoes because she only wore flip-flops?

Would she become soft from everything Seni did for her?

Would she assume she'd always have someone else do the dishes for her?

And clean her room?

And make her bed?

And cook for her and sweep up her dead ants and ... holy shit! Had we become EXPATS? Was our child going to turn melancholy and lead an empty—

"Lisa!"

"What? Why did you stand up?"

"Did you not feel what you just sat in?"

I jumped up and touched my butt. "Oh gross. Victor, how did you not see that before you let me sit down?"

"Before I—? Are you seriously blaming me?"

Black clouds formed over my head, blocking out the blue sky. "How come you just happened to sit on the clean side of the bench?"

"Because I wanted you to ruin your dress. Jesus!" He started walking back toward the hotel, away from the black cloud and unchanged wife.

"Wait!" I ran to catch up with him, rolling the sticky part of my dress into a ball so that I was now more or less wearing a mini dress. "I'm really sorry." Hesitantly I smelled my hand. Sickly sweet. Soda perhaps. Or candy. More like rotting sewage.

"Victor." I touched his arm to make him stop. "I'm sorry."

"Sure. Okay. Whatever. I want to swim some laps before we have to get Loy."

We walked on in silence.

Change or go. Happiness is a choice. It's not what *happens* to you. It's what you make happen on your own.

A couple on rented bicycles shot past after warning us with their bike bells. *Tling-tling! Tling-tling!*

For a second there I was a six-year-old learning how to ride a two-wheeler in front of my gray New Jersey colonial, my father in the driveway shouting me on. "You can do it, Leeka! Relax your hands. Keep your eyes open!"

"Did you know that my dad used to call me Leeka?" I blurted out to Victor who had stopped to re-adjust the strap on his sandal.

"I knew that. I also knew that some mean kids in your elementary school nicknamed you Lumps because you were skinny and flat-chested. And that your old boyfriend Doug called you Pooky."

"Wow. Impressive. Is there anything you don't know about me?"

He stood up, stared into my eyes, and said, "I have no idea what it's going to take to make you happy."

You are?

I cleared the question mark out of my head and tried again.

"You are," I said.

"I'm not so sure about that anymore." He frowned. "I don't know if anyone can."

And then, just before he turned from me, I saw it, plain as day. There. On his face. In his eyes. The sort of sadness you get when something irreplaceable breaks.

He threw off his shirt and dove into the blue pool before I'd even gotten out of my soiled dress. I looked to the right and left. Up. Down. I had no idea if I was supposed to join him in the water or sit there listening to the drone of tourist-speak, go get Loy, or head back to the hotel room and make sure we'd packed everything.

Talk about lacking critical thinking skills.

I went over and sat down on the top step, splashed cool water on my thighs. Victor breast-stroked toward me, then butterflied away from me. Then he crawled toward me and back-stroked away. A very fat man lowered his sunburned belly down next to me and said something in an unrecognizably guttural language. I smiled, threw off my dirty dress, and dove underwater, kicking hard to catch up with Victor on the far side of the pool.

I swam below him, touched his belly, and freaked him out. He shot up, laughing.

"I love it when you laugh," I said, treading water beside him.

"And I love it when you laugh."

"Not a lot of that going on lately, huh?"

"Nope." He side-stroked over to the empty swim-up bar and sat on one of the underwater stools. I joined him. I would have ordered a piña colada, but given the early hour and the ponderosity of the moment, I thought it'd be unwise.

"What's going to make us laugh again?" Victor asked me.

"I stop being an angry bitch."

"Good start."

"We leave Bali."

"Bad idea."

"Just throwing the ideas out there. Brainstorming, you know."

"I know. But I'm not leaving. I'm committed, remember?"

"*Selamat pagi, Ibu!*" Wayan the pool boy kneeled over the side of the pool. "You want I bring you a drink?"

"*Tidak. Suksma*, Wayan."

"*Suksma*! Ha-ha!"

"Where was I?"

"You were no longer being a bitch."

"And you weren't leaving Bali."

"Correct."

"But you hate it."

"No. I don't hate it. It's not working out like I'd expected it to. Not even close, but I've got to do the best I can, right?"

"So much for those three cups of tea," I said as I floated off the stool into the water.

"More like three cups of bitter tea," he said. Victor's attempt at humor. I loved him for that. For once again seeing that half-filled glass of dirty water. For holding onto his integrity through absolute weariness.

He fell off backwards into the water and swam up next to me. I put my arms around his neck. He let me pull him back with me. We floated for a moment, then sunk together. This was his holiday, his too-few blissful days of *not* teaching, *not* sweating in front of children paying $10,000 a piece for the privilege of having him shape their minds. His time to do nothing. To get AWAY.

"I really am sorry," I said as we emerged from the water. "I'm sorry that I dragged us here thinking we'd find love and inner peace and paradise, blah, blah, blah."

"You didn't drag us here. Any one of us could have said no, and anyway, what's done is done. Let's move on and have some fun before we have to go back."

Over on the steps, a young Italian-looking honeymoon-happy couple made out. I still wasn't certain, but my gut told me that Victor no longer wanted me to leave. Maybe he was offering me a second chance.

"Hey, so I was wondering if one of the reasons you agreed to move to Bali was because you thought I would change coming here?"

"What? No—I thought it would be an incredible opportunity for Loy and for me, professionally."

"Oh."

"You know, Lisa, it's not always about you."

"I know."

"At some point, you'll figure out that it doesn't matter where you live—you've got to learn to be happy anywhere."

"I know that. I really do."

"Then let's see you prove it."

"Give me a little time."

He nodded a small closed-lipped nod then ducked under. I wanted us to stop talking about the personal homework I had piling up in front of me. When he came up I asked, "Would you have wanted us to come here on our honeymoon?"

Victor laughed, differently than I heard him last laugh. This time his eyes laughed, too. "Lie on your back. I'll hold you up," he said, putting his hands under me. As I stared up into the cloudless sky he swirled my body back and forth. I smiled and stretched out my arms, letting my body go limp. Feeling him will happiness into me.

He suddenly looked at me.

Looked into me.

Something tilted in him and I leaned into it. Floated into it. Whether because he'd unburdened some of his frustrations and I'd listened, or because he believed that I'd honestly try to change, or because we were at this silly, scraped-clean version of paradise mattered not. All I knew was that this man with the red goatee and strong patient arms needed me to be his true life partner.

I awoke in a fit of sweaty disgust and threw off the sheet, which felt to my skin—after two nights of sleeping beneath 400-count cotton—like a leaf of that homemade hippie paper you find in groovy stationery stores in Ubud or Santa Cruz; the kind with bits of flower and bark and seed embedded in it.

I noticed a small hole at the top corner of the mosquito net and did a quick check of my naked body to see if I had any new bites. I knew I hadn't gotten any at the Hyatt, because I saw the staff there regularly fumigating the garden and pool areas with poisonous clouds. Toxic or no, three days without bug spray on my body felt unimaginably refreshing.

It was hot. Hotter than I remembered it being before we left, and the sun still hadn't fully risen. I leered up at the hardly spinning fan, then eyed the wall switch, which, on our first day here, I'd set to HIGH, and never touched again.

I turned on my side and stared out past the bamboo balcony to the jungly mass of sculpture-still palms beyond. I had to face the fact that there'd be no more ocean breezes to lighten the air; no more glass windows to keep out the bugs; no more air-conditioning. Not for a long, long time.

The sun rose higher, its light and heat slicing through the bamboo wall behind my bed. A dog yarked, then a truck boomed by. I turned on my other side and began mindlessly counting the bamboo slats above my shelves of clothing. One-two-three-four … what was that?

Was that a—? A rat just ran across the wall! I sat up to see where it'd gone but couldn't find it. Was it still in the room? Under the bed? I wanted to scream but didn't want to wake up Loy, so I clenched my teeth together almost to the point of cracking my jaw in two.

Why was I still here again? Oh yeah: because I loved my family. Because only one day ago I'd promised to change; to snap out of this gloomy negative fog of mine so that I could continue being Victor's wife and Loy's mother. And possibly even a writer. Writer? I'd not created squat since moving to Bali. A few mildly inspired emails to friends, but that was it. Did I really think I could continue telling stories for a living? Forget the writer. I just had to be a good Wife and a great Mother. I'd done okay during the holiday—hadn't I?—bonding with my child as we swam and played and explored the beach. She knew I loved her more than life itself. And Victor … well, we were almost there; almost a couple again. If I could just keep my eyes fixed on that proverbial light at the end of the proverbial bamboo tunnel, I'd be able to get through this.

At the thought of such a long dark tunnel running from now until June, I fell back and sneered up at the fan again.

Whoosh. Whoosh. Whoosh.

I heard Victor speaking softly on his cell phone downstairs.

Snap out of it, Lisa. Grow up. You have it so unbelievably easy compared to everyone else on the planet! One lovely child. An amazing husband. A maid who cooks for you. And you live in Bali where you get to sit around on your ass all day writing stories, if only you'd try harder. Dear God, girl.

Whoosh. Whoosh. Whoosh.

I wrapped a sarong as best I could around my waist, then tiptoed downstairs, keeping an eye out for the rat. I found Victor at his usual spot at the breakfast bar, typing away on his computer. A naked Loy lay on the couch inside the mosquito net, a large opened book making a dent across her perfectly flat chest.

"Loy, you're up already?"

"Yeah. Why?"

"A rat ran up the wall and I wanted to scream but I didn't because I didn't want to wake you!" I yelled.

Loy sat up and quickly surveyed the room. "You saw a rat?" she asked excitedly.

While we were lounging at the Bali Hyatt, Aldo had installed a house-sized white tarp over the *alang-alang* roof to help discourage the constant leaks. Unfortunately, the material now kept out much of the natural light that used to stream through the overhanging grass.

"Yes, I did," I announced to the darkened room.

"I'm sorry a rat woke you up," Victor said before going back to his computer.

"Mommy, I'm already on page twenty-four," Loy said.

Apparently, my furry little intruder proved less riveting than I'd anticipated.

"What's going on?" I asked Victor.

"Working."

"But you're technically still on holiday."

"Not really. We have our all-staff meeting this afternoon. Plus, do you have any idea how much I still have to do to get ready for conferences?"

"No."

"Okay, well. A lot." Victor looked at his computer, and added, "Oh, and a bunch of students have lice."

My eyes darted over to Loy. Before I could say anything, he said, "I checked. She's clean."

"That's good." At least lice couldn't kill her.

"Want me to make you some tea?"

"That'd be great," I said, kissing his cheek and heading into the bathroom, where Aldo had also obligingly affixed three artful bamboo hooks on which to hang our wet towels. Before squatting over the compost bucket I gave it the finger, and just for the hell of it, I pushed an imaginary metal handle on the side of the bamboo box after I finished peeing.

As I came out of the bathroom, Johnny and Phillipa's daughter Emily scampered over to see if Loy wanted to join her in a game of dress-up over at her hut. While Loy ran upstairs to put on clothes, I subtly searched Emily's hair for signs of jumping bugs. "Emily, did you go anywhere for holiday this week?"

"Yeah, we did," she replied in her kiwi voice. "We went off for a nice long drive, and we got to see a great big mountain."

"How lovely. Did you, ah, happen to catch any lice?"

"Naw."

"Excellent. Loy, what on earth are you wearing?" Clearly inspired by the most recent episode of *Project Runway*, she had on a pair of brown leggings over which she'd tied a green and gold silk scarf, leaving a slit in the side. On top, she wore a blue halter shirt with a purple lace vest. None of her plastic rings or costume bracelets had escaped notice.

"Ooh, are those real diamonds? May I maybe wear some of your fancy jewelry?" Emily asked.

"Sure!" Loy slipped off her Elizabeth Taylor-sized, purple diamond ring and her dog-and-cat charm bracelet and handed them to Emily. "Bye, Mommy. Bye, Daddy." She tossed an arm in the air like an Upper East Side debutante, pulling Emily with her out the gate.

"Want to go for a walk together?" I asked, cleaning up the dishes and the remainder of the ants. We'd given Seni the week off. When we got home last night, we'd found that our countertop had been transformed into a refugee camp: ants and their cousins and their cousins' cousins, along with their every worldly possession, had, during our absence, come forth to our land of plenty.

All because Loy had left a piece of toast with a smear of strawberry jam on her plate.

But at least the nightly obliteration of those HUGE BITING ANTS would no longer be a part of Loy's bedtime routine.

So much to be thankful for.

"You really can't go for a quick walk?" I tried again.

"Sweetie, I can't."

I hadn't heard him call me *sweetie* in weeks. "You honestly have that much to do?"

A no-longer-on-holiday frown stretched across Victor's mouth. "What did I just talk about for the last three days?"

"How screwed it was."

"Exactly." He took a gulp of his tea. "And like I keep saying, Brad and the Hardys should have listened to the teachers back in August. They should have postponed opening for another year—even six months would have helped. They could have brought the teachers to Bali, put us into regular housing in town, and had us work on developing the non-existent curriculum, order all the supplies. They should have waited for all this goddamn building to be finished," he said with so much force that out of habit I thought it was *me* who'd pissed him off.

Before I could say, "You're right," and restate my pledge to be his supportive wife once more, he continued ranting: "At this point all the administration does is put out fires. When one goes out, another pops up."

"So why do you have to be the one to fix it?"

"Because it needs to be fixed. Every day some more shit hits the fan, and it's all everyone can do to keep their heads above water."

"Why?" I overlooked his muddled metaphor. "Why not just let it stay broken till we leave in June?"

"Because I still believe in this place."

I stopped stirring the honey into my mug. "You do?"

"You know I do. I didn't quit a great job to come here because it's Bali. I came because the school's vision was so incredible. We were all seduced by it."

"But?"

"But what? Do I think it can still be amazing? Yeah, I do, but there has to be less seat-of-the-pants decision-making. And like I keep saying to Brad, the teachers shouldn't have to fight to get every little resource for their classrooms, even if we're working with a limited budget."

"But I thought Brad was pretty much useless."

Just as he was about to answer me, we heard a truck pull up outside our house and stop. I looked out the window hole and saw about ten guys jump out. On the bed of the truck sat a big propane water heater. "Speaking of broken, I think we're about to get gas-powered hot water. So much for being an environmentally sustainable school."

"Yeah, well, that's not what's going to make or break this place. I have a ton of emails from angry parents who are pissed off that the school isn't delivering half of what it promised, and it's not like I can be completely honest with them."

"You can't?"

"You want me to bash the school? No way; not as long as I'm still here."

"That's decent of you. If it were me I'd be letting them all know the truth." I'd want them to know that Kumar and Brad and the rest of the Powers-That-Be were in over their heads, and the teachers were doing their darnedest to keep this idealistic bamboo ship afloat. I guess John Hardy figured since he'd made a wildly successful bangle and bauble business exploiting the talents of Balinese artisans, he could just as easily create a world-renowned school using the talents of willing educators. He'd turned the Bali landscape into silver and expected he'd turn Green School into gold. Only thing is, he forgot that making rings is a tad different than teaching children. Both are precious commodities, but that's where the similarities ended.

I could hear arguing among the men surrounding the propane tank. I glanced out to see a few of them pointing at the ground, the rest up on the truck untying a rope from the tank. A second later another truck filled with half a dozen more men pulled up next to our house. I turned and looked at Victor who had his eyes closed and hands clasped across his bald spot, a posture that signaled some great import to come.

"I'm not ready to tell the parents the truth," he finally said, going back to this laptop, "but I am going to ask to meet with management next week. They need to know that if things don't change soon, the school will fail."

"Why does it have to be you?"

"I've got nothing to lose at this point."

"But what if they—"

"Please, sweetie. Let me go back to work."

So that settled that, and I unexpectedly had a whole morning to, uh, to write. I should find out more about Kallmann syndrome, a genetic disorder that would cause my main character to have anosmia.

Or I could go hang with my sistah, my friend, my bruised brother-in-arms, my distraction from all that needed distracting from, my buddy Sinead.

It'd been days since I'd breathed in her second-hand smoke and I missed the hell out of her. I'd heard nothing from her since she'd flown off to Singapore. Classes started in three days. I wondered what the doctors had found out about her back.

"Be back in a jiff," I lied, skipping over to Sinead's.

"Hello?" I yelled into the obvious void. They'd draped one of those white sheets over her living room roof, too, and the darkness outweighed the brightness by five-to-one. "Hello?"

I looked around and saw no signs of life. Other than the ant wedding taking place around the crumb of food someone had dropped on the coffee table.

Where was she?

Sinead finally returned home on Tuesday, after much speculation by everyone about the reason(s) behind her disappearance. Some folks thought she'd either decided to stay in Singapore, or that Immigration threw her in jail because of her illegal visa.

No one—not even me, her ardent confidant—could have guessed that after she flew back from Singapore—where she'd more or less broken up with her fiance, and learned that she did indeed have a broken vertebrae—she spontaneously decided to get a tattoo to celebrate her newfound singlehood. She'd hailed a cab from the airport to Kuta, where she unintentionally fell for the Balinese tattoo artist who needle-and-inked a pirate ship on her upper back.

"You did what?" I sat up on her kitchen counter watching her alternately smoke a cigarette and check her email.

"I know. I'm a crazy woman, right?"

"What happened? I mean ... Sinead!"

"Christ on a bike. Did you see that Jenna in fourth has typhoid?"

"What? That's way off topic. Where'd you hear that?"

"I'm reading it right now. It's in an email to the teachers."

"We had our typhoid shots."

"Doesn't matter."

"What are you talking about?"

"Listen to this," she said, looking at her screen. "'You and your children may have received vaccinations against some strains, but preventive treatment is not available for all of them. Therefore, we would like you and your household to take extra safety precautions. It is important to be aware that it is possible that your household help, including those who are preparing your food, can be carriers of typhoid without exhibiting the symptoms themselves.'" She stopped reading and smirked at me.

"So Seni could have typhoid and we wouldn't know it."

"Mm-hmm." She puffed on her cigarette.

"Why didn't I know about this?"

"Maybe your hubby didn't want to scare you any more than need be, you being such a wimp and all." She laughed at her own catty observation. I could have gotten defensive about being a wimp, or gone back to my hut to grill Victor as to why he didn't tell me about the presence of a highly contagious, life-threatening disease on campus. But I was in the midst of becoming a less paranoid person and making sure my marriage would last until death did us part.

"Whatever," I stated as impassively as if she'd told me it was raining.

Sinead stopped reading her computer screen. "What's going on, Lisa?"

"Nothing. Nothing's going on." A thousand times I'd come close to breaking down and telling Sinead about the stresses between me and Victor, but for some reason I'd stopped the moment before reaching the door. We'd shared some pretty intimate closeness, but letting her know how scared and sad I'd been seemed a bit of a disconnect. Here, with her speaking of tattoos, while next to me coconut fronds slapped against the white tarp, and the droning of motorbikes clung to the sticky air as if glued there, I couldn't find the proper substrate, the surface, the pedestal on which to place my vulnerable marriage.

"Okay, but if there's anything you want to share. I mean you must know, darling, it's not as if there's anyone else I'd rather talk to. You're the most fabulous thing about this crazy place."

"Yeah?"

"Oh yes. In fact, I just this morning wrote a post about you on my blog. Want to read it?" she asked, turning the computer around.

I'd had no idea she even had a blog and there it was—there I was!

So, my next door neighbour is Lisa. Lisa Kusel. And in between being like a big sister, a listening post, a co-conspirator, nurse, friend, advisor, she is also a writer—where DOES she find the time? She has written two books and I recently borrowed them to read.

"You even put up pictures of my books. That's so cool. Thanks, babe."

She turned the computer back around. "*Ya*, and when I finish reading them I'll post my reviews."

A clutch of ants had gathered to discuss a grain of sugar. I flicked one of them off into the stratosphere. "Enough about me. Take off your shirt and let me see your tattoo."

"Okey-dokey." Sinead took a puff of her cigarette, then did a pretend strip-show with her flimsy T-shirt, removing it slowly and sexily. I got up close and put my finger next to her skin, tracing, but not touching, the black lines with my fingers. The tattoo was still a bit red, but the guy certainly knew how to draw a pirate ship.

"Whooo-hooo," I said. "That is some beautiful picture. What does it say?" The tattoo took up nearly the whole right side of her upper back—a black haunted, haunting ship, sails fully billowing in the wind, clouds seeming to move around it. Below the ship, in an old-fashioned cursive script was written, *Not all those who wander are lost.* … "Wow, Sinead. That is … that's something. Why'd you pick a pirate ship?"

"Because I love pirates. And the sea. I grew up hearing stories about Grace O'Malley. You know who she is, right?" she asked while putting her shirt back on.

"No, but I'm guessing she's Irish."

"But of course. Aren't all the best women Irish? She, my friend, was a truly fearless and very promiscuous Irish pirate who lived during the 16th century."

"An Irish woman pirate?" Loy was going to love hearing about her. "Cool."

"*Ya*, I know."

"So, what happened, Sinead? How did you go from seeing your fiance in Singapore to screwing a tattoo artist in Kuta?"

"I don't know. I got to Singapore and when I saw him at the airport, I knew something wasn't right. It was like something inside me changed. I was happy to see him, *ya*, but I knew right away that I was never going to marry him."

"Did you tell him?"

"No! I mean, I had to give him the benefit of the doubt, right? And besides, I needed a ride to the hospital." She smiled at me then looked over my shoulder at two guys walking by her hut. I turned around and watched them trudge by, machetes in their hands. What on earth needed to be wacked off today? "I'm teasing," she shouted before I could call her a shameless wench. "I wanted to be in love with him, right? So I just kept quiet and decided to give him another chance."

"And?"

"He was with me the whole time I was with the doctors. He was great. I mean, after they told me I had a small fracture in my vertebra, he said I shouldn't come back here. I should just move back home with him again."

"And?"

"I said I needed more time to think about it, and he pointed out that I've already had a few months to think. He wanted to know if were on or we were off."

"And?"

She hobbled over toward the couch. "I'm too hot to stand anymore even though it hurts to sit, but come sit with me."

I plopped onto the white-cushioned bamboo chair, being careful not to touch any of the moldy parts. Sinead stretched out on the small couch and faced me. "I want to be married like you and Victor are married."

What? Did she just place me and Victor up on the Shelf of Great Marriages? "What does that mean, 'like' me and Victor?"

"You're friends, *ya*?"

"I'd like to think I'm his best friend." I tried to keep the doubt out of my response.

"Yeah. I like that. I want to have sex with *my* best friend."

I did too, but first I had to work at Gorilla-gluing that *best* back into the sentence.

"Anyway, I pretty much told him that he probably shouldn't wait for me, and, you know, we hugged and kissed goodbye and then when I got off the plane and I sort of felt like I was free again—I just had to get the tattoo. I had to."

"Of course, you did."

"And the tattoo artist, Wayan, well, I'd heard about him—we'd met once already and I showed him pictures of what I wanted, but I never made an appointment. This time I just showed up. I went to his shop and told myself if he was there I would get the tattoo. If he wasn't, I'd hold off. And, *ya*, obviously, he was there. And I just went for it!"

"And then you had sex."

"No. Not till Sunday morning, after I woke up and he brought me breakfast in bed."

"Women are such suckers for that."

"We are, aren't we?"

"So, you going back to work, or no?" I stood to leave. I wanted to get back to my hut and remember all the reasons Victor and I fell in love in the first place.

And take a cold shower.

"Oh, did I forget to mention they're firing me?"

I sat back down. "What?"

"Alright, I'm exaggerating a little bit, but you know, I can see the writing on the wall."

"What writing? What wall? There are no walls here!"

Sinead laughed. "I wrote everyone from Singapore and told them about the fracture, and that my doctor said I shouldn't have the sort of job that had me bending and stooping, and whatnot."

"And they said, what, 'Fuck off. Don't bother coming back'?" I was worked up now.

"Brad texted me this morning to see how I was feeling, and to make sure I was going to be able to hold my parent-teacher conferences. When I said I was still in a lot of pain, he wrote that it was too bad I'm not well enough to teach."

"And?"

"And I pointed out *again* that if the bloody bamboo hadn't broken, I'd be able to teach."

"To which he said?"

"He said that he was sorry I was hurt, but if I continue to take time off I won't be paid for the days I don't work."

"Wait," I spurted. "So they feel bad that you're hurt, but the school is taking no responsibility for being the reason you got hurt in the first place, and now you are going to be penalized. Right?"

"Right as rain."

"Did you say that was outrageous? Victor is going to be so pissed off. So is Johnny. And Katy and—" In my head I was already forming a class action suit.

"*Ya.*"

We both sat quietly and ruminated on the duplicity of the administration. They were going to replace Sinead if she couldn't get down on the floor at the level of four-year-olds. I had so little to love about Bali, and now I was about to lose my afternoon coffee klatch.

I got up again to leave. "Whatcha going to do?" I asked.

"For fuck's sake, I don't know. Go live with Wayan in his tattoo shop." She grinned at that highly unlikely scenario, then spoke more rationally. "I've already phoned up the Pelangi School. They said they'd be happy to meet with me."

"Isn't that the school that Cynthia Hardy stole Loy's original teacher from?"

"Yeah, so I guess it'd be a fair trade if I went there."

"But how would you be able to teach there if your back is bad?"

"I wouldn't start for a few months. That'd give my back time to heal."

Kadek appeared from upstairs where she'd been cleaning. "I finish. I go," she said succinctly.

She and Sinead exchanged a few quick sentences from which I could decipher all of about six words, *yes* and *no* counting for two.

Suksma: Thank you

Sama-sama: You're welcome

Besok: Tomorrow

Makan: Eat

After she left Sinead said, "Just before you came over I started my resignation letter, just in case."

"Why would you quit if they haven't fired you yet?"

"Darling, you know they already think I'm a blot on this eco-landscape of theirs. They would love to see me leave our little bamboo nation sooner rather than later. They don't want to string this out."

I thought about that. She had been aggrieved from the moment she started teaching here, but so were most of the teachers and their families. But Sinead made her displeasure more pronounced; more in their faces.

She got up and walked over to get a cig. "Think if I promise not to tell the parents the truth, they'll pay me the rest of my salary? Then I can go lay on a beach somewhere for the rest of the year. Doesn't that sound lovely?"

Had Sinead been using her injury as a way to quit?

I got up and shook the suspicion out of my brain. It didn't matter what motivated Sinead. What mattered was that Green School had no right to treat any of its teachers this way. I was so angry I almost asked for a drag of her cigarette.

"I've gotta go home and talk to Victor. See what he says about this." I blew her a kiss. As I was closing the gate behind me I saw Kumar walking down the path toward Sinead's house, his right hand clamped tightly around either a white handkerchief or squashed contract—I couldn't tell for sure. "Sinead," I whispered loudly. "Kumar's coming!" She threw her cigarette in the sink, and straightened out her shirt and sarong.

"Call me," I said, walking out and almost falling into Kumar's chest.

"Good afternoon, Lisa," he said with a lovely smile. "Is Sinead at home? Yes, there she is. Good day, Sinead. May I come in?" He smelled like chai tea and had not a bead of sweat on his smooth and prominent forehead. I wanted to linger, pretend it was taking me a long time to tie my shoes or something, but all I had were a pair of rubber flip-flops to dawdle over.

I heard Kumar saying, "Sinead, I am having some pain with this situation..." as I walked away, thinking about the motto freshly inscribed on my friend's back.

Then I wandered home.

CNN never did show up to do a story on Green School. The crew that had planned to interview John and Cynthia Hardy and a few pre-selected teachers and well-spoken kids, hurriedly flew off to Thailand to cover the Bangkok riots instead. Which meant that the parent-teacher conferences took place as planned, and *Pak* Victor stayed on as the 7th/8th/(9th) grade teacher, much to my non-vocalized dismay.

As I sat on my couch pretending to write a book about a man with anosmia, I silently cursed the Thai people for having problems with their government. But then I remembered the Monkey Forest lessons I learned, as well as our beach holiday where I recognized the beauty of not dwelling on the negative. Of not blaming other people (or other countries) for all that I felt was wrong with my life.

I glanced up to see Seni reaching out past our living room railing trying to grab a banana leaf, but her belly kept her from extending the extra three inches necessary. She gave up, slipped on her flip-flops and tramped to the side of the house, whereupon she hacked off the lowest hanging leaf with a small machete and came back around.

I closed my computer, grabbed the bowl of cut-up papaya out of the freezer and sat up on a stool in the kitchen to watch her. First, she wiped the four-foot-long leaf free of bugs and ambient gunk. Then she held it over the gas flame to soften it before stripping each leaf half away from its thick stem. After that she cut the halves into five separate pieces.

As she scooped what looked like a succulent mixture of tempeh, mushrooms, spices and things like galangal and lemongrass into the leaf sections, she asked me how my writing was going.

"It's fine."

"You are telling stories about Bali?"

"No. I'm writing about a man who can't smell."

"Why he no smell?" she asked as she pinched in one side of the leaf square, then the other, folding over the flap and securing the two ends with bamboo toothpicks. This, in Bali, is referred to as *bungkus,* which more or less translates into "food in packets."

"He was born with this genetic—this rare disease. I mean, he was sick with this thing called Kallmann syndrome, and his pituitary gland—the part of his brain where his sense of smell is made—it never formed correctly. It was broken."

Where was my Balinese dictionary when I really needed it?

"Oh," Seni replied. She placed the packets in the bamboo steamer one by one. After she covered it, she looked up at me and frowned. "If he no smell, then he no taste the food, and that make him be very very sad, *ya*?"

No taste? I'd been focusing so long on my protagonist not being able to smell roses or gas leaks or spoiled milk that I'd not bothered to think through anosmia's other repercussions. "I guess that is true, *ya*," I said, getting off the stool. "Thanks, Seni."

I wandered back over to my computer imagining Miles sitting in a restaurant on an awkward first date. First he has to decide what to order based on texture or look. I assumed he'd hate the look of meat, but love fruit, and maybe noodles. Jell-O, for sure, but who orders Jell-O on a first date? Or any date for that matter. Then Rosemary, his date, holds a forkful of something up under his nose and says, "Here smell this; it's so divine," and he has to make up a reaction because it's no different than smelling a dead cow as far as his nose is concerned.

I typed without stopping. I wanted to tell Victor I'd written a few good pages today like I'd promised. I knew that no matter how he felt, or where he was, or how hung over he was, Jack London always wrote twenty-five pages of prose a day.

Heck, if I could slam out two excellent pages a day I'd be self-smitten.

I found my fingers tapping toward the end of the scene and suddenly Rosemary is saying something to Miles about memories. Smell memories. How they connect her to her past, like the smell of apple pie making her think about her long-dead grandmother. Miles feels none of that poignant bonding with the sacred scape of days gone by. The hot, sickly sweet smell of cinnamon rolls won't, for the rest of eternity, bring the image of shopping malls into his head like it will mine. I would write about that.

Or maybe I should use the smell of hot dogs in New York City, or—

"I go home early today, *ya*?" Seni suddenly appeared on the chair across from me.

"What?" I looked away from the computer. "Okay. I guess. How come? *Mengapa?*"

"I have ceremony."

Of course she did. Ceremonies. Rites. Festivals. How many reasons to take a day off can one culture have? Do they hold them daily? Hourly? It sometimes felt that way. The Balinese have ceremonies for getting pregnant; for being born; for turning forty-two days old; turning six months old; touching the ground for the first time; or getting their teeth filed.

All Balinese adolescents take part in the Teeth Filing ceremony (known as the *Mepandes* ceremony), where a priest/dentist files down the canines and neighboring teeth so that the upper teeth are all level. The reason for this is to remove any animal-like appearance. No wonder everyone's smiles looked exactly the same.

There are also daily rituals for welcoming ghosts or scaring them away. There are purification festivals. Cremation festivals. They have *Galungan, Kuningan, Nyepi, Saraswati* ... "Which one do you have today, Seni?"

"My cousin Nyoman, she three months pregnant. Very important time. We make offerings at the river so baby will be healthy baby."

"Fair enough."

"I make offerings. then I go, okay?"

"Okay," I said, because in Bali a day without offerings is like a day without rice—never going to happen.

All Balinese put out *banten*, or spiritual "offerings" several times a day. The simplest, most ubiquitous ones consist of a small square of woven palm leaf filled with food—a few grains of rice, say, or a mini Ritz cracker or small cookie—a stick of incense, and a flower. The little pallet then gets sprinkled with holy water. From what I'd culled from Seni and others, the food is meant to feed the spirits (but are usually spirited away by stray dogs or wandering monkeys), and the incense is burned to waft the essence of the offering out into the spiritosphere.

There are thousands of Balinese women who earn their living composing and placing offerings around the entire island. Each and every day, the offerings are set in doorways, on car hoods, car dashboards, on floors, in gardens, up and down sidewalks, under trees, on every step of staircases, on the counters at businesses of every kind. The placement of the *banten* has some meaning, depending on whether one hopes to welcome the good spirits or to appease the evil ones. When walking down any street in Bali, you try in vain to step over the incalculable amount of *banten* along the way, but it's almost impossible not to kick one by accident, or flatten one entirely.

Since Seni does not have time to assemble *banten,* we give her fifty cents a day to buy a bundle of pre-made offerings.

Sort of like Holy Lunchables.

At the end of the day, every one of those little, square, spirit soothers gets tossed out into the streets, where they are swept up into huge piles and set on fire. More often than not, people will add their own plastic-filled garbage bags to the burning mass of *banten*, which is why Balinese evenings are often punctuated by the stench of rancid smoke.

Seni came out of the bathroom—she'd changed from her jeans and T-shirt into the traditional Balinese sash-tied-sarong and white blouse—and slowly meandered around the house, dropping *banten* here, waving the spirits away there.

I could almost feel the air getting cleaner.

The scent of spicy incense floated by. Smells … Miles wouldn't be able to smell the incense … how would that be, to live in a world utterly aroma-less … no flowers, no sautéed garlic, no putrefying trash … I stared up at the ceiling fan and watched the bugs accumulate on the mosquito net. I listened to the workers sanding the bamboo floors next door and took in the flood of motorbikes oscillating back and forth on the road next to our house, as time lapped by like tiny ripples tiptoeing ashore from a wind-swept mountain lake … and then I got up to say my good-bye prayer with Seni. By the time I stepped back inside the mosquito net, the ever-rising heat had flushed out any remaining motivation to do anything more than clicking open People. com to see if Clay Aiken really was gay.

"Hi, Mommy! We're home."

"Hello there! How was your day, baby?"

"We learned about sunfish and we made paper airplanes."

"Awesome. Hi, Victor. How was your day?"

"Grand. Want to know what I just discovered?" He threw his back-pack on the counter and ripped off his sweat-soaked shirt.

"What?" I quickly took the jar of ice water out of the refrigerator and poured two glasses.

"The Indonesian teachers are paid shit." He went into the bathroom and turned on the water before I had the chance to tell him there was no water. "Goddammit! There's no water!"

He came out of the bathroom, grabbed the glass from me and poured it right over his head. When Loy saw him do that she squealed,

"I'm doing that too, Daddy," and upended the other glass all over herself.

I thought for sure all three of us would start laughing, but Victor just went on talking as if it were perfectly normal to douse oneself with ice water after work.

"It's bad enough they don't get free housing like we do, or that their health insurance isn't close to as extensive as ours."

"We have extensive coverage?"

"Am I talking about us right now?" he bellowed loudly enough to send Loy scurrying upstairs.

"No, I'm sorry. You were saying?"

"I was saying that I found out that Monique and Ingrid, Veronika— all the Indonesian teachers with *full* teaching degrees are paid like a third of what the western teachers are paid."

"But you're the real teacher," I tried, having no idea why I needed to defend Green School's pay scale.

"Fuck that. If I'd known there was going to be so obvious a … It reeks of colonialism, doesn't it?" Victor, defender of the underclass, declared. Victor, the son of would-be Commies. He, who grew up listening to Paul Robeson, Woody Guthrie, and Bob Dylan. Who went to a clothing-optional summer camp called Camp Thoreau. Who attended Oberlin College and majored in Urban Social Justice or some such right-fist-in-the-air/equality-for-all major.

Victor. Who came to Bali because he believed he could make a difference in the world.

"I don't know," I replied. "Look what we're paying Seni."

"That's not the point."

Katy next door had just turned up the volume on her disco-beat workout music, and I quickly lost whatever point Victor or anyone in the universe was attempting to make. Was it any wonder that most technological advances have historically been made in cold northern climes? I could hardly focus on the music, let alone Victor, in this brain-draining heat and humidity. "Okay," I said, thinking that would suffice.

"Okay, what?" he said through a mouthful of my frozen papaya.

I pulled out a stool and sat down. "I'll talk about anything you want, buddy." I wanted to be comfortable calling him that again, but the moment before I uttered it I felt the word stick sideways in my mouth.

"Nah. I'm done ranting. Oh, by the way, not that I want to go, but we're all invited to the Hardys tonight for a pool-party."

During the drive to the Hardys', Victor asked Sinead how her conferences had gone.

"Pretty good, actually," she said. "Veronika and I put together a slideshow of the kiddies' art work. The parents, I think, really loved it."

I turned around in my seat to see how Loy was doing, squished between Victor and Sinead. "Brad must have been happy, having you show up," I said, trying to join in the conversation.

Sinead's face went dark. "*Ya*, Brad. He just about ruined the whole day for me when he came for *his* child's conference."

"What do you mean?" Victor asked. "What happened?"

"So, yeah, I know he's a busy guy and all, but he scheduled his conference for last, right? And of course there was an over-run on timings."

"Do not tell me Brad gave you shit." Victor already had his *This is so going to get me mad* face at the ready.

"Well, you know, he should have been in parent mode at that point, right? Not director mode."

"Right."

"And *ya*, so I'm finishing up with Sasha's father and my back is really killing me and honestly I want to be done already and go home and lie down, but I'm all smiles and caring—you know—I'm telling

Sasha's dad how he started the year so shy and withdrawn and now he's getting all settled in and starting to open more, like you know, this kid has really changed and I'm so proud how he's joining us in circle time and such. And then Brad was there, and I was running maybe, I dunno, maybe ten minutes late. But rather than just wait outside like any other parent, Brad walked into the classroom and said straight out, 'Are you going to be much longer? I have somewhere I have to be and I can't wait around. If you can't see me, then we should re-schedule for another time.'"

With Loy in his arms, Victor pushed back against the car door as far as he could manage, as if literally repelled by what Sinead had said. "Christ. What did you say?"

"Well, you can imagine that I was appalled. I mean, you had to hear the tone of his voice, and that he said it in front of both Veronika *and* a parent. It felt really degrading to be spoken to like that by the director of the school."

I could imagine Victor imagining what he would have done.

"It was embarrassing, Victor. Really embarrassing."

"I bet."

"*Ya*, and I could see that Sasha's father was really uncomfortable. I turned to Brad very calmly and said, 'No, we do *not* need to re-schedule. We're almost finished here. I will see you in a moment.'"

"What did Brad say?" Loy suddenly hollered. Who knew the kid was listening! Victor looked at me and I looked at Sinead, who patted Loy's leg.

"He walked back out and waited. But Sasha's father immediately stood up and started apologizing for being the reason we were running over time. He ran out of the classroom, not even looking at Brad when he passed him."

"Son of a bitch."

"What do you mean, Daddy? Whose son do you mean? Are you talking about Sasha?"

Victor shook his head and said nothing, as did Sinead. We three sat quietly letting the scene play out in our minds, while Loy continued on babbling about Sasha. "Hey, I think I know Sasha. He's the little boy who was always crying…."

Some fifteen minutes later, after driving through many villages and many rice fields, the driver turned down a long narrow lane, finally coming to a stop in an enormous courtyard. In front of us was a towering unlocked gate.

"That's the front door," Victor said from the back seat.

"Nice," Sinead replied. "I bet they feel pretty safe behind that."

We pushed it open and found ourselves inside the Kingdom of Hardy.

Wow.

"You never told me the view was this outrageous," I said to Victor as one of the servants greeted us with a tray of chicken saté. I took a stick and thanked her, then made my way to the bar area where I quickly downed a bamboo mug filled with an ice-cold *arak*. *Arak* is one of the national drinks of Bali—think Balinese gin made from coconut palms. The best thing to do with *arak* is to mix it with honey (*madu*) and lime juice and you get an *arak madu*. It goes down like an ice-cold margarita on a beach in Mexico.

It goes down pretty easy in your husband's boss's backyard in Bali, too.

I picked up another mug and made my way over to the pool where most of the other teachers and their children were already swimming, eating, laughing, socializing. It wasn't really a pool so much as a man-made river complete with a black bottom and store-bought fish. I finished the last of my second drink just as Cynthia Hardy appeared looking as sun-kissed, yoga-fit, and hotel-rested as she always did. Behind her, as if a painted scene were placed just to make her look that much more regal, a magnificent river gorge spread out for miles in a wash of green undulating hills.

"Thank you for having us," I greeted her.

"Thank you for coming. Hello, Victor. Nice to see you."

"Hi, Cynthia. Come on, Loy, let's jump in." Victor took Loy's hand and made for the pool.

I replaced my empty mug with one from a passing tray and followed the small group of teachers who were about to be led on a tour through the exotic, over-the-top, Hardy home.

Because she could still hardly walk, Sinead and I stayed back a few lengths and let everyone pass us by. "Go on. We'll catch up," I said to Katy and Andrea.

We wound slowly through the two stories of wondrous open-walled architecture. Everything was made from wood, but not, I noticed, bamboo. Downstairs the big open living area was filled with sculptures and antiques, with tasteful saffron-colored furnishings contrasting nicely against the dark wood and golden bowls. Upstairs, we passed an office with glass doors which could be closed—CLOSED—off against the outside elements. Was that an air conditioner? The cozy den had gorgeous built-in book cases and old Persian rugs strewn about and—"Oh, look," I said, pointing to the far wall. "A great big television."

The bathroom had a stone bathtub the size of a baby elephant. And a flush toilet.

I felt like a kid from The Fresh Air Fund.

The Hardys' two children lived in their own five-story tower across another man-made body of water. At first I wondered what kind of parents relegate their children to their own house, but then discovered that each of the girls had their own personal *pembantu* who slept in the room with them.

No wonder there were so many *pembantu* milling about. Everywhere you turned another beautiful Balinese woman appeared. "*Suksma*," I said thankfully to the one who appeared with a tray of freshly filled *arak* mugs.

"They have *pembantu* coming out their ears," I whispered conspiratorially to Sinead as we sat down together on a hillock overlooking the view beyond the pool.

"I think I heard he has thirty-five."

"What for?"

"One picks out his clothes." She rearranged her pained lower body sideways.

"I betcha he has one just to transcribe all those important thoughts he splooges into his tiny tape recorder all day long," I said, picturing him as he walked through campus, talking into his hand.

Sinead laughed. "*Ya*, and they probably have two *pembantu* just to take care of his $700 dogs."

"He has purebred dogs?"

"*Ya*. Some small shitty things."

"When there are so many strays in Bali? That's outrageous. Where is he? I've got to go say something to him. I've got to tell him—"

"No, you don't, my friend," Sinead said grabbing my arm. "Stay here with me and enjoy the view."

She was right; you don't go insulting your hosts just because they don't choose to save a stray dog. Or because they don't use compost toilets. Or because they have hot water.

John Hardy appeared out of nowhere. He exchanged hellos with a couple of the teachers then sank down on the grass, Indian style, only a few feet away from us. He always sat that way, with his back erect and his hands in his lap—like he was about to start meditating.

But then, instead of closing his eyes and listening to his breath, he scratched at his crotch and looked our way.

He asked after Sinead's class, as if her back injury hadn't happened. She said that she had had really good parent-teacher conferences. He nodded then scratched at his crotch again.

I tried to get up the nerve to ask him why he thought it was okay to own a television and air conditioning and a stable of cars, but I didn't think Victor would speak to me again. Instead, I gulped the rest of my drink and complimented him on his fantastically gorgeous and well-designed house.

He thanked me and again went after something between his legs. Like a nervous twitch, he dangled his hand down there over and over again. In fact, as I thought about it, he did that while walking around the school, too, or whenever he gave one of his marketing speeches to the parents. I finally understood the appeal of wearing sarongs and almost fell over laughing, but instead held tight to what little sobriety I had remaining in a tiny corner of my head.

"Will you be coming to the *Melaspas* Ceremony?" he asked me.

I had no clue whatsoever what he was referring to. "Of course," I replied as I leaned back onto my elbows and admired my own toes.

"If you don't already have them, you and your family will need to get traditional Balinese clothing."

"Sure. Sure," I said with a smile. Then I got up to go find me another drink.

I had no idea how many *arak madus* I'd drunk, until I woke up with the room spinning in the opposite direction from the ceiling fan and my stomach in heaving knots.

I had to throw up so I fell down the stairs, trying to be quiet but failing. I got to the bathroom, opened the compost toilet, then—WTF? I couldn't throw up into that heap of pee and poo-loaded sawdust!

I slithered back upstairs and rocked Victor side to side through the mosquito net.

"What?" he moaned. "Why are you waking me up in the middle of the night?"

"I have to throw up."

"I told you not to drink so much."

"I think I ate something bad."

"No, you didn't. You just drank too much. Now leave me alone."

"But I have to throw up."

"So go throw up and let me go back to sleep. I have to go to work in a few hours." He started to turn over but I grabbed him before he left me for good.

"I can't throw up in the sawdust. All that shit will fly around. Oh, that is so gross I may have to throw up right now." I hurried out of the room, down the stairs and out the door gate, barefoot and naked, over toward the coconut palms, where I stuck my hand into my throat and purged my body of the rest of the semi-metabolized *arak*.

I fell back onto the damp dirt and gazed up into the spiraling darkness. I prayed no machete-bearing security guard would come around, and briefly closed my eyes. I felt something crawl across my shin and almost enjoyed the tickle of its tiny legs, but when a swarm of mosquitoes circled my defenseless body I had no choice but to get up. I got as far as my hands and knees before I collapsed down again.

"What am I doing here?" I voiced into the buzzing air.

If you really don't want to be here, just leave. What's stopping you?

"Victor and Loy need me."

Victor told you to go back to California, remember? And Loy seems pretty good, considering how useless you are as a mother.

"No, I'm changing."

Are you? Maybe Victor would be happier without you.

"No, he wants me here. We're good again." I thought of the pool. Floating beneath his hands. His smile. The fact that he was sleeping in the same bed as me.

Do you honestly believe that? When was the last time he kissed you on the mouth?

I couldn't answer that. Off to my right I heard the faint drone of a walkie-talkie. "You're right, whoever you are. I'm useless here. I am the rain on their parade."

Then go.

The radio voices moved further off into the distance. The sky above me began to lighten. A bat swooped by close to my face, its high-pitched cry sounding more like a human baby in pain than a small creature in search of bugs. Was it a vampire bat? I pictured it turning into a dolled-up vampiress, sucking what was left of my pathetic life out of me.

Really? You call this pathetic? I call it weak-kneed. Since when did you become such a scaredy-cat? Such a paranoid mess? You used to be self-assured. Positive. Present. You made a promise not too long ago. If you can't come through, then get the hell out of Victor's way and let him get on with his life.

"You're right. I can't leave." I pushed my defiled body up and stumbled toward the gate. "Because this is where I live."

Two days later I learned why Green School was having the *Melaspas* ceremony John Hardy had spoken of at his party. Back in July, the husband of Brad's administrative assistant had died of massive head injuries after swerving his motorbike to avoid a street dog. He'd gone out to the *toko* (shop) down the street, supposedly, for a box of milk, or a pack of smokes, and neglected to put on a helmet.

Not long after, the same sort of accident befell one of the Hardys' *pembantu*. He had stayed late to help clean up after one of his master's parties and fell asleep while motorcycling home, *sans* helmet, only to be side-struck by one of the thousands of bullying drivers who crowd the roadways of Bali every moment of every day.

He died on the spot.

As reported by Johnny at one of our *cumi-cumi* parties, a fifty-foot-long bamboo pole being used to build Heart of School fell on a Balinese classroom helper. Thankfully, she survived with only a headache that lasted several days.

Last Monday, Edie, the young Balinese boy who sweeps leaves and branches and dirt and mud and plastic bags and dead bugs and candy wrappers from the many paths the students use to get around campus, crashed his motorbike on his way home and fractured his helmet-less skull.

And days later a young Javanese worker dropped a heavy piece of stone on his toe, causing him to shriek so loudly that I stopped not writing my novel mid-almost-sentence and went running. Phillipa had gotten there three beats ahead of me and had a hand on the screaming man's bloody appendage.

"Gosh, what next? It's like this place is cursed," Pip said. Two of the workers were sent to fetch her medical kit and a towel from the closet-sized hut that served as the infirmary. The nail-less toe was quickly cleaned, wrapped, and the young man sent on his way.

To those unfortunate incidents, I add:

1. the near-disastrous ceiling fan fiasco.

2. Sinead's accident.

3. Seni's burn while frying bananas for dessert using our metal tongs. She thought she'd closed them before setting them in the boiling hot oil, but had only closed them partway. They popped open, spraying the lower portion of her face with hot oil. Seni screamed, ran across the road to the forest, yanked out a handful of aloe plants and immediately doused her burning face with the plant's oozing gel. The next day she showed up at work, her lips and chin smeared with a turmeric/coconut oil concoction. Within two days her face had magically healed.

If you're in Bali, and you put all those accidents into one superstitious, ghost-groveling pot, you get a stew of native nervousness. After the last mishap, the workers on campus started to talk. Maybe Green School *was* cursed. It was, after all, built next to a cemetery.

Anyone versed in Balinese lore/culture/ritual, believed that, after so many bad things occurred, some serious cleansing had to take place.

Cue *Melaspas*: a traditional Balinese purification ceremony used for expunging negative energy from a building. Or, in this case, campus.

Since it was a traditional ceremony, we were instructed not to attend the ceremony unless we wore traditional kit, which, thankfully, we'd bought when we first arrived in Bali.

As I stood in front of the bathroom mirror on the day of the ceremony, I wrapped a colorful *kamben* (a sarong worn only for rituals) as best I could around my waist, then tied it in place with a red and gold *selempot* (sash), thinking how special it felt to dress in something other than a worn sarong and yellowed T-shirt. That feeling subsided after the fifteen minutes it took to fasten the innumerable hook-and-eye closures on the delicately embroidered *baju kebaya* (blouse dress).

I rolled my sweat-streaked hair into a bun and ran down to join the gathering. As we assembled under a large tarp, I looked at the white-skinned adults and children dressed in their Balinese-style formal best. We looked ridiculously out-of-place next to the locals, who wore their clothing with such elegance they made the rest of us look like kids at a Halloween party.

I settled myself on the ground next to Loy's class, where I kept getting touched by stray arms and legs and elbows and feet. I gently removed a small moist hand from my thigh and adjusted my sarong so the flap faced forward. I noticed Victor sitting next to Sara with their class. Victor had on his new white *udeng* (traditional male Balinese headgear that sort of looks like the inside pleated part of an accordion). I waved to them and they waved back.

I saw Kumar, dressed in his traditional Indian businessman costume—smooth black slacks, white stainless shirt. No one was making *him* leave for not wearing the right clothing. After his visit to Sinead's house the other day, she had told me and Victor about how he'd been cordial and respectful. He'd downplayed the school's threats to withhold her pay and added that if Sinead wanted to resign, he'd understand.

She said that maybe she would quit, and asked if the school would be willing to pay her salary (and insurance coverage) for the remainder of the year.

Kumar had said he would think about it, but added that she would have to sign an indemnity letter releasing Green School from further responsibility. In fact, he just happened to have one in his hand.

Victor had gone ballistic over that. "Did you tell him to go fuck himself?" my normally balanced husband asked.

Sinead hadn't told him that, no.

Nothing had been decided and Kumar had left her house, I presumed, as cool and collected as he'd been when I almost fell on him.

I watched him now, talking on his cell phone, his stoic face giving nothing away.

He caught me staring at him, and I quickly looked to the far side of the pavilion where John Hardy and his family had just come in, wearing their best Balinese frippery and their—what was that in his ears? Was he wearing iPod ear buds? John Hardy was listening to an iPod! He, who insisted that we honor the Balinese ways on this holy day.

In the corner, I saw Daniel, the school's videographer, with his camera pointed at the Hardy clan. Would Hardy order Daniel to Photoshop out those white strings hanging from his ears before he posted pictures of the ceremony onto the school's website?

Beneath my *kebaya* I fumed and felt a worm of anger begin to crawl through my heart. I ceased seething when the village high priest began chanting and praying and talking to the spirits, all of which sounded exactly the same.

A few of the locals danced to gamelan, and incense wafted in our general direction. A pretty, young Balinese woman walked among us and sprinkled our heads with holy water. Just when I thought the ceremony was over, someone tapped me on my shoulder. I turned to find Phillipa kneeling next to me. "You might want to close your eyes for the next part," she said.

"Why?"

"They sacrificed a dog for the ceremony. They'll bring it out in a minute, and I know how you feel about dogs."

"Thanks a lot for telling me now, Pip. Why didn't anyone bother to mention that small detail in the email they sent out?"

Phillipa shrugged and smiled her serenely calming smile. "Guess they didn't think it was important enough."

"The children are going to freak when they see a dead dog. I know Loy will. She loves dogs. Jeez." I was more miffed at this than the iPod on Hardy's head.

"No one will know it's a dog."

"Huh?"

"Don't ask me why, but they skin it first. I think the kids will just assume it's a lamb or something."

"What? That's less bad?"

"Shhh!" came from Loy's teacher. "Go talk somewhere else."

Before I could blink, the priest held up a smallish skinless mammal-like creature, then placed it out of sight, continuing on with his spiritual entreaties. "We killed this animal for you, oh generous and wise spirits. Now stop letting heavy objects fall on our employees!"

Or at least I assumed he said something like that.

As he chanted I couldn't get the image of the pink fleshy thing out of my mind. Where had they gotten the dog from? I wondered if it was that cute dog I tried to save the other day. Ever since my skirmish with the monkey, I'd been trying out different walking routes. While I was wandering through some of the farms past the east side of the campus I'd come upon a dirt-road-side *toko* selling bottled gasoline, white bread, rice, beer, coconuts, live birds—the usual 7-11 sort of fare. Chained up in front of the store was a small blonde dog with fluffy ears and a pushed-in face. She looked like a Pekinese gone bad.

She had a scant three-feet of chain, no shade, and no water in sight. It had to be in the 90s with 134 percent humidity. Granted, I was panting harder than she was but I knew she had to be beyond miserable. I knew this because she tried to bite me when I leaned over to pet her, but neither her heart nor her teeth were into being much of a watchdog.

I was well aware that there was no love lost between the Balinese and dogs, but I beseeched the owners to help their reincarnated sinner, pantomiming "hot" to the teenage girl and her father, who held out a plastic water bottle to me. "*Tidak*," I said. No, not me. The dog. The dog. Don't you people see that she's "*pedas*!"

"*Pedas*!" I said again, not realizing at the time that I was telling these people that their dog was spicy—as opposed to *panas* (hot)—which is probably why they just stood there smiling blankly at my crazy arm-waving antics.

I pointed to a bowl on one of the shelves filled with plastic crap, then pointed at the water bottle, flipping my wrist over, pretending to pour THAT into THAT. The young girl finally got my drift and filled a disgustingly oily bottom half of a plastic jug with water and put it down on the ground. The dog drank it gone in four seconds.

"*Suksma*," I said to her, hoping she'd make this benevolent act part of her daily routine, but doubting it. The rehydrated dog yarked at me, as if to thank me. I was about to go on my way with a wave goodbye, but took a step backward, and asked if I could please take the pooch with me for a little *jalan-jalan*; a little un-chained walk. I did this by pointing to the dog, then to my chest, then making believe my two fingers were a little person walking.

Surprisingly, they agreed, unhooking the dog and handing me the end of the metal chain. I pulled her with me, making the standard kissing sounds. When she stayed rooted to the spot, I gave a little airy girl-whistle. Still nothing. No one in Bali would ever make a friendly overture to call a dog to them so what would she know from kisses and whistles? Finally, I just dragged her along. She got the idea and began to trot along beside me, her tail wagging.

We walked for a few minutes, she constantly looking up at me, a smile on her dog face, her tongue hanging out, her yellowed teeth shining.

Freedom, she seemed to be telling me with her eyes, tasted really good.

We walked together for another ten minutes or so, but then her little body all but gave out. The walking was just too much for her unused muscles. She dropped to the ground, panting. I noticed a year's worth of dried feces stuck to the fur around her butt.

I squatted down and petted her filthy, matted body.

And then I started to cry because I knew I couldn't take this knotted waif home with me. I knew I'd have to bring her back to that *toko*, where she'd be chained up again. Where she'd be used as a watchdog to ward off malicious spirits, at least until the owners got tired of filling a dirty water dish for a worthless once-and-future sinner.

Where she'd soon be handed over to the village priest, who would come around one day looking for some help in cleaning the bad karma off a white man's school.

"That was not a good meeting," Victor said to Kumar, after taking a bite of his hamburger. Loy, Kumar, Victor, and I were sitting at a table in Kafe, an eco-groovin' restaurant in Ubud. Around us was a potpourri of customers, including yoginis on a dinner break from their yoga retreat; deeply tanned European expats typing away on their laptops; and a few starry-eyed tourists taking in the whole *Eat, Pray, Love*-ness of it all. On the sales shelves in the corner next to the many bottles of Bali-scented soaps and shampoos, organic bug juice, as well cleansing/detox kits, were a dozen copies of Elizabeth Gilbert's memoir, signed by the author herself. Now that I'd lived in Bali, I had to wonder how it was that two food-loving American women, both looking for something more out of life, could have had such strikingly different experiences on the same small island.

"Mommy, you've got to try my pasta. It's so good."

That's why. Elizabeth Gilbert hangs out with jetsetters at posh dinner parties. I share bites of peanut-ty noodles with my six-year-old. She spends spiritually rich days with a Balinese medicine man who sees into her future. I hang with a Balinese maid who fries up seriously soul-satisfying squid. She finds true love with a Brazilian businessman. My marriage to an American schoolteacher teeters on the edge of ruin.

"Yes, I know, Victor. It is not what I would have expected to occur, given the present situation." Kumar, a lifelong vegetarian, sat across from me nibbling on a *mezze* plate. I looked from my bowl of bland lentil stew to his assortment of hummus, babaganoush, tabouli, feta cheese, kalamatas, and toasted pita bread, and wished we could swap plates.

"Victor, let's trade for a little."

"No way. I told you not to order mush," he said, but then immediately offered up his burger to my pouting mouth. I took a walloping big bite, momentarily satisfying my need for salt and fat and hollow calories.

Kumar had suggested having a quiet dinner together, away from the school, the drone of sanders and insects, Victor's colleagues. Victor had agreed to the dinner meeting because after the meeting that he'd had this afternoon with Brad and the rest of management, he'd come home more discouraged than ever. He was supposed to have told *them* what he thought needed fixing. They'd told him that they thought the teachers whined too much.

"You know that we wish very much for you to be happy," Kumar said.

"Of course."

"And it is unreasonable for you to be spending so much time with these frustrations. They must understand that the teachers are our most important part of this project," he said, stuffing a mini feta-and-hummus sandwich into his mouth.

"Yes."

"We need for all the teachers to be happy, on every level, beginning with where you live."

At the table next to ours, a young woman with dreadlocked hair wrapped up in a batik headband was telling another woman about some cute guy she'd met at yoga class. I couldn't decide which conversation to listen to.

"Maybe you and Lisa can tell me which part of your house I can help change to make you more comfortable."

"It's not so bad."

"What?" I said more loudly than I'd intended. I wanted to kick him under the table. Or pinch him. Or throw my arms out wide in an exasperated expression of total confusion. "What?" I repeated, choosing the third option.

"What's your problem?" Victor said. "You hate it, but I don't. I hate the mold and—you can put your arms down now—and the smoke, but no, I think it's pretty. The structure itself is gorgeous. I love the bedroom. And hey, the kitchen is great."

The bedroom? "We were promised that we'd have an oven, but we don't," I said. I knew how much Victor missed making pizza and thought this might improve our lot considerably.

From the blazer he had thrown over a chair, Kumar took out a small notebook and wrote something down. "Yes? What else?"

I looked at Victor who had the most tight-lipped scowl on his face. He wanted to talk about the school, and here I was about to ask Kumar to build us an enclosed space with air-conditioning. "Nothing else," I said, grabbing a French fry from his plate. "It's fine."

Kumar shrugged and turned back to his star teacher. "Then I must ask you if you would consider becoming our Head of Curriculum."

"No, thank you. I came here to teach."

"What if it should come with a substantial increase in pay?"

I could tell Victor was starting to get antsy. He didn't need Kumar offering him pizza ovens or promotions. He needed him to get the

Hardys and the others to stop trying to market Green School like it was a high-priced piece of artwork, and instead start focusing on the kids.

"You going to eat those fries?" I asked him.

"Have 'em."

Loy looked up from the outline of a Bali beach scene she'd been filling in with focused crayon strokes. "I want them, Mommy."

"Okay. Here. Let me have one. The rest are yours."

"Thanks."

"*Sama sama.*"

"Again, I appreciate the offer, Kumar, and defining the curriculum would be great, but it won't change the big picture. Other things are more important right now."

"Like?"

"I brought it up twice at the meeting today. There are too many secrets; there's an utter lack of transparency with the people in charge. When you try to tell John and Cynthia what's wrong, they blame Brad. When you try to get Brad to make changes, he says his hands are tied because of the Hardys."

Kumar nodded. I watched a tall, leathery, sixty-something man stroll in with a copy of *The Bali Advertiser* in his hand and a hand-rolled cigarette hanging from his mouth.

"You know," Victor continued on as calmly as ever, "this is the most dysfunctional management team I've ever worked with. They talk about each other behind their backs, and the teachers hear it all. At this point they have no credibility with any of the staff."

"It is perhaps because this school has been created by business people?"

"Even as business people, you have to have a systematic approach to how you're going to do things. They don't. They're reactionary."

Kumar took notes as Victor spoke. I waited for someone to bring up the Sinead debacle but thought it best to keep my mouth hushed. "Please give me a specific example," Kumar said quietly.

"The school is trying to portray itself as a *sustainable* organization, so our power gets turned off for an hour every day to save energy. Maybe that works for workers in PT Bambu, or the people cleaning the paths, but teachers and students can't work like that. Not if we're trying to be innovative."

"Yes, I myself would also like this idea to go away."

"And why did no one think through the fact that textbooks aren't going to last in this kind of heat and humidity?"

"Can I get a dessert?" asked Loy.

"Sure, sweetie. What sounds good?" Victor said.

"Oooh. Chocolate mousse."

"What else?" Kumar asked.

"I could also eat the apple pie."

"No, Loy, I was asking your father."

"Oh. I want the pie, Daddy."

"I just want tea," I said, standing up to go to the bathroom. "Loy, you want to come, too?"

We wandered behind the counter to the stairs leading out back to the toilet. As I waited for Loy, I read a poster about an upcoming fundraiser for the Sumatran Orangutan Society. The toilet flushed—its watery gurgle a reassuring sound—and Loy unlatched the door. "Your turn, Mommy."

"Wait for me here, please." I went in, lifted my skirt and sat, thinking about the orangutans. Years ago, I went to a reading by Birute Galdikas, the anthropologist and conservationist who wrote *Reflections of Eden: My Years with the Orangutans of Borneo*. I got so fired up by her talk, that I, too, wanted to go live in the jungle and save apes. While waiting in line to have her sign a copy of her book, I planned how to convince her that I'd be an amazing addition to her cause. By the time my turn came, I chickened out. I didn't really want to move to Borneo. I didn't want to rescue endangered animals. I wanted to write novels.

By the time we got back to the table, Kumar and Victor had more or less wrapped up their list-making and airing-out of grievances. We ate our dessert, said our goodnights, and texted the nice I Made to please drive us home.

In the car, as Loy leaned tiredly against his chest, Victor distilled his dinner talk with Kumar down to this: "They're fucked."

After we were let off at the bamboo security pole, Victor and Loy went on ahead and I skipped over to see if Sinead was around to share a beer and a bit of gossip. She wasn't, which bummed me to no end. She still hadn't made up her mind whether to quit, wait to get fired and sue the school, or try to teach with a bad back.

As I flicked off my flip-flops at the front gate of our hut, I saw Victor and Loy looking up the staircase toward the top of the tree.

"What? Are the ants back?" I asked, panicked.

"No. Shhh. Come here. Look."

I came in and followed their heads. "Oh. Wow. What is that?" A moth the size of a catcher's mitt had its purplish-colored wings spread open on the side of the tree. "That is the biggest freakin' thing I've ever seen."

"I know."

"The markings are beautiful. All those white spots and see how the edges of the wings are almost pink? I'm gonna go do a search. I want to find out what it is."

Victor grabbed my arm before I could go over to my laptop. "Sweetie. It's here now. Who knows how long it'll stay there. Why don't you wait until it flies away?"

"You're right." I needed to stay present.

I moved over and stood between him and Loy and marveled at the gigantic creature that had decided to grace us with a visit. After a few minutes, Loy sat down on the floor and we followed suit, finally lying on our backs with our heads in our hands, staring up at the moth as if it were a sky full of stars.

It was still there when Loy fell asleep. Still on the tree as we carried her past it up the stairs and undressed her and tucked her inside her netted bed.

Still there as we watched it while brushing our teeth.

Still there when we at last lost interest. "You gonna stay here for the night? I hope you do so we can see you again in the morning," I said to it on my way upstairs. Figuring it'd probably be gone, I wished it a final *bon voyage* and climbed into bed and found Victor on his computer.

"So, our friend," he said, looking up from his laptop with a smile, "is an Atlas Moth, and it is the largest moth on the planet. And listen to this: 'Throughout their one to two-week adult life, they survive entirely on larval fat reserves that they build up while they are caterpillars.'"

"Two weeks?" I fluffed my pillow and fought the urge to go stare at it some more. "It lives for only two weeks?" I repeated.

"Yup. Only two weeks."

"That's not enough time."

Victor closed the computer and yawned. "Not enough time for what? Not enough time to write a novel? Or to learn to speak Chinese?"

"I don't know," I said. "The world's a prettier place right now because that moth is out there."

"And in two weeks? What's the world going to look like then?" he asked, turning over without waiting for an answer.

"Less pretty?" I uttered quietly.

He turned back toward me and put his hand on mine. "No, not with you in it, it's not."

I felt tears fill my eyes. "That is the corniest thing I've ever heard you say."

Victor sat up and held me in his arms. "I love you, you know."

"You do?"

"I do." And with that he let go and turned over. He'd had a long hard day. He'd sat through two meetings with people who professed to be walking down the same road, but couldn't for the life of them agree on which map to use.

Kumar had asked him to be patient, to wait for changes to happen.

I'd been asking him, for what seemed like forever, to wait for me to change.

All that waiting and wondering and wandering would make anyone dizzy with exhaustion. No wonder he was already snoring.

I turned off my light and let the moth take my thoughts away on its wings as light as dust.

Victor at our front-door gate

Victor and Sara planning curriculum

Our bamboo castle

Victor teaching in his bamboo classroom

Teacher Sara

Looking out our bathroom "windows"

Halloween in Bali

Our master bedroom

Our living room

Playing dress-up

Loy and her babies

The one and only Seni

Part 3:
Bye-Bye Bali

Victor had gotten plenty pissed off about the last meeting he'd had with Brad and the Hardys. He was disheartened by the increasingly fragile state of the school, as well as the volatile attitude of the people who ran it.

But it took an acetylene torch to get him to finally say ENOUGH.

A few nights after having dinner with Kumar we were lying in bed together, talking about this and that, watching various insects land on the outside of the mosquito net.

"We've got a newcomer tonight. Ever seen one of those before?" Victor asked me.

"Yeah, I know that guy. It's a multi-winged coconut roach," I said, making up a name.

"No way. It's too pretty to be a roach." Victor grew up in New York City where there is no such thing as a comely roach.

"It's prettier than that thing over there. What's on his head?"

Victor sat up to get a closer look. "Horns?"

"That must be a Balinese horned cicadydid."

"I'm tired," he replied, not amused by my cleverness. "Mind if I turn off the light?"

"It's only 8:30. Want to watch a movie?"

"Sweetie. I'm too hot to do anything. Just let me go to sleep, okay?" He'd given me a whopping thirty minutes of his attention since coming home from school, and I wanted more. I wanted to talk about his day. About Sinead's decision to sign the indemnity paper and quit.

But his eyes were already glazing over, so I kissed him on the mouth and read a chapter of Richard Ford's *Independence Day* before falling asleep myself.

I dreamt of fireworks exploding over and over in front of me, their bright lights flashing before my eyes—POW! POW! POW!—and awoke to bright lights flashing before my eyes.

What the hell? I sat up in bed. A flash of light ricocheted off the opposite side of the room. I yanked my earplugs out and listened for fireworks, but instead heard a sizzling, popping sound.

I pushed Victor awake. "What? Why are you—what is that noise? What's that light?" He pushed through the net and looked out the window hole. "You have got to be kidding me," he said. "They're working on the water heater."

"Now? What time is it?"

"It's time for us to get the hell out of this place. I'm done."

Did he just say he was DONE? Was he messing with my head? I sat frozen as I watched him go downstairs. I heard him outside, talking to the workers but couldn't tell what was said. A few moments later he returned with his laptop, got into bed with it, and began to type.

I said nothing. I whispered silent prayers, one after the other. I flashed back to being in bed with Victor in our blue house in California and he's holding *Three Cups of Tea*, talking about wanting to go off to find an adventure while I egg him on. As I watched him type, I felt that same frizzling promise of potential snapping its fingers in front of my face. What was he going to do next? What? What?

The minutes passed. The excruciatingly bright light outside our hut flickered, and the smell of burning metal filled the room. I went to check on Loy, waiting for the next glow of torch light to be sure she was still asleep. She was.

I came back to bed. Victor had stopped typing. "Here," he said, pushing the computer toward me. "Read what I sent."

"You already sent it?" I was incredulous. Victor never sent anything of import without letting it sit and simmer for a minute or two. I'd once gotten myself in deep doo-doo at a former job for impulsively firing off an angry, insult-filled email. When I told Victor about it, he'd advised that I never send an email in the heat of the moment. Write it. Then wait. Then read it again. "You don't ever want to act on emotion only."

And here he'd ignored his own warning. Dizzy with anticipation, I adjusted the screen and read the letter. When I finished, I looked at him, my mouth agape. "You really began a letter to your bosses with the line, 'This is totally fucked up'?"

"It *is* fucked up. Why does the work need to be done right now, at one o'clock in the morning?"

"Because John—"

"Because John Hardy said it had to, that's why." He shook his head as if in disbelief over the obvious. "I'm fed up."

"You certainly made that clear." I glanced again at the email, the phrases "dysfunctional organization" and "total reactive stupidity" and "unsustainable" shining out like neon lights on a dark desert highway.

"You mean this, buddy?" I asked.

"I do. I'm done being treated like a child. I'm tired of it."

"We're really going to leave?"

"No, Lisa. Did you not read the letter? I said I want to take the weekend to reevaluate our place here."

As if anyone in their right mind couldn't translate that into "I quit!"

"Okay, fine. You want to—"

"What I want, sweetie, is to go to sleep. We'll talk about it this weekend. Good night."

The next morning I went skidding across the wet rocks to Sinead's to share with her my prospect of escape. Victor had asked me not to tell a soul until our decision was final, but shoot, I had to tell Sinead!

First, I had her swear up and down that what goes on in the bamboo hut *stays* in the bamboo hut.

"What?" she exclaimed, stirring two heaping teaspoons of palm sugar into her instant coffee. "I'm supposed to quit first. You can't quit before me. When would you leave?"

"*If* we leave, it'd be as soon as they find a replacement, is my guess." I put on some water for my own cup.

"But what if I'm still here? You can't leave me here alone."

"Actually." I looked in her fridge for milk and, except for a damaged muffin, found it empty. "I can," I said.

"Well, shite."

"Knowing Kumar, he'll get you the rest of your salary and insurance paid for." I sipped my bitter coffee and felt my core temperature rise two degrees.

"He'd better. I signed that damn letter saying Green School had nothing to do with my back getting hurt."

"You're not asking for a whole lot of money. They have to go for it. Then you can go lie on a beach and have Wayan draw more pirates on your body."

"Har har. When will Victor make his final decision?"

"Dunno. This weekend? I know this sounds sick, but I hope something bad happens at school today so he won't change his mind."

"Did he tell you about the snake search they're doing tonight?"

"Snakes?"

She clicked on an email and read: "Dear Teachers, In order to secure the residence, classroom, and camps, we are going to do the snake hunt tonight. It is going to be done by professional and accompanied by our security personnel all the time during this. He will start at the teacher residence area before move to other area. He will be seen around your house with security personnel. *Pak* Kobra catch only the snake that potentially dangerous for human."

"*Pak* cobra is the name of the snake catcher? It does not say that!"

"It does. Here, look."

It did. *Pak* Kobra. Mister Snake.

"So darling, is that fucked up enough to make your hubby sure?"

I thought about the snake threat. "Nah. We had loads of rattle-snakes in California. One slithered right by Loy on our driveway when she was three years old. Victor and I watched it come out of the grass. We didn't want to scream and panic her, and it was like instinctively she knew to keep totally still."

"What'd the snake do?"

"It rattled by her and went into the garage. I grabbed Loy, and Victor grabbed the biggest piece of metal he could find and bashed its head in."

"Lovely image that. Thanks."

"*Tidak apa apa.* I gotta go," I said, heading home to eat lunch. I found Seni talking out the window to two gardeners digging in the dirt next to our hut. When she saw me, she smiled so big I thought her mouth would break in half.

"Lisa! You home. I just now telling my friends why I love you so much."

"What? Why?"

"Everyone who work here, they think you mean, you always with bad face, always mad." She tried to scrunch her smile into a frown in a comical attempt to mimic my persistent madness. "But I say, 'No, my Lisa so good. She good to me. And she a good mama. And a good friend. She take care of everybody. She no mad. She right to hate this place. This house, it's bad here. Really really bad. But she has the biggest heart. I love her,' I say."

"Thanks, Seni. I love you, too. And thank you for telling people I'm not so bad."

"No. You good. You very good woman. You want lunch? You want I make you a big salad?"

I didn't want her to, not really. She never quite made it the way I like it. She never tore the lettuce the right way or put in the correct proportions of extras, like carrots and broccoli and dried fruit and nuts.

"Sure, Seni," I said in spite of certain disappointment. "That would be great. *Suksma*," and then I stopped halfway across the room because it hit me that if we quit, SENI WILL LOSE HER JOB.

Instead of checking email, I sat up at the counter and watched my beloved *pembantu* wash and peel and chop, with so many appreciative nods that my neck began to ache.

"Sinead not so happy, *ya*?"

"Yeah, I think she's going to work somewhere else. Or take time off till her back gets better."

"*Ya*, good idea she go. This place no good. So many mold. So many bad things happen."

"You think so? What would you think if we left, too?" I let just a toe touch the water.

"Oh, I cry so much if you leave. I love you. I love Victor. I love Loy. You my family."

I said nothing.

"Lisa. I go make offering now, okay?"

"Totally okay," I said, taking a bite of the best big salad I'd ever eaten.

We were low on DVDs and that was never a good thing. Especially when the school's Internet went down every other hour, and I'd been able to download just three of the eight parts of *Project Runway*'s next episode. When Saturday night came around with nothing to do, we decided to venture into Ubud to grab some dinner and snag some cheap flicks.

After the nice I Made dropped us at the bottom of *Jalan Raya Hanuman* we wandered north, reading the menus posted outside the restaurants, repeating "*Tidak. Suksma*," again and again to the young women who stood out front, beckoning us inside. When we came to

an alleyway we spotted a small cardboard sign painted with SONG'S
CHINESE FOOD and an arrow pointing into the darkness.

"You want to go check it out?" Victor asked the two of us.

"I don't care," replied Loy, the child who didn't care if she discovered the next best thing. "I just want to eat already."

We walked down the stone alley, following it further into the stillness. At an artist's studio, we peered through the glass at the many
half-finished tropical scenes bulging with bare-breasted women in
sarongs. We passed a Laundromat, where inside, two young tourists
slouched against a wall. A dog ran by us, stopped to stare, then disappeared into an opening between two gates.

"Where is this place?" Loy whined.

We finally found it: a small, open, three-sided room, like a stage set,
raised off the ground, with five tables and Chinese lanterns swaying in
the flimsy breeze of a lone ceiling fan. We took off our shoes, climbed
up the steps and sat down. A white man and woman drank beers at
another table. While Victor and Loy read the menu, I tried to figure
out where they were from.

"Are you Australian?" I hazarded. Why did I want to engage them?
Because talking to people was fodder for my books? Because I collected their stories like other people collected stamps? Whatever the
reason, I'd opened my mouth and now it was too late.

"Indeed we are. You ever eat here before?"

"Nope," Victor said, looking up from the menu. "Our first time."

"Well, it won't be your last," the tipsy woman said. "This place is
the best kept secret in Ubud! We've been coming here for three years."

And then they talked without stopping for another ten minutes.
We learned that Michael and Deanna had a house in Ubud and another
in Australia, and still another in London. That they were childless and
newly married; third marriage for him, second for her. He was retired.
She was a—I didn't quite catch it, and didn't make her repeat what
she'd just said. I wanted to ask them by what means they'd acquired

their fortune, or if they'd like to join us for a drink, but I felt Victor's big toe poking my ankle. He had a love/hate thing with my need to consume strangers whenever I encountered one.

"Well, thanks for chatting," I said, turning my attention away from them, "but we need to order before this one passes out."

Loud laughter and beers raised high. "Sure. Sure. Enjoy!"

"Mommy. There's no Chinese food."

"What?" I opened the plastic menu.

"It looks great," Victor said, "but it's really Balinese with some French thrown in."

"Darn. I have no interest in eating Balinese food."

"Well, the only thing on the menu that isn't Balinese is chicken."

We ordered chicken: I the pan-fried chicken with tarragon cream sauce; Loy the fried chicken with lemon; and Victor the simple grilled chicken. All three dishes came with the same salty string beans, perfectly cooked turnips and potatoes, and a side of lettuce covered with a mustardy vinaigrette. If Loy's watermelon juice hadn't been on the table in front of us, and bats hadn't kept swooping by throughout the meal, and legions of red ants weren't crawling up the wall behind us, we could almost have imagined we were in a bistro down some Parisian alleyway.

Although in Paris the bill wouldn't have come to ten dollars.

"That was good." Victor downed the rest of his beer. "I'd come back here every week."

"See! We told you," said the eavesdropping Australian woman through a mouthful of chicken.

I could tell they saw Victor's comment as an opening to continue their personal tales and that Victor wanted no part of it. He smiled at the lady, stood up and went over to the kitchen to pay the bill.

We cut over to Jalan Monkey Forest and made for the huge DVD store. "Aah, air conditioning," Loy said before zeroing in on the kids' section. Victor and I fingered through the semi-recent releases.

"Johnny gave notice today."

"What?" I looked up from reading the back of *The Dark Knight.*

"I didn't want to tell you in front of Loy, because I know how much she'll miss Emily. Johnny's mother is sicker than they thought. The cancer's spread to her brain."

"That's awful. Poor Johnny."

"Yeah." Victor put the movie back on the shelf. "They won't actually come out and say it, but they're thrilled to be leaving."

"They seemed to be pretty happy here. Is that not true?"

Another westerner came over to the D section, so we moved further down to the L's. "Johnny's like me that way. He loves teaching, loves the kids. One of the main reasons he took the job was because Brad told him Green School was going to be fully Waldorf. He has no interest in teaching an International Baccalaureate curriculum, if that's what they finally end up with. Johnny is the quintessential Waldorf teacher."

I often wished Johnny could have been Loy's teacher. He'd brought all sorts of Waldorf-y instruments and props with him from New Zealand. Johnny had the merriest classroom of any teacher in the school. Music seemed to pour out from the space even when Johnny was standing in front of the children just talking.

"And the money thing really got to them," Victor added.

"Money thing?"

"You know they're paying tuition for Emily, don't you? Well, half-tuition, anyway."

"Shut up! They are not."

"I'm not kidding." Foreigner guy began to loiter near the L's, so again we moved, all the way to the T's this time. "They thought both Elliott and Emily would be free. It wasn't until after they arrived that they were told they had to pay for Emily."

I peered over the aisle at Loy, who had about ten DVD cases clutched precariously in her small arms. "When would they leave?" I asked.

"As soon as possible. He wanted to stay until the end of the term, but they don't think his mom has much time left."

Loy came over with her stack of movies. "You can't have all these, Loy," Victor said in a patient voice. "Let's narrow it down to five. How's that sound?"

Loy shrugged while I fretted. Would Johnny's departure make it harder for Victor to leave? What will happen if someone gets hurt and Philippa's not around to nurse them well again? How would Loy take the departure of her best friend in Bali?

"Will this change your decision about whether or not we're leaving?" I followed the two of them over to the DVD player in the back of the room. We'd already learned our lesson about buying pirated DVDs. They cost less than a buck, but more than half of them didn't work. Some were videotapes made by someone who filmed the movie on his personal video camera. We figured that out when we heard the people sitting next to him laughing. Some DVDs would only play in Arabic or Russian. Others played just one frame at a time.

One of the clerks came over and put in the first DVD—*The Incredibles*—and pressed PLAY. I think he remembered us from our last visit when we made him play every DVD for a minute or two. He looked down at the stack of Disney films and Bugs Bunny cartoons, handed Victor the remote, and went back to the front of the store.

"No, it has nothing to do with my decision. What Johnny does has no bearing on me," Victor said.

I almost clutched my chest with relief but knew it would be too dramatic, even for me.

"This one's fine, Loy. Hand me the next one." He loaded the player, crossed his arms and looked at me. "I still have to think it through. I'm not one hundred percent sure."

"Um," I mumbled. "I thought you were pretty sure you wanted to leave ... and ..."

"I told them we were going to take the weekend to reevaluate our place here and I will, Lisa. It's a big decision and I take it very seriously." He popped out the DVD and put in *Chicken Little*.

Loy sat up on the table with her head in her hands, and I twirled my hair around my finger as we waited for it to play. After the opening music, the camera zoomed in on an animated chicken screaming, "Run for your lives! Everyone run for cover! SOS!" from the top of a tower. Loy laughed. I snorted, thinking how poetically coincidental it was to our present lives, when the frame suddenly froze on the face of the frantic chicken.

"Aw! Try it again, Daddy."

Victor pressed PLAY again but nothing happened. "It's broken, sweetheart. You have enough movies to get you through a few weekends. Who knows," my valiant mate speculated as the broken disc slid out of the machine, "you might end up watching them in New York City."

The email about the lice showed up first in Bahasa:

Yth. Seluruh Orang-tua
Kami belajar dari pengalaman adanya masalah kutu rambut dari beberapa siswa-siswa kecil. Banyak dari siswa ini memiliki kutu rambut di kepala mereka . . .

And since I didn't have my pocket dictionary with me, I ignored it and went back to writing. A few minutes later, the English version appeared:

Dear Parents,
We are experiencing a head lice breakout in several of the younger classes. A number of our children have active lice in their heads . . .

"Shit, Seni. There's another lice outbreak."

Seni looked up from the stove where she was frying some *kroket kentang* (potato and pork croquettes), Loy's favorite meal. "*Ya? Kutu?*"

"That's what they're called? *Kutu?* Oh, like cooties. I wonder if that's where the word comes from."

Unphased by my warning, Seni went back to frying while I answered my ringing phone.

"Sweetie. I'm not coming home after school, so do you want to come get Loy or send Seni to walk her home?"

"Why?"

"Can't say right now. Hey, Sara. What? You do? Oh shit." I hated when he did that: kept me on the phone while he spoke to someone else. Could he not have asked Miss Sara to wait?

"Hello?" I said loudly into the phone.

"Hey, so Sara's going to walk Loy home. I've gotta go. Bye," he said and hung up before I could say another word.

I frowned at the phone, threw it on the couch and looked at my computer. I opened *The New York Times* and read a few articles about the upcoming election. Sarah Palin said something lame again. "Really, John," I said aloud. "Sarah Palin?"

"Lisa. Why you are talking about Sara? She come for dinner?"

"What? No. Well, maybe she is," I said, fumbling from Sarah the candidate to Sara the teacher, who I could now see coming down the path toward our hut, my daughter's hand in hers.

"Sara!" Seni yelled more loudly than she needed to. "Come in."

"Hi, Mommy!"

My baby was home. My clean, bug-free child had come through the gate, looking sweaty and tired and as beautiful as a tawny fawn. I leaned down to kiss her face and just as I made contact with her lips, she uttered, "Sara says I have bugs in my head, Mommy."

I flicked my head up so quickly I gave myself whiplash. "What? You have lice?"

"Yeah," Sara replied. "We both do."

"Oh, no."

Seni looked up from her splattering croquettes. "What, Lisa? Loy have the *kutu*?"

"She does, Seni. So does Sara."

Seni came over and looked at Loy's head, pushing her fingers through that baby fine red hair, sussing out the situation. "*Ya*, many lice here. So many."

The very notion of it depleted whatever resolve I had left in my day. I wanted to go upstairs, part the net and throw myself down on my pillow. But I had of late been little more than a pallid presence in Loy's life, and now she needed me to be a stay-at-home, hands-on, helicopter-hovering mother. She needed me to pick nits.

"What about me, Seni? Do you mind?" Sara said, holding out her blond head as if a present.

Seni meddled through Sara's curly locks, declaring after a moment, "Not so many *kutu*. Sara not so bad as Loy, no."

"Well, aren't you lucky," I said. "Come on, Loy, let's get you a snack before we get to picking."

"Lisa. Is okay I pick for Sara?"

"Huh?" I turned to look at them from the open refrigerator. They were waiting for me to give Seni *permission* to pick the lice from the beautiful head of my husband's co-teacher. After all, Sara had no *pembantu* of her own. She and the other western co-teachers lived in one-room yurts across campus. They all shared two large bathrooms and one big kitchen and were paid about $1,000 for the whole year. The least I could do was offer her free lice-cleaning.

"Of course. Yes."

After tying my own hair back into a tight bun, we sat Loy and Sara down on our mold-backed dining room chairs facing one another while Seni and I positioned ourselves up on our high barstools behind them. We combed lots of coconut oil through their hair first: the Balinese secret for better lice extraction.

Loy opened her book and Sara opened her MacBook.

Then we started to pick nits.

After a few minutes, Seni broke the silence. "The lice here live in trees so it's very very easy for bugs to get into the hairs," she said, feeding my growing dislike of all places tropical.

"That's good to know," I replied, pulling nit after bug after nit through Loy's individual strands.

"I always thought teachers didn't get lice," Sara said with a smirk. She looked as pretty with a grease-soaked head as she did with airy curls. Oh, to be thirty and buoyant again ... I resented her beauty and youth a little more than I should have. Certainly, I was in good shape, for my age, but at that moment I couldn't help but suck in my post-baby belly to the point that I had trouble breathing. After stealthily twisting the stiffness out of my lower back, I discreetly pulled a few strands of hair from my grandmotherly bun so that they fell provocatively down my face.

"Miss Andrea doesn't have lice," Loy offered. "And I don't think Daddy does."

"Daddy doesn't have enough hair for the bugs to cling to," I said.

Seni and Sara chuckled. I let my arms drop to my sides, giving them a rest for a moment.

"Victor said you guys haven't decided anything yet." Sara met my eyes and made a quizzical look over her shoulder toward Seni. She had no idea what Seni or Loy knew about our possible departure, and I appreciated her wanting to be circumspect.

"Yeah." I gave a small shake of my head. "How come he stayed after class today and you didn't? What's going on?"

"He didn't tell you? Brad showed up outside our classroom just as we were ending class."

"Why?"

"He asked Victor to go for a walk with him." She fiddled her eyebrows enough to communicate that she found it rather suspect. I knew no one wanted Victor to quit and wondered what sort of cards Brad had hidden under his sleeve.

By the time Seni finished with Sara and she went home, I was only halfway through Loy's scalp. Seni offered to take over. "Lisa, you not so good. You slow. Here, you move. I do."

"No, Seni. I'm fine."

"You move."

I stood up and wondered if Victor had agreed to stay on. A wave of anticipatory angst, like the line of red ants above the sink, crawled up my back.

"Mommy. If I have to sit here for so long, would you at least read me *Black Beauty*?"

"Yes, baby. I can." I would have to accept whatever Victor decided, even if it meant staying in Bali until June. And I'd have to be content doing so. I'd promised.

"Mommy, you said you would read to me."

"Oh yeah, sorry." I got the book, tossed a salty shrimp cracker into my mouth and pulled up a chair in front of Loy. As I opened the book I looked at her innocent face. She asked for so little, my child, and now she wanted nothing more than for me to share a good story with her while a woman who wasn't her mother plucked insect-laden eggs from her slithery hair. Soon her best friend Emily would be leaving for New Zealand; and Loy would have no one to play dress-up with other than me, and oh dear lord, but I hated playing dress-up.

"'One day she bit James in the arm and made it bleed, and so Miss Flora and Miss Jessie, who are very fond of me, were afraid to come into the stable,'" I read, half-listening to the intermittent click of eggs being crushed between Seni's nails. "'They used to bring me nice things to eat, an apple or a carrot, or a piece of bread, but after Ginger stood in that box they dared not come, and I missed them very much.'"

"Hello!"

"Daddy!"

"Victor, you home!"

"Victor!" I looked at his face for a sign.

"What's going on? What, Loy has lice, too? Jesus, everyone has it." He leaned over and gave both Loy and me a quick kiss.

I unconsciously scratched my head.

"*Ya.* But you no worry," Seni said, beaming. "We make them all dead, *ya* Loy?"

Loy shrugged. "I guess. Mommy, keep reading."

Victor grabbed a glass of water from the fridge. "Mommy needs to come for a walk with me for a few minutes and then she can read, okay, pickle?"

"Yeah, alright."

Before Loy could pout even more, Seni said, "We all finished with *kutu*, Loy. You help me cook *kroket kentang*, okay?"

"I love those. Yum."

Victor and I were all of four feet outside our gate before I asked, "What happened? What did Brad say? Are we leaving?" to which Victor replied, "Let's head over to the Wave House. I don't want anyone to hear us."

I kept my mouth shut for the few minutes it took us to reach the west side of the teachers' village and the vacant Wave House. Long before Aldo took over as lead bamboo hut designer, John Hardy let some famous German architect have his way with the empty plot of land. He'd designed a thoroughly beautiful and thoroughly uninhabitable dwelling. No teacher wanted to live in it, and as we approached the empty shell, I remembered why. It had an abundantly overgrown shaggy roof that kept the interior in virtual darkness. Even though the other huts offered little privacy, the front of the Wave House opened, like a giant yaw of a mouth, to the trails everyone used coming and going to campus. Also, like that one-bedroom hut we were offered when we first arrived in Bali, the bottom floor of the Wave House had been built flush to the ground. As we stepped around a pile of rotted leaves and an abandoned nest of some sort, I threw silent kudos to Aldo for at least building our hut above the dirt.

"So? What?" I asked, squatting down on the dusty bamboo floor.

Victor paced back and forth before speaking. He had his hands in his pockets, and he tilted his head from side to side as if replaying a conversation in his mind. I looked past him at the magnificent view across the river. Someone who cared little about darkness and exposure and animal droppings should really move in.

"We're done here," he said, finally looking at me.

"Okay. Cool." I tried to sound nonchalant; like whatever—if you want to leave, sure, but if you want to stay, I'll hang by your side. I tried, but I knew he could hear the banging sounds my heart made as it leapt for joy. "What made you decide?"

"So Brad meets me after school and is really calm and nice and says he wants me to go for a walk with him, just to chat a little."

"Mm-hmm."

"He stops half-way across the bridge and we stand there for a while, looking out at the river. 'It's beautiful, isn't it?' he says and I say, 'Yeah, but a beautiful campus isn't enough to keep me here.' I ask him to just come out and say what he has to say and he spreads out his arms—you know, like the whole Buddha thing he has going, like he is open and vulnerable and has nothing but goodness to offer."

Victor spreads his arms and imitates a man who is open and vulnerable and has nothing but goodness to offer. "He tells me that with Johnny leaving, it's going to be really hard on the school. I tell him it's not my problem."

I nod vigorously.

"And then he repeats his concern over how long and how difficult a process it will be to find not one, but two replacement teachers in the middle of a term. And I tell him, 'Wait a minute, Brad. Haven't you been saying all along that for every position at Green School you've got a hundred people who want the job?'"

"You said that? Awesome."

"Come on! He's been threatening to replace us for months, and now when he needs to find one of those hundred people, they no longer exist."

Directly behind his head the sun had begun to sink so low in the sky that I had to shield my eyes from the glare. "That's it? That's why you're quitting?" I wanted to run home and pour an ice cold beer and call my mom and write my friends and break the news to Seni and—

"God, no. It's what happened next that convinced me."

What happened next was that Brad suggested they keep walking because there were too many people around the bridge. He proposed they continue their chat on the *bale* out in front of the administration office. Victor said sure and followed along, waiting for Brad to counter or comment on Victor's last observation. But Brad said nothing. It wasn't until they turned the last corner by the building that Victor saw that John and Cynthia Hardy and a woman named Amelia were waiting on the *bale.*

"Can you believe it? How fucking belittling. How dare he lie about wanting to talk to me and then spring the Hardys and this stranger on me."

A pair of construction workers, done for the day, wandered by the front of the house. They must have heard our voices because they stopped for a second to stare in at us before continuing on their way. It made me think of Robert Frost's poem, "Two Look at Two."

"I don't know. Maybe they thought if they asked you to come to the meeting you'd say no." I surprised myself for defending the rulers of Green School.

"Are you kidding me? I've come to every meeting. I've—I'm the one who asked for most of the meetings. No, this was plain and simple manipulation."

"Who was the woman?"

"She's some kind of facilitator or bullshit life coach or something. They said they wanted an objective observer to hear my complaints about the school."

"And did you tell her what was wrong?"

"Oh, you bet I did. But after I listed off what needed to change, I made it very clear that being ambushed into a meeting is exactly why I won't stay. I said I would no longer work for a management team that belittles and disrespects its employees."

"And what they'd say to that?" The sun had set and the mosquitoes were beginning to swarm over to my sweat.

"Nothing. The whole idea of the meeting was that I would talk, they would listen, and Amelia would take notes. When I was done talking, I walked away."

I pictured Victor jumping down from the *bale* and striding defiantly away, wiping his hands clean of the whole dirty affair. "I know how scary John and Cynthia can come off. You're pretty brave, standing up them."

"Nah. They're just people and it's just business." He pulled me up and put his arms around me. "But this is personal. This is what really matters." He kissed me deeply on the mouth.

After the kiss I stared into his eyes. Was that it? Had we moved past the ugliness that had been plaguing us and become a loving married couple again? "Wow, you haven't kissed me like that in—in a long time."

He let me go and walked over to the railing. "That's because I haven't wanted to," he said, not looking at me but at the pale orange light sweeping across the horizon like an impulsive swatch of paint.

I didn't move.

"Do you have any idea how relieved I am?" he said.

I wasn't sure if he was referring to us, or the job, so I simply nodded.

"I didn't realize until just now—I knew it, but I didn't really get what it was doing to me, to us—that I have been surrounded by stress and total dysfunction. Completely surrounded."

"I know. I'm sorry for that. I really am."

"Are you?"

"I am." Now was my chance to start with a clean bamboo slate. "I really am sorry," I repeated. "I should have been more supportive. I should have seen what they were doing to you instead of just focusing on my own shit."

"Not that you didn't have a lot of shit, too." He sounded almost happy that I had shit, too.

"Nothing like you did."

"Okay, we both had shit, but let's not make it a contest, okay?" He grabbed my hand and started to lead me out the hut toward our house. Darkness in Bali descends quickly and we had to walk slowly over the unlit lava rock path, being careful not to trip or slide. Up ahead, the lights of our hut glowed against the dark jungle. I could just make out the silhouettes of palm fronds dancing in the small breeze.

I stopped before we got to our gate, pulling up on Victor's hand like the reins of a horse. "Wait," I whispered. "I've gotta know. Are we okay? You and me?"

"Seriously? How can you ask that after all we've come through together?"

A few feet behind me, I heard Katy talking on her cell phone. She sounded anxious about something. "Because other than that kiss you gave me back there, we've been living like roommates. I haven't been a particularly pleasant person to live with, and you said yourself you haven't wanted to touch me. And not too long ago you told me to go back to California."

"That I did."

"So, are we gonna have to divvy up our stuff when we pack to go home, or not?" I said with a small hopeful smile.

He laughed so loudly that Loy heard him and yelled across the gate, "You guys are back? Come on already! I'm really hungry and Seni's making me wait for you!"

"So, tell me," I said not letting go of him, starving child or no.

"Tell you what?" He took his hand from mine and held it against my lower back. Then he pressed me hard against him. "Tell you that you are the love of my life? Always have been … always will be?"

"Guys! I'm starving!"

"Yeah," I replied a little breathlessly, "tell me that."

"Kumar is really bummed," Victor said as we headed into Ubud together, the nice I Made at the wheel.

"You mean about your decision to leave sooner rather than later."

"He really wants me to wait, give it another month. He said that he didn't think I was giving him enough time to make changes."

"Of course, he says that. You're the best teacher they have here."

"I told him it wasn't just about the school's disorganization. At some point I'd like to believe they'll get their shit together, and Green School might actually end up being amazing, from a pedagogical standpoint. But the living in the jungle part, I don't know. If I were thirty and single I could see sucking it up and staying, but the heat and smoke. The mold. It's exhausting." He sighed, then stared out the window at the passing crowds lining the roads, the pigs being driven to slaughter, the rice fields dotted with ducks and farmers.

"I feel bad for him," he added, still watching the world pass by.

"Bad enough to want to stay?"

"Funny. Hey, I Made, drop me off at Kakiang first, please."

"*Ya*, okay, Victor. I go there now."

I watched I Made smile in the rearview mirror and thought guiltily about the fact that a good percentage of his driving wages would soon be drying up. Our five-dollars-a-pop rides to town now and then supported his smoking habit, at the very least. It also probably allowed him to take his fiancée, Ketut, out on dates. Not that she had much time off—Ketut worked twelve hours a day, six days a week, in one of the least popular restaurants in Ubud, cooking, cleaning, waiting tables. Out of respect for I Made we ate dinner there once, but the food was so bad we surreptitiously fed most of it to a stray dog that stood quietly near our table, waiting for something to drop. He'd enthusiastically scarfed the tasteless noodles and overly salty egg sandwich.

"Want to know what else Kumar said?" Victor said, breaking my reflections.

"Yeah."

"He said if I stayed he'd pay for a house off-campus, one with walls."

"You mean it'd have air-conditioning?" I latched onto that vision with my claws.

"It would. And a pool. Oh, and he'd also pay for a driver."

AC? A pool and personal driver? Could I Made be our driver? Would we still get to keep Seni? "Wow," I replied, speechless.

"Yeah, but like I said back in May, I have no interest in commuting to work. Part of the point of teaching here was being able to live on campus."

"I know you said that." And look how *that* turned out!

I Made pulled up in front of Kakiang, our favorite French/Balinese bakery—owned by a Japanese woman. Being that it was our fourteenth wedding anniversary, we'd left Loy with Seni and decided to partake in a little self-indulgent adults-only time before meeting up for a dinner date out. Victor would spend an air-conditioned hour enjoying a perfect latte and a cream puff while catching up on email and reading any English-language newspapers he could find at the *toko* next door, and I would take a yoga class at The Yoga Barn.

After I Made let me off, I shuffled down the long alleyway to the yoga studio and, upon seeing the rate card, asked if I could pay the LOCALS/KITAS $5 rate (as opposed to the general drop-in rate of $9).

"I need to see your KITAS," said the skinny American girl at the desk.

"We haven't gotten it yet, but my husband teaches at Green School and, I mean, we do *live* in Bali, but they haven't gotten our paperwork done yet," I said, flubbering through my lame explanation as to why I had no legal documentation.

Come to think of it—why exactly was that? Why were we still here under false "social" visas rather than real work visas? What was going to happen when we tried to leave Bali without having had proper visas all these months?

"Sure," she sighed with resignation. "Just pay the 50,000 rupiah."

"Sweet. Thanks." I walked up a flight of stairs to a beautiful room overlooking rice paddies. Deep chant-y, gong-y, ohm-y music played softly on a boom box in the corner. A sleek woman with fantastic skin coloring sat on the floor at the front of the class, her legs spread apart and her body in a forward bend.

The other mostly American-sounding students were in various states of stretching and socializing. I threw my purse against the wall and unrolled a mat, sat down and waited for class to begin. The teacher introduced herself as Rain, and got us going right away with a sort of flowy, stretchy ashtanga/vinyasa hybrid format—exactly the kind of class I could fall in love with and want to take all the time. I breathed in the smoke-less breeze. I held the cobra pose with such precision that my picture could have been on the cover of *YOGA* magazine.

What was it going to be like living in the States again? Before we left California, we'd talked about one day trying out New England since we loved it when we visited friends in Vermont. We'd checked out the job market, housing prices, and schools, but it felt premature, almost irrelevant since we were moving to Bali. New England, at the time, seemed like light years into the future.

Now that a new future loomed, I wasn't so sure I could leave California, my friends and family, the Pacific Ocean. And if we moved to a new state where we knew almost no one, would Victor be able to find another job before our savings dwindled down to nothing? Would Loy mind changing schools yet again?

I stretched forward into pigeon pose, letting those questions weigh my head all the way down to the floor. When the music on the boom box changed to grating gamelan, I looked up and laughed.

The end of the class came too soon, and we were instructed to lay flat with our eyes closed for *savasana*—corpse pose. I tried to clear my mind with little success. Just for the fun of it, I envisioned the three of us living in a house with walls and windows and flush toilets.

I took a deep breath and let gravity take my body. I thought about Lindsey and her friend from the Monkey Forest, and the lessons I was supposed to have learned: I must stop looking to others for happiness. It's right here, always available for the taking, and I have to stop blaming Victor and the rest of the planet's inhabitants for any and all that goes wrong.

There was only this one moment. This now. And I needed to embrace it.

Victor looked up as I opened the door of the café, as if he sensed I was there before I was there. I sat down across from him and knew that no matter where this man wanted to go, I'd follow him.

"Hi there," I said, leaning over to give him a long kiss.

"Hi. How was yoga?"

"Primo. How was your treat?"

"Delicious. Here, I saved you the last bite."

"Thank you," I said as he fed it to me.

"Kumar keeps texting and emailing me."

The door opened and two Japanese couples came in. We watched them peruse the desserts inside the glass cases. I thought about spoiling my appetite and ordering my usual green tea ice cream-and-red bean parfait. "Yeah? What's he saying?"

"He says he's working on getting Brad to leave so that I'll stay."

I whipped my head over from the cream-filled display cases. "Are you kidding me?"

"Nope."

"Damn. He must think you walk on water."

"Not necessarily, but he must think that Brad is sinking the school. He forwarded me an email from Cynthia about some major organizational changes they're about to make."

"Oooh. What'd she say?"

"They're basically not going to let him have anything to do with hiring and firing staff, or anything to do with curriculum. Listen to what she says in the email: 'Until now Brad has been responsible for 100 percent of staff recruitment. I would like to consider between all of us if this is the best policy going forward ... I say this because though we have recruited great people they have come with many issues and we seem to have a hard time retaining them.'"

"They've come with many *issues*? What the hell does that mean?"

"Whatever. Forget it. The point is that Brad is no longer going to be in charge of the staff."

"So, what will he do? Become a security guard?" I expected him to laugh but he didn't. Even when his worst enemy is down for the count, Victor would never be the kind of opponent who jumps around the ring with his fists in the air.

"They're making him the Development Director," he said. "The Hardys expect him to raise a million dollars."

"Yikes."

"It's their way of getting him to quit is my guess. There's no way he'll stay if he has no power. He's too arrogant for that."

"What are you going to tell Kumar?"

"I already told him that I thought his heart was in the right place, but we're not changing our minds."

"You hate letting him down, don't you?"

"For sure. I mean, I trust him, but there's been too much second-guessing. I told him I'm done. Period." The waitress walked over and cleared his cup and dessert plate. We exchanged a few pleasantries in Balinese, Bahasa and English, all of which amounted to:

"How are you?"

"The cake was awesome."

"It's nice and cool in here."

"Thank you."

Victor folded up the *Financial Times* he'd been reading and smiled at me. "I tried to explain to him that the school would ultimately succeed with or without any one individual missing."

"Do you really believe that?"

"I don't know, but what else could I say?"

What else, indeed. "How long you think it's going to take them to find a replacement for you?" I asked, suddenly a little panicked about how many more $2 desserts and $3 pizzas and $5 yoga classes and $8 massages and $1 beers I was going to be able to squeeze in before our departure.

"I'm not sure. They'll post the position right away. I'll put out some feelers, too. Most likely three, four weeks, give or take."

"And what, we'll fly to New York first?"

"I assumed so. All our winter clothes are in my parents' basement."

Bali to New York City.

I pictured the three of us bundled in our coats and scarves, gloves and hats, strolling Central Park on a weekday afternoon when you almost feel as if you have the park to yourself. I made a mental note to check the upcoming schedule for the Swedish Cottage Marionette Theatre. Loy loved those performances—all those glass-eyed fairytale characters prancing around the stage bursting out with songs and stories.

"Here's your card."

"You made me a card?" He handed me a piece of blue construction paper folded in half with lots of pink and orange and green "14"s all over the cover.

"Loy helped me decorate it," he said with a smile.

"I could tell. So many rainbows. It's very pretty."

Inside was a poem:

Rain. Burning garbage. Too many dogs. Dirt and dust.
Banana trees. Frangipani. Shimmering rice fields. Peeks at volcanic peaks.
Insects.
Mosquitoes. Flies. Ants—red, black, large, tiny.
Bug spray—every day
and all day.
Bamboo. Bambu. Mold, mold, mold. Compost toilets. Lumpy beds
and leaky roof. Seni, "You so funny, Lisa!" Sambals. Soto Ayam. 20 ways, but
all essentially the same. Pedas, but rarely penas. Fern tips, water spinach,
and salads to remind us of home. Manggis. Sweat.
Walks through garbage and less garbage. Right, left, right, left, right.
Trooping monkeys. Pip and Co. The River—flowing, peeing, pooing,
laundry, naked teeth brushing. Cold showers three times daily. Rain, rain;
torrents of rain.

Mosquito net nights of reality TV to take us far from this reality.
Priorities—you, me, Loy.

Walking the length of Manhattan, the circle of Central Park.
Vermont? Trying the new in New England.
Hiking. Camping.
Rex. Books. Cold. A real toilet and tub. Cuddling under thick quilts and
swimming in icy lakes.

A hard place, this place. For this I am
sorry, while hoping we changed for the good somehow from it.
I could not have survived this without you. Ultimate support and
protection. A clear demand that we had to get out.
Soon. Let's celebrate 14 years again somewhere else.

I looked at him. "That is the most romantic thing ever. I love you.
Thank you."

"I love you. Happy Anniversary." He reached over the table, put
his hand behind my neck and pulled my mouth onto his. The smell of
sugar filled my nose.

He sat back and folded his hands. "You *are* still up for moving to
Vermont, like we'd planned to someday, after—"

"After staying in Bali for one to three years?"

Victor laughed at the absurdity of that idea, stopping mid-giggle
to frown. "It's more sad than funny, isn't it? Such a big fantasy we had,
living here for a few years, then—"

"Then we'd move to Vietnam or Thailand or India and create more
schools just like Green School." I filled out the rest of the dream we'd
talked about while packing up our house in California.

"We're not going back to California, right?" he asked.

"I don't know. We have all our friends there, and it's so familiar
and—"

"It's safe. That's why you want to go back. Because you know the
dentist and the vet. Loy's pediatrician." He crossed his arms in front
of his chest. "You only want to go back because it's safe and it's easy."

"What's wrong with safe and easy?"

"It's boring."

"After living in Bali don't you want boring?" I know I did. Maybe
not so much *boring* as less unpredictable.

Instead of answering me, Victor slid his hands around the smooth clean table as if pushing together invisible crumbs. "Did you know that Burlington is a federally designated refugee resettlement site—which means they welcome displaced people with open arms?"

That would be a plus for Victor. He lived to help others. "No," I said, thinking that one more displaced family moving to Vermont might not be such a bad idea. "That's pretty cool."

"And that only 600,000 people live in Vermont as opposed to 38 million in California?"

I snipped the marionettes' strings in New York City and flew over to New England, landing my thoughts on the shores of the postcard gorgeous Lake Champlain. If we moved to Vermont, we'd be closer to Victor's parents. And Montreal. If we moved to Vermont we'd learn how to tap maple trees, and I'd write my next great book during one of its famously long dark winters. At my maple desk. In front of a roaring fire. With Rex curled up next to my keyboard.

Would I get by okay in Vermont? Me, who in the last few months had been kicked out, sent home, shut up, attacked, yelled at, and altogether fired? If I could survive all that, couldn't I survive wearing snowshoes six months a year?

"Ben and Jerry's ice cream is headquartered in Vermont, isn't it?" I asked.

"It is."

"Yeah," I said. "Let's move to Vermont."

"Okay, but first let's go eat dinner. I'm starving."

Lordy lordy, we're losing Loy

Posted by *Pak* Glenn • Category: Year 1 - 2

We have laughed our way through our last lunch and last lecture with Leopard Loy. She and her family are labeling luggage in preparation of leaving Bali and landing back in the states. We will labor through our lessons and need to label all the lyrics to our songs without Loy to remind us. We wish them all the luck in the world and send them all of our love. We will miss them all large!

Don't go changin' Loy!

Andrea, Glenn and Desak

Selamat Jalan Pak Victor! *Kita Akan Merindukanmu!*

Posted by *Ibu* Sara • Category: Year 7 - 8

Bittersweet. That's the word that best describes what today felt like. It was *Pak* Victor's final day as our classroom teacher; we all agreed he is one of the very best teachers we have ever had. We are thankful for the way he made us feel: enthusiastic to come to school every day, engaged in our learning of even the most difficult lessons, optimistic about our future, empowered by being treated and respected as unique individuals, and renewed by the faith that truly great teachers really do exist; his presence in our lives is proof of that. We all wish you the very best, *Pak* Victor, as you and your family carry on your journey. Know that you have left us all an important gift: the gift of understanding what it feels like to be treated with respect.

To: Putu [the Putu who worked in Human Resources]

Cc: Kumar

Subject: Our expired Visas

Hi *Ibu*,

As you know our flight leaves next Sunday at 1:05 AM (in the morning, just after midnight). We are very concerned that we will be stuck at the airport, with nobody to assist us since we have now stayed long past our most recently stamped visas. The Indonesian government website makes it clear that we will either be fined $20-$25 per day for each day of an overstay; or that we can be IMPRISONED. Can we be absolutely certain that we will not run into a problem? Will someone from immigration be there to meet us where we check in our luggage? Do we tell them we were in Bali for pleasure? Work? What will they actually know? If things do not go well, who is going to assist us from Green School?

This is making me really uncomfortable, especially as it involves not just me, but my family as well.

I really wish these visas had been in order as I requested over one month ago.

Please respond today.

Victor Prussack

Dear Victor,

It will be alright, Putu will accompany you. It is a very normal process for people overstaying. And there is no legal reason for you having any discomfort.

Kumar

Kumar,

I am cc-ing Putu to clarify:

Putu will meet us at the airport at 9:30 PM on Sunday evening.

She will be out front and introduce us there to someone from immigration.

She will pay him for the overstay.

He will then escort us to check-in and wait for us.

Then he will escort us through the immigration section to the waiting area.

Putu, please let me know if this is correct or not.

Thank you.

Victor Prussack

We were leaving Bali. Now all we had to do was get us and our belongings out in one piece. Seni had, through a constant stream of tears, helped us pack. We'd acquired quite a few things; lots more than what we'd brought with us in our original nine boxes and suitcases. Deciding what to take home and what to leave for Seni took days. We had to include Loy's new golden-colored butterfly quilt. And those intricate baskets we'd bought to hold her clothes and toys. And the fifteen-dollar whimsically painted bookshelf in the shape of a canoe would have to come along. As would the seven pairs of fifty-cent flip-flops and my cheap yellow sun umbrella and the chair hammock we impulsively bought during our beach holiday.

Then there was the matter of the many green dishes that we'd bought from Tamin down in Ubud. I wanted to use them in our new home in Vermont. I asked Seni how to best pack fragile goods and she told me, "Lisa, I work for shipping company many many years; I know good way for shipping. You trust me, Lisa. I do good job."

When all was said and done and sorted and packed, we ended up with thirteen boxes, in addition to our suitcases, and the canoe book-shelf. After the Javanese man in the brown UPS uniform and broken scanner came and took the boxes away with the promise they'd make it safely to New York City, I looked around the empty hut. No more photos on the fridge. No more plastic bins taking up the bathroom floor. No more freshly washed shoes drying in the sun.

Seni had gone upstairs to deal with the spirits. I heard the swish of her sarong as she went from room to room, wafting the incense, pray-ing for our safety. We'd gotten her a job with a very nice Australian family of five who lived in Ubud. She was excited, yes, because now she would have three lovely *perempuan* to take care of.

What else (besides the visa worry) could possibly stop us from leaving? The Bali Bombers, that's what. The infamous Bali Bombers who'd blown up two nightclubs and burned hundreds of tourists to death, had been in jail for years and sure enough, just as we decided that we were truly leaving Bali, the Indonesian government decided it was high time to execute the lot of them. That decision pissed off a lot of terrorist groupies who vowed revenge if the executions happened, which made me freaked about flying out of Denpasar.

The first thing I did every morning was check the status of the impending executions. *Wait until we're gone. Please wait until we're gone,* I chanted as the home page of *The Jakarta Post* downloaded.

On the day of our departure, I awoke happy and optimistic, sliding down the stairs with a smile on my face, stopping short when I saw Victor's face.

"The positive thing to remember is that we're flying Japan Airlines," he said.

"What are you talking about?" I said, pushing past him toward his laptop.

There it was. The headline:

INDONESIA ON ALERT AFTER EXECUTION OF BALI BOMBERS
And another:

INDONESIA EXECUTION OF BALI BOMBERS SPARKS CLASHES, TENSIONS HIGH
And this chocolate-covered cherry:

REPRISALS FEARED AS BALI BOMBERS EXECUTED
I moaned. "Why today?"

Victor came up behind me and put his hands on my shoulders. "They have no beef with the Japanese. If we were flying Northwest, say, or Qantas, even I'd be worried."

I let it go, because I was getting the hell out of this hellhole and Victor was right: if it was Americans they wanted to kill, they'd find far fewer flying from Denpasar to Osaka on an Asian airline than from Denpasar to Cleveland on an American carrier. I had to stay positive and not let slip "bombing" or "hijacking" or "religious fanatical fucks" when Loy was in the room. We were packed, and everything but our visas were in order.

Later that morning, Seni showed up with her husband, Ketut, two other men, and a truck. They hauled away boxes of toys and clothing, a toaster (her first!), glasses, silverware, food, and every single piece of furniture we'd bought to replace the ever-moldering stuff Aldo had removed from the house. While Ketut was loading the last bookshelf, I handed Seni an envelope with the rest of her year's salary, plus an extra month. Then she hugged us, one by one, smiling bravely as we made promises to see her again someday.

Our neighbor Katy threw us a going-away dinner party that night. A couple of the teachers showed up: the ones who didn't resent us for leaving, and were, in fact, contemplating their own resignations; as well as those who were always up for a free meal. We sat around Katy's big, round bamboo table bitching about the school and reminiscing over a time too short while eating spaghetti topped with jarred marinara sauce. It was an utterly unfitting dish for our last night in Bali, but I was grateful it wasn't *nasi goreng*. I'd eaten enough Balinese fried rice to last me three lifetimes.

Sitting there with those people, some of whom had become real friends, I did my best to conceal the profound relief igniting the chakras up and down my spine. I felt like the straws had been extended and I'd pulled the long golden one.

"So, what's Tom like?" Sinead asked Sara, referring to Victor's replacement teacher, an Australian guy who'd arrived a few days ago.

Sara looked at Victor who shrugged, raised his eyebrows, and smirked, all in one act. "Well." Sara looked at her bowl of sweet red noodles. "He has a habit of addressing the kids as boys and girls, as in 'boys and girls, please have a seat in the bubble.'"

"Ewww," Andrea said. "They must hate that."

I glanced at Victor, who looked at his watch for the fifteenth time since dinner started. I saw that he had it on his wrist instead of in his pocket, as if anticipating skin cool and dry enough to once again accommodate leather.

Sam pushed back from the table to get more pasta. "Did you guys hear what Brad did when Tom arrived?"

A collective grunt of unknowing went around the hut.

"So, after he gets picked up at the airport and comes here, he remembers that he'd checked his toiletries last minute and is a bag short." We waited while Sam sat, took another forkful of food, then washed it down with many loud gulps of beer. "He tells Brad that he's gotta go back to the airport, right? But Brad says, 'Hey, it's not our fault you didn't keep track of your personal belongings,' and Tom's gotta foot the bill for the taxi ride to Denpasar. Green School's not paying."

Katy slammed her hand on the table. "You're shitting me."

"Shitting you not."

In the middle of talking about new teacher Tom having to retrieve his toothpaste, I Made showed up to take us to the airport, formally bringing our last meal at Green School to an end. While he packed the van, we all stood around hugging and crying and sweating. Sinead and I walked over to her hut so she could give me a letter and made me promise not to read it until I was on the plane. The last few weeks had been an employment roller-coaster for her. Kumar had told her he needed more time to work out her contract details and asked if, in the meantime, she'd stay on; work as much as she could, even a few hours a day.

"I need to keep teaching till they agree to continue my insurance, right?" she'd asked me when she came to me with the news.

"I can't answer that," I'd replied most unhelpfully. I mean, I wanted her to leave so she could remove herself from all this drama—it couldn't be helping her back. But I had no idea what Green School would ultimately do for—or to—her.

At her house, I took her letter then hugged her against my chest. "I will see you again, Sinead," I said to her, with not even a dust mote of doubt in my mind. I heard I Made honk and said I had to go.

I hurried inside our hut and went into the bathroom for one more obsessive-compulsive check to see that we'd grabbed all *our* toiletries. I ran my hand along the inside of the smooth stone sink—my favorite thing in the whole house. I said, "Fuck you," one last time to the bamboo toilet. I said, "Goodbye, mold," to the chairs. "Goodbye, dog" to the pregnant stray chewing on something brown outside the living room. I raised my head and stretched my arms out wide, like Julie Andrews in *The Sound of Music,* breathed in the palpably hot, non-Austrian air and whispered, "Goodbye, Bali dream," before closing the gate behind me for the last time.

As I approached the fully loaded van, I saw Loy's face looking out the window from the back seat, but she wasn't looking at me—she was looking up at the tree that grew through the roof of our hut. I got in and slammed the passenger door. "Whatcha thinking about, baby girl?" I asked.

"Nothing. Those ants that used to come every night."

"You going to miss your room here?"

"Nah. Maybe just a little."

Victor took her hand in his. "What else are you going to miss?"

"I'm gonna miss Emily even though she's gone anyway. And watermelon juice. And some of those cool bugs that live here, like that gigantic moth."

"I'll miss that moth, too," I said. As we passed under the big bamboo pole, I gave a last wave to the two security guards. One of them waved back. The other adjusted his sarong. "What won't you miss?"

Loy waited until we were past the barricade before she answered. "Um. Being hot all the time?"

"I hear you there, sister." I turned around and smiled at her, then looked back out the window.

"The smell of that poison spray you had to put on my clothes."

"The DEET. Yeah. Awful."

"I don't ever want you to spray me with that stuff again, okay?"

"Deal." I again turned in my seat, flashed her a two-fingered scout's-honor, and turned around again.

"You and Daddy fighting all the time."

I kept my eyes on the road after that one. Victor said nothing either, but I could tell from the sounds behind me that he pulled her closer into his arms.

In silence, we continued on into the village, and just as we reached the outskirts where the jungle began, I Made slowed the car down to a crawl.

"Why are you slowing down?" Victor asked from the back seat.

"I no want to hit the peoples, Victor," I Made replied, pointing out the enormous crowd lining the east side of the road.

I watched the throng spreading out like slow-moving liquid into the trees. I opened the window and the rollicking timbre of gamelan flooded the car. "What's going on?" No one was wearing their elaborately adorned ritual dress. "Is there a ceremony or not?" I asked, confused.

"I think maybe a child or old person must be lost. This is why many people here. You see they are looking. I can hear they are calling a name."

"Oh. Are they playing loud music to help the person to find his way back?"

"No," I Made said, driving on. "It is very possible a ghost steal the person and is holding him tight. The men play the gamelan to make the ghost dance. When the ghost dances, he lets go and the person, he run to get away."

"Huh." I looked back at Victor who had an amused expression on his face. "That makes perfect sense," I said, relieved that we were leaving a place where being kidnapped by dancing ghosts was always a possibility.

An hour and a half later we pulled up to the departure terminal at Denpasar airport as planned, and Putu, as planned, was there, looking bitter and tired. Standing next to her at the curb was the immigration "officer," or at least the Indonesian gentleman who would be bribing the real people with whatever resources he used for such illicit activities. Putu informed us that she had already paid him off, gave us a cold, "*Selamat jalan*," and disappeared into the night.

I Made stood on the curb next to our luggage, his hands in his pockets. He looked sad, and I knew from his face that it wasn't just those five-dollar trips to Ubud he was going to miss. We'd gotten to know him as intimately as you can get to know someone who hardly speaks English and is usually behind the wheel of a car. We'd heard about his family. Met his sweetheart. Shared a few meals with him.

He reached out to Loy who threw her arms around his waist. They hugged for all those times when I Made would take me and Loy to Bintang Market and Loy, without fail, would crow into the hot air, "I don't want to go shopping!" so I would hand I Made 10,000 rupiah and tell him to buy ice-cream cones from the vendor by the parking lot. One for him and one for Loy. And when I'd come out—fifteen, twenty, thirty minutes later, my cart full of expensive jams and cheeses and cereal—I'd find the two of them sitting on the curb, shoulder to shoulder, an ice-cream moustache around Loy's babbling mouth, and I Made focusing intently on her stories, as if he believed she held all of life's most important answers.

Immigration Dude (ID) sounded off an anxious throat-clearing. We gave I Made five times what we usually paid him for a ride, grabbed the overloaded luggage cart, and made for the check-in counters, ID hot on our trail.

Once inside the terminal, I expected to find a battalion's worth of police because of the Bali Bomber executions, but as we made our way to the Japan Airlines ticket counter we passed only two armed security guards.

"I guess the newspapers overreacted about the threat to western-ers," I noted to Victor.

"Screw the bombers: at this point I'm just worried about getting out of the country." He handed our tickets to the smiling man.

The $15 painted canoe bookcase was deemed OVERSIZED, and the agent informed us that we'd have to pay $150 if we wanted to check it on the airplane.

Take it.

Leave it.

Take it.

Leave it.

I could see ID waiting in the lobby, tapping his fingers on his leg as he watched my quivering mass of indecision. What if he got impatient and left without helping us?

"Let's just pay for it!" I shouted too loudly.

"Okay!" Victor shouted back, also too loudly. We were both nervous. We'd overstayed our visas. We could be thrown into prison. We were at the mercy of a government which killed stray dogs and marijuana dealers with abandon.

We paid. Our bags went on the carousel. We turned to follow ID but he was gone! He'd taken Putu's money and left the airport without bothering to help—oh dear God, there! There he is. Quick let's go!

I grabbed Loy's hand. Victor grabbed our carry-ons and we raced to keep up with him. He never looked back. He assumed we were there, behind him. It would be fine. Fine.

Up the escalator we rode, ID in front, the three of us a subtle five steps below. Then down a corridor, following arrows, following other tourists, Japanese, British, Australian, American, the animated (and considerably relaxed) voices a whirl around us.

Up ahead we came to a podium.

PAY DEPARTURE TAX HERE.

Okay. A quick 300,000 rupiah handed over. On our way.

"Was that it?" I asked Victor, who was reading the third text message Kumar had sent him since we left campus:

Victor, Please reconsider. It is not too late. Stay and teach the children.

"Christ. You should have just left it on the car seat," I said, almost ripping the phone out of Victor's hand and throwing it across the airport.

"We may need this phone. Shhh. Here we are."

We'd arrived at IMMIGRATION.

ID approached us. "Passport. *Ya?*"

"He wants our passports. Give him our passports," Victor said in more of a high-pitched voice than I'd ever heard come from him.

We handed them over. ID pointed to some chairs and ordered us to "*duduk.*"

We sat.

He went inside a room. We waited. Through the door we could hear talking. Yelling. Screaming. All completely unintelligible.

He came out of the room wiping a dirty rag across his sweating forehead. He approached us, shaking his head, said something neither of us could make out. Then he said, "*guru*?" and pointed to Victor.

"*Ya*! *Suami saya guru!*" I shouted. Yes. My husband is a teacher and he's been working as one in Bali all these months, yes! Or, no, he wasn't! Was he *not* supposed to have been working? Were we here on tourist visas? Which one were we supposed to say? Why didn't Putu tell us what to say? "Loy, stop kicking the chair! Victor? What should we tell him?"

Victor looked as panicked as I did. Should we admit that Green School had hired him but didn't give him the proper visa? What?

What?

"*Apa*?" I asked, stalling.

ID wiped his face again and rattled off a string of Bahasa declarations, gesturing his head toward THE ROOM after every other word.

"*Tidak mengerti*," I admitted. We do not understand.

He nodded, but said nothing. A passing threesome of Australians, giddy with holiday spirit walked by. I wanted to be giddy with them. I wanted to browse the Duty Free shops and buy last-minute souvenirs and drink cheap beer. I kept my eyes peeled on ID. He paced two steps toward the door of THE ROOM. He returned, sat down on the chair next to Loy and looked at his watch, then he stood up again. I watched his eyes dart back and forth between us and THE ROOM. I could almost see our freedom dissipating into the cold stale air.

"He's losing his patience, Victor. What should we do?"

"And I know, why?"

"Wait. Here." I reached into my purse and pulled out a small white bag. Inside was the rust-colored beaded necklace I'd bought for my mother. "For you?" I handed it to him. He looked into the bag and smiled, stood up, went back inside THE ROOM where there was still more indecipherable yelling.

Again he came out with a worried look plastered across his slick face.

"You have my mother's necklace. What now? *Apa*? *Apa*?"

"Fuck this," Victor said. "I'm calling Putu." He dialed.

While praying that Putu answered her phone, I imagined the yelling men in THE ROOM coming out and ordering those armed guards over there to arrest us. Would Victor and I get separated? Who would take Loy? Would she get arrested too, or would they let her go? Should I call someone now and have them come to the airport just in case? Who should I call? Sara? Sinead? I had to call someone right away. I reached out to grab the phone from Victor, but—

"Putu, thank God. It's Victor. It's not working. The guy you paid isn't doing anything and he's still holding our unstamped passports." ID paced back and forth, my mother's carefully chosen present bribing a hole in his pocket. "Yes? Okay. Here," Victor said, handing the phone to ID, who took it, and listened. Then yelled into the phone. Then took the phone with him back into THE ROOM and then more yelling. Then quiet talking. Then the door opened and ID walked over to us.

"*Ya*, okay," he said. "Come."

We followed him.

"Victor? What did Putu say? Where is he taking us?"

"I don't know, but he better not be taking us to the police."

"Why would we go to the police, Daddy?"

"Shhh, Loy. You have to keep up. Walk faster."

We followed him down a long corridor past a line of tourists waiting to get through immigration, to one of those cords that you have to unhook to get past. Above it was a sign:

CREW ONLY.

He unhooked it, gave a respectful nod to the guard with the machine gun, and waved us through. Then he handed Victor his phone as well as our stamped passports.

"*Selamat jalan,*" he said, fastening the hook behind us.

"*Selamat tinggal,*" I replied with the weightlessness of a freshly sprung jailbird.

And with that he was gone.

And so, at last, were we.

Loy slept stretched out between us while I read *SkyMall* and Victor stared anxiously out the window, as if expecting Kumar or John Hardy to suddenly materialize on the plane's wing.

I closed the page of fancy kitchen gadgets on my finger. "Why are you so worried?" I asked him quietly.

"I'm not worried."

I let the magazine fall to the floor and shifted Loy's feet from my knee to my thigh. "You don't trust them, do you? You think because they're so pissed off that you quit, they might do something to mess with us, like what happened at the airport."

"You're kidding me." He gently swept Loy's bangs off her sweaty forehead and smiled at her perfect sleeping face. "I forgot Bali existed the moment they turned the seatbelt sign off."

"Then why do you look so nervous?"

"Because I really have to pee and I don't want to wake this little one."

I laughed so hard I woke Loy, who, for a disorienting second, had no idea where she was. She sat up and rubbed her eyes. I expected her to whine on about how loud we were and how tired she was, but instead she looked at both of our grinning faces and said, "We never ever have to live in Bali again, right?"

"Never!" we cried, squeezing her between us.

Not until we were flying from Osaka to Detroit did I begin to relive those anticipatory twitches of delight that I get when traveling "someplace else." We were on our way back home, and much of my joy stemmed from being that much further away from Bali; but I still felt that "leaving here and going there" sense of freedom, adventure, escape.

With both Loy and Victor asleep beside me I stared out the window, thinking how crazy it was to be leaving a tropical paradise, yet feeling like I was going on vacation. Visiting someplace else is way different than *living* someplace else. Typically, when you go away on a short holiday, you unpack a few belongings, spend some moment-to-moment time tasting the new; peeking at the strange; marveling at the different.

If, instead, when you get to your destination, you unpack your books, stock the fridge, hang family photos, and decide to stay awhile, the exoticness eventually evaporates and you're left with the same issues you had back home. Life in Bali was just life somewhere else. For the first couple of weeks it felt like a vacation. But once we moved onto the campus at Green School, real life started up again. I not only had the same routines—give or take a few bugs thrown in—but the same challenges, as well as the same small victories.

"Whatcha thinking about, sweetie?"

"What? Oh, nothing." I smiled and put my hand on his lap. He picked it up, kissed it, then closed his eyes again.

Thirty-three hours later, we touched down in New York. With a spring in our step and a canoe on our cart, we raced outside to breathe in real air.

And oh, what air it was. The air was—it was cacophonous.

Yes, the air smelled NOISY.

And cold and clean and dirty and crazy familiar. We were oh so glad to be sucking it into our lungs.

In the van on the ride to the city, we marveled at the lack of greenery. Everything in Bali had been green. Every shade of green, too, from the black-green of our ever-present mold to the peridot green of the banana trees outside our hut to the blue-green sea of rice paddies blanketing the countryside to the iridescent green of the dead beetle inside Loy's backpack. (She announced that wherever she went to school next, it'd be her first Show-And-Tell.)

There was not much green in New York City, but brownstone can be just as pretty when you pull up and see your father-in-law standing on the stoop of one with a bottle of champagne in his hand.

Hugs. Kisses. Sighs of relief.

"When did you get so tall?"

"How were the three flights? Did you sleep?"

"You're so tan."

"Thank God you made it out of there alive."

"Who's hungry?"

"A toast," said Victor's father, Charlie, as he raised his glass to the three of us now sprawled out on the couch. "Welcome to America!"

At my mother-in-law's insistence that we eat something, I dragged my jet-lagged body over to the table and ate a bowl of her heavenly mussel and bean stew. Victor dunked slabs of crunchy bread into the steaming broth, exclaiming, "Oh my God, bread. Real bread," over and over again. Loy took two slurps and more or less fell face-first onto the table.

The next morning, after six hours of fitful turning and tossing, I found Loy still deeply asleep on the futon and Victor at the dining room table, reading emails. "*Selamat pagi,*" I said to him, kissing his cheek.

"Screw you," he replied with a smile. "So, Kumar sent another letter. He says we should know that a group of parents are offering to pay for a house on the beach for us."

I poured myself a cup of tea and sat across from him. How bizarre it was to have my feet touching cold slate instead of splintery bamboo.

I looked around the apartment at the walls. At the gorgeous plumb walls with flush corners and perfectly smooth plaster. The squareness of the room comforted my sense of balance and order and symmetry. "They really think it's because of the housing that we left, huh?"

"All I told the kids was that I left for personal reasons. Period," Victor said with his typical *laissez-faire* shrug. "Let them think what they want."

I knew most of the families assumed Victor quit because of me. Because I'd whined about the school. About the housing. About the mold and the bugs and about being so far from town. They probably believed that Victor left a dream job at a dream school on a dream island because of his bitch wife.

Victor had never let on to his students or their parents how unhappy he was. Ever. He never would have complained about Green School's wily ways, or the garbage and the smoke and the noise and the pollution and the gamelan. Even if he did hate it.

"Did you hate gamelan as much as I did?"

"What? Where'd that come from?"

"I don't know. Did you ever get sick of all that gamelan music?"

"No, not really. I mean, yeah, it got old, but how can you hate something that's so much a part of a culture?"

That's so Victor to say.

"It's incredibly beautiful outside," he said. "Let's take a walk in the park."

"Won't Loy freak if she wakes up and we're not here?"

"No, because A, she feels completely safe and comfortable here, and B, I guarantee she's going to sleep for another four hours. My mom will give her breakfast if she gets up before we get back."

After I got dressed, I tiptoed downstairs to the basement bedroom and looked at her sleeping rash-free body, appreciating more than I could say that I didn't have to watch her through the cloudy gauze of a mosquito net.

"Okay," I whispered to Victor, who stood next to me, loving that kid of his as much as a person could. "Let's go."

We strolled lazily along the rows of drooping Korean chrysanthemums and fainting grasses under a blue sky in Central Park's Conservatory Gardens. I had on my down coat, but the morning's chill crept through the feathers. We wandered over to the south garden and plunked down on a bench by the Burnett Fountain, with the bronzed figures of Dickon and Mary from *The Secret Garden* in the middle of it.

"I feel like it's been two years since Loy and I read *The Secret Garden* together."

"You read it just a couple months ago, right?"

"I think so," I said, reaching out to time as if I could snatch it from the air like a floating leaf. In that moment, Bali was in my past. But what of this unknown future that hung out in front of us? What were we going to do now? I suddenly felt dizzy and had to put my head between my legs.

"What's wrong?"

I moaned. "I'm really jet-lagged. That's all."

He rubbed my back. "Want to go back?"

"Yeah, in a sec." I sat up and cuddled into his outstretched arm. Not since the air-conditioned room at the Bali Hyatt had I wanted to get this close to my husband. I'd almost forgotten how well I fit into that crook, that special curve that evolution carved out so that one lover could fit inside the other while sitting side by side.

"You're my hero, you know."

"Yeah, me. The big hero," he said half-laughing.

"Dude. You totally rescued us. You got us out of there."

"That I did."

"Thank you."

"No, thank you for pushing me to get us out."

"Do you have any regrets about leaving?" I asked.

"None."

"Regrets about going in the first place?"

"None," Victor said. "As much of a disaster as it was, it's part of our lives now. I mean, I'm glad we got out, but we met some great people, and we learned a lot about another culture, and that's always a good thing."

"Yup."

"I know I'm going to be a better educator because of it. I know now what it really takes to effect change."

"That's cool."

"And we both got a new perspective on us, right? Our marriage?"

"You can say that again." I almost laughed, but the observation felt too keen; too relevant.

"What about you? You wish we'd never left California?"

If I looked at our lives, had we not gone to Bali, where would we be? Hanging out in California in our blue house. Wondering if perhaps a better life awaited us beyond the oaks.

I'd moved us to Bali to find paradise; but now that I knew paradise wasn't what my imagination had cracked it up to be, I could stop trying to find the new, the better, the different. I had needed to move to Bali to know that. To discover more of my own creaks and crevices, ugly and beautiful. Far from the soft tropical breezes and limitless supply of papayas, it turned out I'd gone to a place where I couldn't have been any more vulnerable; a place I had no control over. I had no walls to hide behind. No insulation to muffle my voice, the one inside my head as well as the one coming from my mouth. My home was open to all creatures; a space where anyone could enter. Oh, boy, did they.

As if reading the Sunday paper, I skimmed through our time in Bali, turning pages, glancing over the many faces of the people we met, rereading their stories. I browsed the Green School section before turning the page and reliving my short but lovely friendship with Sinead. I licked my finger and flipped through the ants and the heat and the monkeys, the images flashing out at me like giant movie ads.

I closed the paper. Folded it. Looked up at an old couple passing by, arm in arm.

Yes, Bali had been crazy and horrible and terrific. What else could it have been? To think that I survived it all with my self and my marriage and my family ultimately un—

"Are you going to answer me or what?"

"What?"

"Do you wish we'd never left California?"

"No. Not at all. I realize that I had to move to Bali so I could learn that the bamboo isn't always greener on the other side," I said, tunneling further into him.

He chuckled. "Nope. It ain't."

"And to learn that happiness is here." I put my hand on his chest.

"No, sweetie." He took it off and placed it on my chest. "It's here."

I closed my eyes, feeling ineffably grateful. Grateful for the here and now. Grateful for Victor's patience and love. Grateful for all the wacky wonderful pleasures I'd been lucky enough to be spoiled by.

"I'm glad we went," I said again, more sure than I had been five minutes ago. "But I'm even more glad you got us out of there."

"It's good you think that. Just don't forget about all those promises you made."

"Promises?"

He pulled me to my feet. "Yeah, remember everything you swore up and down you'd do from now on if I quit?"

"Yes," I said, realizing how far I still had to go to be a better, more positive person, and how much more that mattered to me now. "Don't worry; I'm on it."

"I know you are. Let's get back."

Loy didn't wake up for four more hours, as Victor had predicted. She awoke bright-eyed, bushy-tailed, and starving. As she and the rest of the family scarfed down bagels and lox and cream cheese, I read a new email from Sinead saying that all Kumar could offer her was three months' salary—plus $600 out of his own pocket—and her health insurance paid for another year.

> I wish you were here right now. I could so do with talking to you. I sure miss our coffee breaks. As for what Kumar is offering me I don't think there is going to be anything else from them … so I figure just agree and be done with this place … and get out of here with my pride and integrity intact. I'm so drained. I have nothing left … I just want to lie on the beach and let the waves roll over me and wash away this whole experience from my skin and from underneath my finger nails … I feel so dirty, so infected with the lies and deceit and bullshit …

I thought about calling her on Skype, to tell her that it would turn out fine; that ultimately it wasn't about the money, but it was already past her bedtime in Bali. Instead, I went to join the others at the table.

Two days later a UPS truck pulled up in front of the house in the pouring rain. As the nice man in the brown uniform brought in box after box and set them down on top of one another, we could hear the sick, crunchy sound of breakage in each one.

Thirteen boxes had made it.

Hardly any of the dishes did.

We sliced open one box after another, unwrapping what we thought was a whole plate or bowl or platter or cup, only to watch helplessly as most of it fell back into the box, shards of shattered green-leaf pottery scattering everywhere.

I burst into tears.

"Mommy, why are you crying?" Loy asked, coming into the room to see if her favorite dolls had made it home safely.

"Because Seni didn't do such a good job packing our dishes, sweetie," Victor told her.

"No, it's my fault, too. I helped her pack them."

She walked over to the box I was crying into and looked in. "Can't you just glue them back together?"

I was *this* close to laughing at her ridiculously futile question, but then I saw on that beautiful and totally trusting face of hers that she was seriously expecting me to answer.

I knew from Victor's silence behind me that he, too, was waiting.

I wiped my sleeve across my face. "Sure," I said to my family. "I guess we could always give it a try."

Tidak apa apa.

About the Author

LISA KUSEL HAS BEEN PUTTING WORDS TO PAPER EVER since the sixth grade. After earning her Masters in Anthropology from Brown University, she wrote for the Environmental Protection Agency, Seattle Solid Waste, and Microsoft, where she was creator and editor-in-chief of the company's first online magazine, *Matter.*

In her thirties, she left the professional world behind to pursue fiction writing, publishing her first collection of short stories *Other Fish in the Sea,* followed by the novel *Hat Trick.*

She has lived in many parts of the world, including Russia, the Czech Republic, and Bali. Lisa and her husband, Victor, recently moved to Burlington, Vermont, where they adopted two cats, and promised their daughter, Loy, not to move again until she graduates from high school. Victor is an administrator for the Burlington School District. Lisa writes full time at her desk overlooking Lake Champlain.

CPSIA information can be obtained
at www.ICGtesting.com
Printed in the USA
BVHW092230121118
532890BV00021B/940/P